THE PINAKOTHEK

MUNICH

BY

WOLF-DIETER DUBE

CURATOR OF THE
ALTE PINAKOTHEK, MUNICH

HARRY N. ABRAMS, INC. · PUBLISHERS · NEW YORK

Frontispiece: JOSEPH STIELER, *Ludwig I of Bavaria*

TRANSLATED FROM THE GERMAN BY J. WOOD

STANDARD BOOK NUMBER: 8109-0409-8
LIBRARY OF CONGRESS CATALOGUE CARD NUMBER: 74-117932
ALL RIGHTS RESERVED
NO PART OF THE CONTENTS OF THIS BOOK
MAY BE REPRODUCED WITHOUT THE WRITTEN PERMISSION OF
HARRY N. ABRAMS, INC., NEW YORK
PRINTED IN WEST GERMANY BY K. G. LOHSE, FRANKFURT AM MAIN
THIS BOOK IS PUBLISHED IN FRANCE BY
ÉDITIONS AIMERY SOMOGY, PARIS

CONTENTS

INTRODUCTION: THE BUILDING

Page 7

THE BEGINNINGS: WILHELM IV, DUKE OF BAVARIA,
AND HIS SUCCESSORS

Page 11

MAXIMILIAN I

Page 19

MAXIMILIAN II (EMANUEL)

Page 31

THE PALATINE COLLECTIONS

Page 38

THE AMALGAMATION OF THE GALLERIES UNDER
MAXIMILIAN I, KING OF BAVARIA

Page 50

LUDWIG I

Page 54

THE LAST HUNDRED YEARS

Page 61

GERMAN SCHOOL

Page 72

EARLY FLEMISH SCHOOL

Page 114

ITALIAN SCHOOL

Page 128

FLEMISH SCHOOL

Page 185

DUTCH SCHOOL

Page 218

SPANISH SCHOOL

Page 244

FRENCH SCHOOL

Page 262

LIST OF ILLUSTRATIONS

Page 291

INDEX OF NAMES

Page 301

INTRODUCTION: THE BUILDING

On 7 April 1826 the foundation stone of the Alte Pinakothek was laid by Count von Armansperg, Minister of the Interior and of Finance. Thus work began on the project outlined by the General Director of Galleries, Georg von Dillis, in his report of 19 March to King Maximilian I of Bavaria:

Although the present Hofgarten building would have been adequate for the purposes of accommodating the gallery transferred from Schleissheim, when Your Majesty also later moved the Mannheim and Zweibrücken collections to Munich, the present building was felt to be too small, and the administration was forced to send a great many excellent pictures out to various annexes. This important and valuable expansion of the collection has, naturally, led to a desire among art-lovers and artists to be able to see all the best paintings together in one central gallery. Your Majesty alone has the prerogative of ordaining measures to promote the flowering of the arts: namely, the construction of a museum in a classical style, in which would be assembled all the valuable and notable items from the various galleries, organized into a systematically arranged exhibition. For such a building, the following matters would have to be taken into account: choosing a site, deciding which halls should have skylights, situating small rooms on the north side, ensuring a regular temperature to permit viewing all the year round, establishing security measures and fire precautions. May Your Majesty graciously deign to accept this proposal for the building of a new gallery.

On 20 April 1822 the court architect, Leo von Klenze, was ordered to draw up plans for the new building. It was to house 226 paintings of the German school (both old and modern), 724 of the Flemish school, 44 of the French school and 306 of the Italian and Spanish schools – a total of 1,300 paintings. Klenze built a gallery in an elongated H-shape, 127 metres long and 37 metres wide. The exhibition halls were situated on the upper floor along an axis. Twenty-four small rooms were built on the north side, and on the south side a loggia with

The Alte Pinakothek in 1836

twenty-five separate doors, to allow individual access to each room, without one's having to go through the whole gallery. The great masters were displayed on the walls and ceiling of this loggia. Klenze himself explained his conception of the building:

An art gallery must be situated in an open space, protected from fire, dust and vibration. It must house under one roof every aspect of the graphic arts. It must make the right impression on visitors to put them in a suitable frame of mind; for it is intended for the whole nation, not just for artists who will be favourably disposed by their nature. The paintings must be set out chronologically in schools, but one must be able to reach each room directly, so as not to be distracted by the previous sight of other works. Large and small paintings do not mix: the large ones will overpower the small ones, while the small ones will spoil the effect of the large ones. They must be displayed separately in different halls, particularly since the large historical paintings must have roof-lighting only, while window-lighting is better for the small paintings. Roof-lighting will avoid too bright a light, while window-lighting will take advantage of the constant light from the north. Moderate heating is necessary both for the conservation of the paintings and for the visitors' comfort. Our project for the Pinakothek fulfils all these conditions in every respect.

Interior decoration →

The building will be erected in a large open space, set out with gardens, flowerbeds and fountains, and surrounded on all four sides by roads. It will have an east-west axis, one façade looking south and the other, which will have windows, to light the small paintings, looking due north.

As commanded by our most illustrious patron, the decoration of the halls housing the large paintings must be lavish, and we must therefore choose a decorative style which is at once sumptuous and grandiose but does not jeopardize the pictures. The halls and rooms of the Pitti Palace in Florence, which houses an admirable collection, offer a model in matters of proportion and ornamentation.

Work on this great project was completed as early as 1830, and on 16 October 1836 the galleries were opened to the public. Dillis wrote in a letter to Ludwig I: 'This magnificent and unparalleled monument is now completed. It bears witness to the profound passion for the arts which Your Royal Highness inspires.'

In this gallery were exhibited the greatest masterpieces from the Bavarian collections which had been built up over a period of 300 years by the dukes of the Wittelsbach family.

THE BEGINNINGS: WILHELM IV, DUKE OF BAVARIA, AND HIS SUCCESSORS

The nucleus of the Alte Pinakothek – as the visitor to Room I on the upper floor can still see today – came into being during the years 1528–40, thanks to Wilhelm IV, Duke of Bavaria from 1508 to 1550.

In 1565 the Dutch doctor and historiographer Samuel Quickelberg referred to Wilhelm IV's important commission of paintings on subjects from ancient and Biblical history as follows: 'Before I end, I must tell our illustrious art-lovers of the esteem in which great works of art were held by Duke Wilhelm IV, father of the present Duke Albrecht. By means of a kind of competition he had the best German artists produce brilliant works of art, the dimensions for which he himself proposed. Even to this day, foreign visitors, attracted to Munich by its exceptional location, view these paintings with awe and admiration.' These paintings exalt manly virtue and courage, and celebrate the great deeds of famous heroines. Albrecht Altdorfer rejected the office of Mayor of Augsburg in order to be able to paint his marvellous *Battle of Alexander* (1529). Other Augsburg artists included Hans Burgkmair, who painted *Esther and Ahasuerus* (1528) and the *Battle of Cannae* (1529), Jorg Breu the Elder, painter of the *Lucretia* (1528) and the *Battle of Zama* (around 1530), and his son Jorg Breu the Younger, among whose works is *Artemisia's Conquest of Rhodes*. Barthel Beham of Nuremberg, court painter to Wilhelm IV and to his brother Ludwig X, executed the *Invention of the Holy Cross* (1530); Melchior Feselen of Ingolstadt, the *Porsenna before Rome* (1529) and the *Caesar before Alesia* (1533). Munich painters were represented by Abraham and Hans Schöpfer, with their *Mucius Scaevola* (1533) and *Appius Claudius and Virginia*. The commission was completed by the four paintings of Ludwig Refinger: *Susanna and the Elders* (1537), *Horatius Cocles* (1537), *Marcus Curtius* (1540) and *Manlius Torquatus*.

BARTHEL BEHAM *Wilhelm IV of Bavaria*

The considerable difference in quality of the artists commissioned to paint these works shows clearly that the royal patron attached far more importance to the execution of his programme than to artistic merit.

This commission of paintings – to which must be added the now lost works depicting the *Queen of Sheba* and *Judith and Holofernes* – is in the true spirit of the Renaissance. The court humanists almost certainly had much to do with it. But not only does it reflect the Duke's humanistic tendencies, it also illustrates his feelings towards his wife Jacobäa von Baden, whom he married in 1522 when she was fifteen. Their joint coat of arms figures in the majority of these paintings, no doubt indicating their desire to eternalize the communion of their souls. Jacobäa also set up a small gallery with portraits of her ladies-in-waiting, which led Wilhelm IV to get Barthel Beham to paint a whole series of portraits of nobles. Their aim was not to create a collection of paintings in the modern sense, but rather to decorate their residential seat to make of it the kind of 'pleasure palace' described by Caesare Gracio in a letter of 13 June 1530 addressed to Mantua.

Gracio, who was among the Emperor Charles V's retinue when he was given a ceremonial welcome in Munich *en route* to the Diet of Augsburg, recounted his impressions of the clean, beautiful and busy city, its wonderful cathedral and elegant inhabitants. He described a dinner reception held in gardens outside the town and mentions in particular a house on pillars, 'built round a marvellous fountain, overlooking which are some apartments with magnificent paintings depicting hunting scenes, battles, dances and landscapes.' Contemporary admiration for these paintings, although it may seem somewhat excessive today, was shared by later generations. In 1632 the Swedes carried off a large number of them, three of which are still in Stockholm; and in 1800 the French took away Altdorfer's *Battle of Alexander*, Napoleon's favourite painting, which remained at Saint-Cloud till 1815.

Other paintings of note owned by Wilhelm IV were the portraits of himself and his wife by Hans Wertinger, Altdorfer's *Susanna* and Albrecht Dürer's *Death of Lucretia*.

But it was Wilhelm's son, Albrecht V, Duke of Bavaria from 1550 to 1579, who first took a really active interest in collecting. This was all the more surprising since his main taste was for music. He summoned to his court the famous Orlando di Lasso – with Palestrina, the most celebrated composer of the day – to conduct the royal orchestra, on which he lavished enormous sums of money. Between them, they made Munich the musical capital of Europe. In 1572, Albrecht V bowed to the admonitions and pressure of the Provincial Assembly to

HANS MUELICH *Albrecht V of Bavaria*

cut court expenditure and declared that henceforth hunting and his choir would be his sole amusements.

Albrecht's passion for art accounts for a major part of the Munich collections. He aroused such enthusiasm in the court humanists that they went to any lengths to amass all the works of art, *curiosa* and books they could find for their patron. So strong was this urge to find paintings to fill his galleries and to possess rare and precious objects that the acquisitions often did not stand up to critical examination, even at the time. But, for all that, this was not a matter taken lightly. One of the key figures in the acquisition of treasures was the banker Johann Jakob Fugger, whose father Raimund was the first great German collector of antiquities. Albrecht bought part of this collection, together with antiques, coins and the library belonging to Johann Jakob Fugger. Another figure was the renowned connoisseur and accomplished artist, Jacopo de Strada (Titian's portrait of him is in Vienna), who had helped Johann Jakob Fugger build up his collection and who was now summoned to serve at the Munich court, while continuing in the service of the Emperors Ferdinand I and Rudolf II. Albrecht's policy was, in fact, to bring to Munich not only collections of works of art, but collectors and connoisseurs as well. Also engaged was the devoted engraver and collector Hubert Goltzius. Similarly the services were procured of Samuel Quickelberg, till then superintendent of Johann Jakob Fugger's collections, and with him Fugger's librarian. Finally, in 1587 Johannes Fickler, Canon of Salzburg, entered the service of the Bavarian court, after having presented to the art gallery his extremely important coin collection.

Albrecht decided to erect a special building to house all these treasures that were streaming into Munich. The art gallery – today the Mint – was built between 1563 and 1567, and the decoration of its interior was completed in 1578. The items in this gallery were not selected by reason of their value, but were intended as specimens of the gigantic *theatrum mundi* that the collection was to be. The tract entitled *Inscriptiones vel tituli theatri amplissimi . . .*, published in 1565, shows Samuel Quickelberg's scheme of classification. The fifth and last part of this catalogue was subdivided as follows:

1. Oil paintings by great masters, all types;
2. Watercolours, arranged according to artistic value;
3. Engravings and drawings, set out in albums as in a library;
4. Schedules, historical and chronological catalogues, large geographical maps;
5. Genealogical tables of kings, dukes, counts and nobles, both printed and manuscript;

6. Portraits of illustrious men, as many as possible;
7. Coats of arms of families, counties and estates;
8. Silk, brocade and woven tapestries, hung as paintings.

This systematic arrangement of the collection, aimed at furthering knowledge of man and the universe, was fully put into effect on the completion of a second building. The rapid increase in size of the antiquities collection led to the erection of a special building to house it. The Antiquarium was built into the Munich Residenz between 1569 and 1571 by Jacopo de Strada and Wilhelm Egkl, the latter having previously designed the art gallery. In order to procure a uniform decorative effect, all the antiquities displayed there were painted yellow or black. Fifteen years later the floor of this long vaulted building was lowered to convert it into a banqueting hall.

Despite the range of Albrecht's interests as a collector – by the time he died, his library rivalled that of the Emperor – he did little to further the Alte Pinakothek. He did, however, add some portraits of famous men and a set of portraits of ladies of the court – a kind of collection of court beauties. But for the most part he contributed bizarre objects, such as the *Salvator mundi* whose eyes could be made to move by pulling a string, or paintings of notorious criminals and monsters. A good illustration of Albrecht V's attitude is the case of David Ott, agent for the Fuggers, who was dispatched to negotiate with Titian not over the latter's paintings, but merely to buy from him a glass casket which the Duke fancied.

All in all, Wilhelm IV's and Albrecht V's activities as collectors were fruitful, but they came to a halt immediately after Albrecht's death. The inclinations of his successor, Wilhelm V (the Pious), Duke from 1579 to 1597, were of a totally different nature. His main achievement was as a great builder, on behalf of the Jesuits in particular. For them he erected the Church of St Michael and its college, more like the palace of some powerful king than the dwelling of the humble followers of Jesus. All available funds were poured into this enterprise, and Wilhelm was thus prevented from making any valuable additions to the collections of his predecessors. In 1580 an annual sum of 400 florins was granted out of the budget for the acquisition of paintings, but when the Provincial Assembly voiced its objections in 1583, the grant was withdrawn. It is worth noting by way of comparison that the Duke's personal physician had an annual salary of no less than 500 florins. The Provincial Assembly normally took advantage of changes of government to get court expenditure reduced. As early as 1579, the first session of the Assembly not only deplored the money lavished by the Dukes on fashions, but even demanded a reduction in the expenses of the orchestra, as well as an end to those unfortunate purchases of bizarre, useless objects, and to the construction of buildings intended for entertainment purposes. The Duke was also advised to sell part of his art collection to help pay off state debts.

The Wittelsbach art treasures therefore remained as Albrecht V had left them. In 1595, disillusioned with power after fifteen years of rule, Wilhelm V appointed his son Maximilian as Regent, and in 1597 finally abdicated in his favour.

NICOLAUS PRUGGER *Maximilian I, Elector of Bavaria*

MAXIMILIAN I

Maximilian was Duke of Bavaria until 1651, and in 1623 was the first Bavarian ruler to become Elector. The most remarkable German ruler of his age, Maximilian stands out as one of the few people to have foreseen the political developments that led to the Thirty Years' War. He devoted all his energies to strengthening and maintaining the Catholic Church and the Empire. During the Thirty Years' War – which he was the only ruler to live through from beginning to end – he emerged as the Catholic leader and defender, a role for which the large-scale reforms carried out in his own state had well prepared him. The power of the Provincial Assembly was broken, the administration of the state was conducted in the most exemplary manner, a strong army was created, and the law was formally defined by his *Codex Maximilianus*, which was to remain in force until 1751. Although Maximilian's political activities extended all over Europe, they by no means exhausted his energies. In this young Duke – he was barely twenty-four – Bavaria found herself with a ruler who was a refined and passionate collector in all spheres, and who himself dabbled in painting and amused himself with lathe-work. In 1611 the Augsburg art-dealer Philipp Hainhofer wrote in his report to the Duke of Pomerania: 'The favourite entertainments of this duke, and the things on which he spends the most money, are good horses and stud-farms, falconry, art and painting, and lathe-work – a field in which His Highness has created some objects of remarkable beauty. Feasting and carousing, gambling, hunting, tournaments and other amusements and vain occupations hold little interest for him.'

It appears that the young Duke's natural inclinations were cultivated by the jurist and collector Johannes Fickler (mentioned above), who in 1587 accompanied him as tutor to Ingolstadt University. In the course of putting into order the affairs of state – a task made extremely necessary by the Treasury deficit, since expenditure exceeded revenue by half as much again – an inventory of the collections was drawn up. Johannes Fickler began to catalogue the contents of the art collection in February 1598. The first catalogue lists 3,407 items of all types, including 778 paintings. Due to the special nature of the collection, there were 579 portraits as against only 58 paintings of religious subjects. Only a few of these can be identified today; and it is difficult to say which of them are now in the Alte Pinakothek, since the catalogue gives no indications of measurements and for only nine items are the names of the artists given. The only work from the historical series commissioned by Wilhelm IV whose painter is explicitly mentioned is Altdorfer's *Battle of Alexander*. The present-day Pinakothek has lost most of the great series of portraits of Roman emperors, ancient poets, philosophers and heroes, Dutch women and girls, bearded virgins, madmen and dwarfs, murderers and criminals. Fickler, however, was particularly interested in these portraits, as is seen by his detailed descriptions. His lengthy entry for item number 2891 reads: 'Three paintings of the same format, one the portrait of a blood-stained murderer named Christof Froschamer, of Wangingen in the diocese of Salzburg, who perpetrated with his own hands 345 murders and in connivance with his band of criminals 400 more, condemned to death and executed in the year 1579, at Welss in Austria.'

Maximilian acquired no more of these portraits, nor did he add to the numerous curiosities in the collection, such as the boots 'of unbelievable size' of Duke Johann Friedrich of Saxony, the half skull of a satyr and the 'corn fallen from heaven' – objects still exhibited in later times. Maximilian did not share his predecessors' peculiar interest in objects for their own sake; his criteria were based on artistic value.

At the time of the great rebuilding of the Munich Residenz between 1611 and 1617, Maximilian had a private gallery built on to the stately apartments near his bedchamber. It consisted of a long rectangular room with windows on the north side. The Duke had the most valuable items from the art collections transferred to this gallery, in which were also hung his own acquisitions.

A catalogue begun in 1628 gives a good idea of what this collection contained. It lists all the antiquities, paintings and natural curiosities from the Munich collections, together with the contents of the Elector's personal collection. One hundred and seventeen paintings are listed as being in the latter, sixty-eight of which give the name of the artist. This catalogue begins, not unnaturally, with the works of Albrecht Dürer – even at this time essential items in every prince's gallery. Two rulers in particular went to any lengths to acquire paintings bearing his signature. The first was the Emperor Rudolf II: he had Dürer's *Festival of the Rose-Garlands* carried all the way from Venice to Prague on foot, by men chosen specially for their strength, so as to prevent any damage being done to it. The second, Maximilian, had no qualms about entering into competition with the Emperor. When the latter died in 1612, Maximilian doubled his efforts to acquire for Munich those paintings which Rudolf had failed to obtain himself.

For Maximilian, Dürer was the greatest painter who had ever lived. In 1614 he engaged in lengthy and unsuccessful negotiations to buy a painting by Michelangelo which he had not even seen – he attributed his failure to the fact that 'some people praise Michelangelo even more than Dürer'.

The only work of Dürer's which Maximilian had inherited was the *Death of Lucretia*. Even he found the figure of Lucretia too sparsely clad, and in 1600 additions to the drapery around her body were made. This did not, however, prevent scandal. But Maximilian was so determined to keep this painting in his private gallery that he resorted to the following device. A catalogue of the paintings compiled around 1608–13 has the entry: 'Cato Uticensis by Petro Candido, and when removed, beneath this the nude Lucretia by Albrecht Dürer'. And the next catalogue, begun in 1628, reads: 'Lucretia, life-size, by Lucas Cranach; when this is removed, beneath it is Lucretia, nude, painted by Albrecht Dürer in the year 1518.'

In 1500, Dürer had painted a *Lamentation* for the Nuremberg goldsmith Albrecht Glimm, as we learn from Neudorffer's account of 1546: 'Dürer was on good terms with Glimm and executed for him a fine oil painting which Glimm had hung in the Dominican church, on the pillar to the right of the pulpit, for his own salvation and in memory of his two deceased wives.' This work, which had in the meantime passed into the hands of the important Imhoff family at Nuremberg, had been suggested as a possible purchase to Rudolf II in 1588 Maximilian's earliest efforts were directed towards obtaining this picture, efforts which were eventually successful when he agreed to pay 1000 florins. The painting was speedily transported to Munich.

Maximilian let some time pass before approaching the town council of Nuremberg on 30 September 1612 on the matter of acquiring the *Paumgartner Altarpiece*, at the same time asking for any other paintings by Dürer there might be in the town. He confirmed his request with letters to the Mayor of Nuremberg, Löffelholz, and the councillor Unterholzer. Without giving the council time to consider, Maximilian wrote again on 4 October repeating his request. This put the town in a difficult position. The council replied that, firstly, this altarpiece was the last one left in Nuremberg, and that it was virtually impossible to trace any other works of Dürer's in the town; and secondly, the Emperor Rudolf II had made the same request in 1596 and had been catagorically refused. However, the political situation had now changed, and they could no longer afford to reject outright the demands of such a powerful neighbour as the head of the Catholic League. The council therefore agreed to present the Duke with the centre panel of the altarpiece, after having a copy made, thereby hoping to be able to keep at least the two wings. With his letter of thanks the Duke enclosed a set of gilt goblets for the Mayor, a writing-desk for Unterholzer and a gift of money for the donors, Georg and Nikolaus Paumgartner. But he also insisted that he be sent the wings which he was not prepared to let escape him. This created an embarrassing situation for the town council, who ordered Unterholzer to write to the Duke explaining that these panels were badly painted, not by Dürer, and that it was not worth the trouble to transport them to Munich. Maximilian, however, saw through this excuse, and in March 1613 the complete altarpiece duly arrived at Munich. The Duke had the centre panel, the *Nativity*, hung with the religious works in his collection, and the wings with the secular works.

DÜRER *The Heller Altarpiece*, copy. Historisches Museum, Frankfurt-am-Main

After this success, the Duke next cast his net on a work for which Rudolf had in vain offered 10,000 florins. This painting is the one listed first in the catalogue of the gallery: 'Firstly, the world-famous painting of Albrecht Dürer, the *Assumption* or *Coronation of the Virgin*. For many years the property of the Frankfurt Dominicans, viewed by emperors, kings and potentates; acquired by His Highness in 1614 after considerable effort and expense. Its place on the Frankfurt altar was taken by a copy skilfully executed by a Nuremberg painter. So unmistakable is the excellence of this painting that it has not been thought necessary to give it a number in the catalogue.' Dürer had painted this altarpiece for the Frankfurt merchant Jakob Heller. On its completion in 1509, it was installed in the Dominican church. Although Dürer received a fee of only 200 florins for this work, he preferred to see it exhibited in Frankfurt rather than elsewhere. Frankfurt was the city of coronations and fairs, and his work would be admired there by far more people than it could ever hope to attract anywhere else. A century later, Karel van Mander wrote in his *Schilder-Boeck*: 'It is astonishing, almost unbelievable, how much money this altarpiece brings in annually to the monks of the monastery, just from the donations made by generous nobles, merchants, travellers and art-lovers.'

The negotiations to obtain the central panel of the altarpiece dragged on from the summer of 1613. But the Frankfurt Dominicans could no more oppose the wishes of the Duke of Bavaria than could the town of Nuremberg. In September, a painter was sent from Nuremberg to Frankfurt with a panel, ready to complete a copy of the altarpiece within six months. The original was sent off on 25 September 1614, and was acknowledged by Maximilian on the 20th. Once more, a work for which offers of vast sums had been refused arrived in Munich as a gift. In return, the Duke offered the monastery an annual pension of 400 florins, with the additional provision that the monks should say one mass every day for his soul. But by 1642 the monks were already complaining that they had not received his pension for years. This masterpiece of Dürer's and a Raphael *Madonna* were tragically lost in the 1729 fire at the Residenz.

Having succeeded in acquiring the *Paumgarten Altarpiece* in 1613 while still a mere duke, Maximilian set his sights even higher when he became Elector. What he had his eye on now were the famous *Four Apostles* which Dürer had a hundred years before presented to his native town to hang in the town hall. Nuremberg had rewarded Dürer's generosity with a gift of 100 florins, plus 12 florins for his wife and 2 for his servant. In June 1627, the Elector's chamberlain and steward, Augustin Haimbl, went to Nuremberg to start negotiations for the *Four Apostles*. He was advanced the huge sum of 1000 thalers by the Bavarian treasury – proof of Maximilian's eagerness. The Nuremberg council understood this immediately, having learnt from bitter experience what Maximilian's designs were. The town was at the time in a difficult position owing to the Thirty Years' War, as is shown by the factors taken into account in reaching a decision: 'If the Catholic side were to decide to take some action against Nuremberg, His Highness would not support us just because we had given him some paintings. But, on the other hand, we must accept the fact that Nuremberg and its citizens depend greatly on Bavaria and the Upper Palatinate for food supplies and trade, since the main trade routes to France and Italy pass through their territory – it is well known what difficulties Regensburg experienced in its relations with Bavaria.'

The town's legal adviser, Doctor Oelhafen, was instructed to draw up a report elaborating the points justifying the surrender of the paintings.

Concern, however, for the property of Nuremberg and its inhabitants, for which trade outlets were absolutely vital, finally tilted the balance. Both originals and copies were swiftly dispatched to Munich, with no financial conditions attached. But Maximilian, being the collector and connoisseur that he was, quickly dashed the town's hopes that he might prefer the copies. Even the inscriptions, which they had done their best to interpret as an expression of Protestantism, did not deter him. (Incidentally, there is still discussion today as to whether these inscriptions are pro-Protestant or pro-Catholic.) The Elector simply had them sawn off – they were then carefully attached to the copies and sent back to Nuremberg. The inscriptions were reunited with the originals only in 1922 when they were acquired by the Pinakothek together with the original frames.

The Elector did all he could to keep his promise to protect Nuremberg. He ordered the Bavarian troops, sent as reinforcements to General Tilly, to keep out of Nuremberg territory. But for all his promises, he could not prevent the town's falling victim to the atrocities of war when it was taken by the Swedes. Nuremberg tried to change its tactics for political reasons, and offered the Duke several more original works by Dürer, even going to the extent of buying two paintings from Florence in order to be able to offer them to Maximilian. In compensation, they demanded to be exempted from billeting imperial troops, hoping thus to preserve the free flow of trade through Bavarian territory. There was indeed good reason to fear that, with the outbreak of plague at Nuremberg, her goods might be sent back or forced to take a different route.

Maximilian had an astonishing flair for tracking down paintings. He made use of the stationing of imperial troops in central and north Germany to help him acquire new treasures for his gallery, a task in which he enlisted the aid of Generals Tilly, Aldringen and Pappenheim and of their counterparts stationed in Bavaria. On 31 July 1627 he wrote to Tilly: 'We have been told that in the Frauenkirche at Stendel in the Mark of Brandenburg there hangs behind the organ an altarpiece with two wings, depicting St Jerome, painted by Albrecht Dürer in 1511.' The generals, not surprisingly, succeeded in taking possession of the altarpiece. It was dispatched with a supply train to Munich, where it unfortunately never arrived.

The officers were supplied not just with general instructions, but with detailed suggestions: 'Near Berlin, in the neighbourhood of Bernau, Landsperg and Leibenwalde, is a place called Marzahn. The church here has a painting on wood of the Virgin and Child with Joseph, of which the painter's name has for the time being slipped our memory. This painting is hidden in a long, tall cupboard like a wardrobe, in which are kept the surplices and church ornaments. This cupboard has a false bottom, beneath which the painting was hidden lest the late Margrave von Jagerndorff should carry it off.'

There is not time here to go into detail over all the Duke's efforts to acquire works of Dürer. The final catalogue of his gallery listed eleven paintings by Dürer, including two which, together with the ones mentioned above, are still in the Alte Pinakothek: the *Virgin with the Carnation* and *Hercules and the Birds of Stymphalus* (on loan to the Germanisches Nationalmuseum at Nuremberg).

Maximilian's interest in other German masters was, to say the least, lukewarm compared with his passion for Dürer. He bought only four works of Cranach, although this painter had a great reputation in the sixteenth and seventeenth centuries. Augsburg painters were well represented in the collection: Burgkmair with his *St John Altarpiece* and a small *Virgin* (on loan to the Germanisches Nationalmuseum, Nuremberg), Ulrich Apt with paintings now in Windsor Castle and the Louvre, and Hans Holbein the Elder with his *Fountain of Life* (now in Lisbon). Hans Holbein the Younger is absent from the collection, probably because portraits, except for those of former Bavarian rulers, were excluded from the programme of acquisitions. Most of the works of German masters listed in the catalogue were, in fact, taken from the old art collection.

There were only five paintings from the Italian school, including the Raphael *Madonna* lost in the fire of 1729. Of these, only one is still in the Alte Pinakothek: Bedoli's *Virgin and Child with St Bruno*. There is also evidence of an attempt to acquire a *Holy Family* attributed to Michelangelo (see above). The Duke was put off by the muddled negotiations, and since a higher price was demanded each time, he eventually decided that the painting was not worth the trouble – it may have been a Michelangelo or a Raphael, but to him it was 'just a board coated with paint'. In the spring of 1630, he was offered a Correggio and a Titian by the Mayor of Nuremberg, Holzschuher – who had been instrumental in the Duke's acquisition of the *Four Apostles*. Each of these works must have been worth something like 1000 florins. But Maximilian refused to enter into negotiations since (so he said) the painting attributed to Correggio had been in Munich for a long time and he would not have it even for 100 florins; furthermore, he thought the price asked for the Titian equally excessive.

More attention was given to the acquisition of Dutch and particularly Flemish works. These still form the basis of the Munich collection today. The principal intermediaries in these acquisitions were Maximilian's uncle, Bishop Ernst of Liège, Elector of Cologne, and Maximilian's brother Ferdinand, also an Elector of Cologne. Works acquired included the Lucas van Leyden diptych, which Van Mander mentions as still being in Rudolf II's collection in 1604, an *Adoration* by an Antwerp mannerist, Engelbrechtsen's *St Constantine and St Helena*, the *St John the Baptist Preaching* by Swart van Groeningen, and the *Money Changer* by Marinus van Reymerswaele. Later additions were Willem Key's famous *Lamentation* (then attributed to Quentin Massys), Vincent Sellaer's *Suffer the Little Children to Come unto Me*, the Elder Jan Bruegel's *Jonah emerging from the Whale*, and four paintings by Jan Sanders van Hemessen, one of which, *Isaac blessing Jacob*, is still in the Alte Pinakothek.

The inclusion of Jan Bruegel shows that the Duke was not wholly indifferent to the painting of his own time. Maximilian was also eager to acquire some works of Rubens. His own brother-in-law, Wolfgang Wilhelm of Pfalz-Neuburg, and his uncle, Elector Ernst of Cologne, had previously commissioned works by Rubens (including the five great altarpieces from the Jesuit church at Neuburg and from Freising Cathedral which are all still in the Alte Pinakothek), and Maximilian must have seen these works. A letter from Rubens to Sir Dudley Carleton, British Ambassador at The Hague, informs us that the former's *Lion Hunt* had been dispatched to Maximilian some time before 1618. At roughly the same time, Munich also acquired three other hunting scenes by Rubens, two of which were mentioned by Joachim von Sandrart, the seventeenth-century art historian, as being in the old castle at Schleissheim in 1675. The *Lion Hunt* and *Hippopotamus Hunt* are still in the Alte Pinakothek, but the other two were carried off by the French in 1800. The *Tiger and Leopard Hunt* was lost in a fire at Bordeaux, and the *Wild Boar Hunt* is now in the Marseilles Museum. Maximilian's acquisitions of contemporary German paintings included three works by a friend of Rubens, Adam Elsheimer: *Flight into Egypt*, the *Burning of Troy* and *St John the Baptist Preaching* (this work now lost). Sandrart was also given some important commissions, such as his set of *Twelve Months*.

This enormous burst of collecting came to an abrupt halt in May 1632 when the Swedes occupied Munich. On the town's surrender, it paid out the vast sum of 300,000 thalers to secure a guarantee from the conquerors that they would vouchsafe the safety of private property. But despite this guarantee, the art collection, except what had been hidden, was ransacked. In this pillage, Duke Ernst the Pious of Saxe-Weimar showed his good taste by taking as booty paintings by Amberger and Beham, statuettes by Konrad Meit, and medals inscribed by Jacopo de Strada, among other works – these are still to be seen at Gotha today. The Elector complained bitterly about this pillaging of his collection, which had occurred 'in blatant contradiction to the formal text of the Munich agreements, and against the King's word'. His counsellors told him the extent of the damage; except for a few objects of little value, almost every item had been either ripped, torn down or hacked to pieces. As early as June, measures were already being taken to recover the objects lost. Lists were compiled and circulated, and the whole population was questioned.

The list, which is incomplete, names twenty-five paintings, only five of which were recovered, despite the co-operation of the citizens of Augsburg, Nuremberg, Ulm and Frankfurt. These included Burgkmair's *St John Altarpiece*, Feselen's *Caesar before Alesia* and Hemessen's *Isaac blessing Jacob*. Much later, quite recently in fact, three panels from Wilhelm IV's historical series were successfully recovered. Three other paintings from this series and a Cranach are now in the Stockholm National Museum. Muelich's *Entombment* hangs over a tomb in Solna Church, near Stockholm, while Holbein's *Fountain of Life* is in the Lisbon National Museum, and two wings of Ulrich Apt's altarpiece are now in Karlsruhe and in the Louvre.

This tragic blow, together with the continuing war and financial difficulties, obliged the Elector to forsake his love of collecting works of art. The political conditions which Maximilian had used so well to help him in his acquisitions now, ironically, forced him to abandon all outside interests and to devote himself exclusively to politics.

VIVIEN *Maximilian II(Emanuel), Elector of Bavaria*

MAXIMILIAN II (EMANUEL)

The next Elector of Bavaria, Ferdinand Maria, was totally overshadowed by his famous father. Duke from 1651 to 1679, he emerged from his mother's tutelage only to fall completely under the influence of his wife, the ambitious Adelaide of Savoy. He made scarcely a decision that could be called his own. Italian architects and musicians came to the Munich court, and the court painters included artists from Italy and France. The Munich Residenz was given over to extravagance and ostentation: opera, ballet, masquerades and tournaments, frivolities all spurned by his father, now figured as the Elector's favourite pastimes. An opera house was built, as well as a tournament hall with a capacity of several thousand. The basis of Ferdinand Maria's artistic activity was his sumptous decoration of the Residenz and the building of the Nymphenburg and the Theatinerkirche. From the little information we have he does not appear to have had much interest in collecting, though the decoration of the Residenz and the Elector's country palaces at Nymphenburg and Schleissheim did involve acquiring some paintings. In 1665, a Munich Carmelite friar spent some time in Venice investigating the possibility of buying paintings for the Elector. We do not know the outcome of this mission, but the catalogue of the old castle at Schleissheim, compiled in 1678 and revised in 1692, includes names such as Carracci, Bassano and Veronese, and one can presume that a considerable number of Italian paintings were brought to Munich for Ferdinand Maria and his wife Adelaide.

Although we cannot know today how valuable these acquisitions were, we can be certain that the artistic activity which had grown up at Munich over the previous thirty years of peace was a basic factor in what had become one of the most lavish courts in Europe. It was in this environment that Maximilian Emanuel, who was to become Duke in 1679, grew up. It was he who made Munich the most civilized and sumptuous capital in Germany. Unlike his father, who had managed to avoid any political involvement, Maximilian Emanuel threw himself, and his country, into the midst of the great European upheavals of the time. The political climate seemed favourable for the realization of the most ambitious of schemes. The impending rivalry between the Habsburg and Bourbon houses made both sides court the young Duke's favour. Louis XIV asked the hand of the Elector's sister, Maria Anna, for the Dauphin, and planned a match between the Elector himself and the daughter of the Duke of Orléans. But Maximilian Emanuel eventually came to side with the Emperor, with whom he concluded a defence treaty in 1683. From then until 1688, he campaigned successfully as a general of the imperial army against the Turks, and in 1696–97 against France as Commander-in-Chief, in the dispute over possession of the Palatinate. The Emperor Leopold I linked him permanently to his house by marrying him to his daughter Maria Antonie in 1685, on the condition, however, that she renounce her claim to the dual crowns of Austria and Spain, and that she and her husband inherit only the Spanish possessions in the Low Countries. Maximilian Emanuel became Governor of these in 1691, and subsequently spent his winter months in Brussels, apart from visits to the carnival celebrations in Venice.

The period of his governorship of the Low Countries, which lasted until 1701, was of the greatest importance for the Bavarian art collections. Endowed with powers little less than royal, and with considerable though not unlimited funds behind him, Maximilian Emanuel pursued his natural inclinations by lavishing incredible sums on spectacle and display. His ambitions rose still higher when his son Joseph Ferdinand was appointed heir to the Spanish throne. The great palace of Schleissheim was begun in 1684 to house Maximilian Emanuel's treasures in a gallery to rival the richest in Europe. Maximilian Emanuel became Governor of the Low Countries at a time when the traditions of the Flemish school were still alive and the decorative arts flourishing. And, of course, Brussels and Antwerp were trading centres for works of art, jewels and curiosities from other continents. In the Low Countries, Maximilian Emanuel became a generous patron and a great collector. During this troubled period, many valuable works of art came on the market, and the Duke went after them without a second thought.

He bought items of all kinds in vast quantities and often overstepped his financial means. To continue his purchases, he had to borrow money by pawning objects already bought. At Amsterdam, for example, a gold dinner service was traded in for the amazing sum of 450,000 florins. Maximilian Emanuel did not give his purchases much thought. The Marquis de Sassenage gives an account in his *Memoirs* of a hunting expedition with Maximilian during which, finding themselves in Antwerp, the Duke bought, on the spur of the moment, paintings to the value of 200,000 francs, works which the Marquis thought experts would have valued at under 100,000 francs. The Duke's generosity towards artists is shown by the tax exemption which he accorded the painters' guild. As a mark of gratitude, the Guild of St Luke in 1694 erected a marble bust of Maximilian Emanuel, the work of Willem Kerricx, in their great hall – this bust is today in the Antwerp Museum. Maximilian Emanuel was also an assiduous visitor to great antique-dealers such as Lemens at Brussels, Van Soest and Del Campo at Antwerp and Wisen at Rotterdam, dealers who supplied all Europe with precious objects.

Maximilian Emanuel's largest purchase was made on 17 September 1698, when he bought from the Antwerp dealer Gisbert van Ceulen a total of 101 paintings for the sum of 90,000 florins. Once again, the Duke did not have enough money to pay the sum, having only 60,000 florins at his disposal. Not until 1774 were these paintings finally paid for.

A list of 1763 accompanying a request for payment mentions twelve works of Rubens, including the *Return of Diana from the Hunt* (in Darmstadt since 1819), *Hélène Fourment in her Wedding Dress*, *Hélène Fourment putting on a Glove*, *Hélène Fourment with her eldest son Frans* and the *Polder Landscape*; thirteen works of Van Dyck, including the portrait of *Charles I on Horseback* (now in the National Gallery, London), and portraits of Colyn de Nole, Jan de Wael and Heinrich

Liberti; eight paintings by Brouwer; four by Claude Lorraine; ten by Jan Bruegel; five by Wouwerman; plus still-life paintings by Snyders, Fyt, Boel, De Vos, De Heem; and other works such as Murillo's *Beggar-Boys playing Dice*.

While at Brussels, Maximilian Emanuel maintained close links with Paris. From there, he had sent to him, in particular, marquetry work, furniture, and objects from the Far East. He was an avid collector of porcelain, and in 1693 installed in his Munich Residenz the first porcelain collection in Germany. The Paris dealer Danet supplied him with new works by Poussin, Mignon, and Teniers, as well as bronzes, chandeliers, furniture, rings, buttons, walking-stick handles, and diamond hat- and shoe-buckles, not to mention a commission of several portraits from Vivien.

His close artistic links with Paris paralleled his political links with France. In 1692, on the death of his son Joseph Ferdinand, Bavaria lost its claim to the Spanish throne, which now fell to the grandson of Louis XIV. By way of compensation, Maximilian Emanuel concluded an agreement with France whereby he was guaranteed hereditary sovereign rights to the Low Countries, and French support for claims to the imperial crown. But with the War of the Spanish Succession all his hopes were dashed. In 1701, Maximilian Emanuel was expelled from Munich, where he was at the time, and returned to Brussels as Governor. In 1706 he was banished from the Empire, and could consider himself fortunate to find asylum in one of Louis XIV's palaces. In exile, reduced to the meagre income granted him by the French, his position was a difficult one, becoming critical when, in 1710, the banker Bombarda cancelled his credit. Even in such straits, Maximilian Emanuel continued to surround himself with at least some French artists and craftsmen.

The news from Munich was scarcely more cheering. Maximilian Emanuel complained in a letter of 27 March 1708 to his second wife Therese Kunigunde, daughter of Jan Sobieski, King of Poland: 'I am no longer in a position to be able to think of buying paintings... Besides, when I think of how my beautiful collection in Munich was pillaged, I have no desire to.' Fortunately, it is not true to say that

Munich was pillaged. In 1706, John Churchill, first Duke of Marlborough, not content with receiving the Duchy of Mindelheim in Bavaria and the Viceroyalty of the Low Countries, asked the Emperor to give him some paintings from the Munich collection, in token of his gratitude. He was particularly attracted by Van Dyck's *Portrait of Charles I*. After making forceful demands, Marlborough obtained not only the Van Dyck portrait but also Rubens' *Mars and Venus*, *Lot and his Daughter*, *Venus and Adonis* and a Tintoretto *Last Judgment*. Further demands on his part were, however, refused and no other damage was done to the collection.

The Treaty of Rastatt of 1714 reinstated Maximilian Emanuel as ruler of Bavaria. One of the first things he did on his return was to order the interrupted work on the building of Schleissheim and the Nymphenburg to be started again. Nothing ever broke his nerve; he never relinquished his political dreams or his love of collecting – even with his debts mounting to thirty million florins.

Contemporary sources tell us little about Maximilian Emanuel's acquisitions. Father Pierre de Bretagne said in 1722 that the greatest connoisseurs of the time considered the Munich collections to be the largest, richest and most magnificent in all Europe. The Schloss Schleissheim collection must, indeed, have been an impressive sight in its opulence and splendour. It housed all the magnificent paintings bought from Gisbert van Ceulen, as well as Titian's *Portrait of Charles V*, seven works of Veronese, Rubens' *Portrait of Jan Brandt*, *Return of Diana*, *Mars crowned by Victory*, and *The young Jesus and St John the Baptist*, portraits by Van Dyck, and works by Seghers, Snyders and Boeckhorst. The Duke's preference for Dutch and Flemish painting is shown by the two paintings which hung in his bedchamber: Rubens' *Massacre of the Innocents* and Van Dyck's *Rest on the Flight to Egypt*. The Munich Residenz, the Nymphenburg and other palaces also housed splendid treasures; such was the magnificent heritage which, despite all the political upheavals, Maximilian Emanuel bequeathed to his successors on his death in 1726.

His son, Karl Albrecht, who ruled from 1726 to 1745, did not share his father's great passion for collecting paintings. His interests were in the luxuries of court life and the construction of elegant buildings, as is shown by the lavishly decorated apartments and the Green Gallery of the Munich Residenz, and the palace of Amalienburg. The post of gallery-inspector, created by Maximilian Emanuel for the court painter Domenique Nollet, was soon dissolved as an economy measure. Contemporary documents tell us nothing of Karl Albrecht's acquisitions, except for the purchase in 1733 of the collection of paintings of Baron Malknecht von Muhlegg, for the sum of 12,000 florins. This acquisition was estimated to be worth 35,000 florins. Unfortunately, we do not know the details of its contents, but it must have consisted chiefly of Dutch and Flemish works, following the taste of Maximilian Emanuel.

The Duke's collection suffered several losses in the fire of 1729. The Elector described this terrible event in an entry in his diary: 'On 22 December 1729 at 6 a.m., a dreadful fire broke out in the newly-built apartments of the Residenz. Three rooms were completely destroyed, the family jewels were only just rescued in time, and the whole collection of bronzes was lost together with the castings, most of which melted, although some are still recognizable. Albrecht Dürer's finest paintings, including his greatest masterpiece, were lost, as were several beautiful ivories, the porcelain and, what most upsets me, the ivory casket decorated by my father Maximilian Emanuel's own hand; the universally admired Raphael *Madonna* could not be rescued from the bedchamber – this is the greatest loss caused by the fire. Thanks be to God that the family's jewels were saved and that the whole palace was not burnt down.'

Karl Albrecht continued with the unhappy politics of his father, and was thus unable to make any significant additions to the collection. He succeeded in getting himself crowned German Emperor, under the name of Karl VII, but was later expelled from Bavaria and forced to live in exile in Frankfurt. He returned to Munich only three months before his death.

When in 1745 Maximilian III (Joseph) became head of state, debts had risen to the level of forty million florins. This enormous financial deficit meant that the acquisition of valuable paintings was out of the question. But a systematic arrangement of the existing treasures was made, according to the ideas of the time, for cultural and educational purposes. At the same time, the Academy of Sciences and the Academy of Arts were founded.

A catalogue compiled for the Schleissheim gallery stated that not only were a hundred items missing, but that those paintings that had not been lost, through negligence, suffered damage amounting to 30,000 florins. This unpleasant discovery led to the revival of the post of gallery-inspector, offered to the painter Balthasar Augustin Albrecht. Just how necessary this post had become can be seen from the number of paintings now in the collection: 925 at Schleissheim, 307 at Nymphenburg, approximately 550 at Dachau, roughly 700 in the Munich Residenz, 194 at Lichtenberg and 170 at Schwaige Laufzorn, not to mention those scattered in all the smaller palaces. Albrecht was succeeded in this post by Johann Nepomuk Edler von Weizenfeld, whose qualifications for the post were questioned since he had previously been in charge of the palace linen. It is to Weizenfeld, however, that we owe the first *Description of the gallery of paintings of the Elector at Schleissheim*, printed and published in 1775, and listing 1,050 paintings. This figure means that the collection must have been growing steadily. In 1760, Maximilian III bought five paintings from the Chancellor of the Exchequer, Dufresne, for the sum of 750 florins, including Bruegel's *Four Elements*. Some valuable works entered the collection in 1768 with Dufresne's bequest, which included Murillo's *Domestic Toilet* and *Little Fruit-Seller*, Rubens' *Susanna and the Elders*, and the *Portrait of the Van Dyck Family*, a large painting by an unknown Flemish painter of about 1630, then attributed to Frans Hals.

THE PALATINE COLLECTIONS

On the death of the Elector Maximilian III in 1777, the Bavarian House of Wittelsbach came to an end. To avoid new dynastic conflict, Karl Theodor, Elector Palatine, was hastily married into the family and assumed joint rule over Bavaria and the Palatinate. Having resided at Mannheim since 1742, he now moved his capital to Munich. The direct result of this new succession was an enormous increase in the riches of the Bavarian collections, since the Mannheim and Düsseldorf galleries were now added to the Munich collection. This amalgamation did not take place immediately, for the new Regent still preferred Mannheim to his new official residence. In Mannheim he had greatly contributed to progress in science and the arts. In 1763 the Academia Teodoro Palatina was founded (Lessing was one of its members), and in 1775 the Deutsche Gesellschaft, which was instrumental in the establishment of the first German national theatre. In 1757 an academy of arts was set up, and in 1758 a collection of engravings which formed the nucleus of the present Munich Staatliche Graphische Sammlung. A collection of antiquities and plaster casts, largely transferred from Düsseldorf, was similarly established – this collection was, incidentally, a source of inspiration for Goethe and Lessing.

Karl Theodor undertook to play this role of enlightened prince in Munich too. In 1780–81 he had Lespilliez erect the first building designed specifically as a gallery – the Hofgartengalerie. To it were transferred the most valuable paintings from Schleissheim, Nymphenburg and the Residenz. Seven hundred paintings were displayed in eight halls, arranged for the first time in accordance not only with aesthetic but with historical considerations as well. The decisive step had been taken towards converting what had up to now been the court

POMPEO BATONI *The Elector Karl Theodor*

art collection into a public gallery. Rittershausen wrote in his *Vornehmsten Merkwürdigkeiten der Residenzstadt München* (*Most Notable Sights in the Capital of Munich*) of 1788: 'It is wonderful to see so many young scholars, both men and women, at work in this gallery. Everyone is delighted that it is now open to the public; Theodor could not have set up in the whole of Bavaria a more worthy monument to the arts.'

The nature of the collection was not changed by the new acquisitions, for Karl Theodor shared his predecessors' taste for Dutch and Flemish paintings. New additions included landscapes by Van Goyen, Everdingen, Hobbema and D'Artois, a still-life by Pieter Claesz, and Pieter Janssens' *Woman Reading*, then attributed to Pieter de Hooch.

The Elector moved his Mannheim gallery to Munich some years before his death in 1799, the threat of a French occupation of Mannheim at the time leaving him no alternative. The Mannheim gallery had been first set up by the Elector Palatine Karl Philipp, who came to power in 1716 on the death of his brother Johann Wilhelm. He moved the Palatine capital from Düsseldorf to Mannheim, where he died in 1742. Karl Philipp likewise had a preference for Dutch and Flemish painting. The first catalogue of the gallery in 1756 lists over 200 items, including great names such as Rembrandt and Rubens. Many of these works were not acquired by Karl Philipp but came from Düsseldorf, for example, Rembrandt's *Erection of the Cross* and *Descent from the Cross*. His chief agents were the court architect, Nicolas de Pigage, and the painter Lambert Krahe. The latter, a native of Düsseldorf, was given commissions and bursaries by the Elector, as well as the directorship of the Düsseldorf gallery in 1756. Krahe was himself a great collector, and his treasures were bought by the Berg Assembly to form the nucleus of the Düsseldorf print collection. Krahe was responsible for the acquisition of Rembrandt's *Abraham's Sacrifice*, which he had originally bought for himself in 1760 at Amsterdam. He had at the same time also bought Rembrandt's *Holy Family* for the Elector, at the price of 1,600 florins but he was always careful to present himself as a private collector. Krahe also bought paintings at auctions. We know of five works acquired in this way at Amsterdam in 1761: they are described by Krahe as 'a large journey on a calm sea by J. de Capelle;

FRANS DOUVEN *The Elector Palatine Johann Wilhelm*

a sea storm by Backhuisen; a return from the hunt by Michelangelo delle Battaglie; a banquet with figures by Aelbert Cuyp; and a family group with three figures, life-size, of Willaerts.

The catalogue compiled when the Mannheim gallery was moved to Munich gives a final figure of 758 paintings. Besides the Rembrandts mentioned above, these included Aert de Gelder's *Jewish Bride* (bought at an Amsterdam auction in 1749), portraits by Ravesteyn, Verspronck and Nicolaes Maes, landscapes by Aelbert Cuyp, Adriaen van de Velde and Jan van der Heyden, peasant scenes by Van Ostade and Jan Steen, Ter Borch's *Boy picking Fleas from a Dog*, still-life paintings by Van Beyeren, Jan van Huysum and Rachel Ruysch, genre paintings by Gerard Dou, Mieris and Netscher, and Karel Dujardin's *Sick Goat* (also bought at an auction in 1789). Of the Flemish paintings we need only mention a few: Rubens' *Pastoral Scene* and *Portrait of a Young Man with a Cap*; Van Dyck's *Martyrdom of St Sebastian* and *Portrait of Snayers*; four paintings by Brouwer; and several works of Jan Bruegel and Hendrick van Balen. German paintings included, among others, Hans Holbein the Younger's *Portrait of Derich Born*, Elsheimer's *Burning of Troy*, and Rottenhammer's *Last Judgment* and *Wedding at Cana*. The Italian and Spanish schools were represented by two paintings by Giordano Bruno, two by Cavallino, a large Magnasco, Zurbarán's *St Francis of Assisi* and Murillo's *Pie-Eaters*.

The Düsseldorf gallery was smaller than the one at Mannheim, with only 384 paintings, but in quality it was one of the richest in Europe, with masterpieces by Rembrandt, Rubens and Van Dyck. It had originally been founded by Johann Wilhelm, Elector Palatine from 1690 to 1716, and the only one to make Düsseldorf his permanent capital. His energy and love of art were responsible for the Düsseldorf collection, whose reputation almost eclipsed that of all the other eighteenth-century German collections. In 1678, on his first marriage, Johann Wilhelm became ruler of the Duchies of Jülich and Berg, and rapidly proceeded to make his first acquisitions, despite the limited funds available to him, particularly later with the destruction of the Palatinate and Heidelberg, and the War of the Spanish Succession. Their ruler's artistic aspirations were viewed with dismay by the Provincial Assembly, and his councillors also reproached him for excessive expenditure – an act which provoked Johann Wilhelm to call them 'a load of asses and idiots'. These reprimands suggest that vast sums were spent, but, in fact, if Johann Wilhelm set to work as energetically as did Maximilian Emanuel in his time, he also exercised a great deal more caution.

His first agent was the court painter Jan Frans Douven, summoned to Düsseldorf in 1682. It is said that it was he who first awoke this passion for collecting in Johann Wilhelm. Douven was offered Rubens' *Battle of the Amazons*, but the Elector would not even look at it. So Douven had it secretly installed in the Elector's chamber; Johann Wilhelm was so entranced by it that he bought it. He then sent Douven to the Netherlands to try to acquire all the works of Rubens he could find. We know that Douven negotiated the sale of some paintings in Brussels in 1684, but Johann Wilhelm postponed the matter, funds not being available until January 1685. At the 1684 Amsterdam auction of the Earl of Arundel's collection, the Elector acquired Rubens' *Portrait of a Franciscan* for 39 florins. Other works were later bought at auctions, such as Carl Loth's *Death of Seneca*, purchased in 1693 for 121 florins. In addition to his diplomatic representatives and agents in all the important towns of Europe, Johann Wilhelm also made particular use of his family ties in adding to his collection. In 1691 he took as second wife Anna Maria Ludovica, daughter of Cosimo III of Tuscany. Her dowry included Raphael's *Canigiani Holy Family* and Andrea del Sarto's *Holy Family*. In the following years, further exchanges of gifts took place between the courts of Florence and Düsseldorf, partly for political reasons. Horses and falcons, wine, marbles, plaster casts and paintings crossed the Alps in both directions.

These family ties with Italy brought to Munich the altarpiece Rubens had painted for the Elector's grandfather, Wolfgang Wilhelm von Pfalz-Neuburg. In 1690 the Elector claimed Rubens' *Last Judgment*, which hung over the high altar of the Jesuit church in Neuburg, but had since 1653 been covered by another painting because its nude figures were considered indecent. When the Neuburg Jesuits refused his demand, the Elector turned to Rome, where his case was taken up by Cardinal Francesco Maria Medici. The matter was speedily resolved, on condition that the Elector provide Neuburg with a substitute painting of the same value. He therefore commissioned Cignani to paint an *Assumption of the Virgin*, but he liked the painting so much that he kept it for his own collection. His failure to supply the Jesuits with a substitute painting did not deter him from demanding from them two other altarpieces in 1700. Negotiations were protracted, and in May 1703 Johann Wilhelm finally used the War of the Spanish Succession as an excuse to demand the immediate surrender of the altarpieces. The Jesuits had to give in, but their fears were justified; neither Johann Wilhelm nor his successor, Karl Philipp, had settled the debt when the Jesuit Order was suppressed in 1773.

At the same time as his negotiations with the Neuburg Jesuits, Johann Wilhelm also tried to obtain paintings from churches in Liège. He had no difficulty in acquiring two works of Gerard Douffet, but the Franciscans would not relinquish Douffet's portrait of *Pope Nicholas V at Assisi*. Negotiations dragged on from 1701. When in May 1704, the Franciscans finally yielded under pressure from Rome, they did at least escape the fate of the Neuburg Jesuits – the remaining half of the price still due was paid to them by means of taxes levied in Liège.

In 1711 the Elector had less difficulty in purchasing two works by Rubens belonging to the Church of Notre Dame de la Chapelle in Brussels: the *Assumption of the Virgin* (later hung at Düsseldorf because of its size) and the *Martyrdom of St Lawrence*. In 1693, the church had suffered war damage, and the community was obliged to sell off its paintings in order to raise funds for the restoration of the building. Johann Wilhelm paid 4,000 florins for these works, but, yet again, forgot to supply the promised copies.

In 1690, one of the Elector's sisters married Carlos II, King of Spain. This opened up new possibilities of adding to his collection by means of exchanges of gifts. The Elector tried to use the Queen's confessor as intermediary, but the latter pleaded ill health to avoid getting involved. One of Father Gabriel's letters of 22 November 1696 does, however, tell us something about the Elector's designs: 'I am afraid that the same applies to the Veronese as to Rubens' *Adoration of the Magi*, which hangs in the King's lower apartments and is therefore rarely seen. My Gracious Lady, moved by sisterly love for Your Highness, some considerable time ago approached the King about this matter, but his Majesty replied that he could not grant her request.' Nothing came of this matter, despite all the Elector's efforts.

In Heinrich von Wiser he found a more successful intermediary. As the Elector's diplomatic representative, he accompanied the Queen to Madrid as secretary. Wiser was an active buyer. On 6 August 1694, he announced the purchase of a Rubens, a Bruegel, a fine portrait by Velázquez, a Paul Birl and a Paris Bordone which he despatched with works by Luca Giordano, also purchased for the Elector, as well as a present from the Spanish King: Rubens' *Reconciliation of Jacob and Esau*. The paintings arrived safely at Düsseldorf, judging from the twenty-one works by Giordano in the Elector's collection, and the Velázquez and the Rubens, which can still be seen in the Pinakothek.

The Elector was apparently not satisfied with the number of works exchanged as gifts. On 14 February 1691, he wrote to the Marchese Ariberti, since 1698 his representative at the Spanish court: 'When Her Majesty the Queen decides to send us horses and paintings, we should like you to choose the paintings yourself, if possible Brigel's [*sic*] little landscapes with figures (I enclose the exact measurements). We should also like a Veronese, a Raphael, a Correggio, an Andrea del Sarto, a Rubens and a Van Dyck. We should be pleased if His Majesty would also send a barrel of good Alicante red wine; twelve pairs of pigeons would also be appreciated, as well as a brace of good hunting dogs, not just for hunting but for breeding purposes.'

The future Elector Karl Philipp also tried to procure paintings for his brother Johann Wilhelm. In July 1712 he offered him three works for the sum of 2,000 florins. Johann Wilhelm's reply was as follows: 'I appreciate your concern for my interests, but it is shameless to ask such a price for paintings which are so bad and so absurd that, even if they were originals, which they are not, I should not want them though I were paid to have them. These two portraits are not worth a quarter of the price you ask, and as for the third, which is supposed to be a Van Dyck, it has never even seen Van Dyck. I am consequently returning them to you, and beg you to spare me your impudence in offering me such wretched paintings in future.' Not surprisingly, this correspondence between the two brothers was not continued.

Johann Wilhelm probably did not buy any complete collections. Documents do refer to some, but it is highly unlikely that he was able to raise the considerable funds required for such a transaction. He did once show interest when his representative in Rome, Count Fede, told him of the sale of the collection of Duke Odescalchi, previously owned by Queen Christina of Sweden. The negotiations for this lasted five years. The price asked was extremely high and, with the War of the Spanish Succession going on at the time, no one was willing to spend 600,000 crowns on paintings. In the summer of 1715 the Elector officially withdrew from the negotiations.

Among the painters of the time, apart from Luca Giordano, the Elector was particularly fond of Adriaen van der Werff. In 1697 he was appointed court painter and in 1705 received a title. Twenty-three of his works were displayed in the Düsseldorf gallery, which the Elector started building in 1711. The first inspector of this gallery was the painter Gerhard Joseph Karsh. In 1719, three years after Johann Wilhelm's death, he drew up the first catalogue. It lists 54 paintings, exhibited in five halls. The nucleus of this gallery was the forty-six works of Rubens, which filled a whole room. Apart from the paintings mentioned above, these were: the *Fall of the Damned*, the *Small Last Judgment*, *Christ and the Penitent Sinners*, the *Crucifixion in a Nocturnal Landscape*, the *Virgin in a Garland of Flowers*, *St Christopher*, the *Rape of the Daughters of Leucippus*, the *Drunken Silenus*, the *Death of Seneca*, the splendid portrait of *Alathea Talbot*, and *Rubens and Isabella Brandt in the Honeysuckle Bower*. Other works in the collection were twenty-five paintings by Van Dyck, including the *Susanna and the Elders*, the *Martyrdom of St Sebastian*, two *Lamentations of Christ*, three full-length portraits, the portrait of the young artist and the portrait of the sculptor Georg Petel. The outstanding Dutch works were Rembrandt's set of scenes of the Passion and his *Adoration of the Shepherds*.

After Johann Wilhelm's death, artistic activity at Düsseldorf came to a halt, and the collection was, as we have said, partially moved to Mannheim in 1731. Not until the time of the Elector Karl Theodor was there a new artistic flowering in Düsseldorf. In 1754, the general inspector of Louis XV's collections, Collins, was summoned to Düsseldorf to 'study all the paintings, examine their condition, restore those which proved to be damaged, take measures for their proper conservation and indicate what should be done to look after them in the future.' Lambert Krahe was appointed Director of the gallery, which then consisted of 297 paintings. But more difficult times were ahead. In 1758, when the Prussians besieged Düsseldorf, the collection had to be moved to Mannheim. It did not return to Düsseldorf until 1763, enriched by the addition of several works which had been transferred to Mannheim from Düsseldorf at an earlier date. In 1794, due to the advance of the French troops, the paintings had once more to be hastily packed up and moved to safety. They were sent via Bremen to Glückstadt in Denmark. Fearing that the French might demand the surrender of the collection as part of the terms of the peace treaty, attempts were made – in vain – to insure it for two million thalers. In 1801, the paintings returned to Düsseldorf, but not for long. In 1805 war broke out again. It was decided to move the collection permanently to Munich, where it arrived safely on 7 February 1806.

Meanwhile, in 1799, on the death of the Elector Karl Theodor, the Palatine branch of the Wittelsbachs became extinct. The throne passed to Maximilian IV (Joseph) of Pfalz-Zweibrücken, who, by the Treaty of Pressburg in 1806, became King of Bavaria, under the name of Maximilian I. The way was now clear for the transfer of the Zweibrücken gallery to Munich. This collection was a relatively recent one, the old collection having been auctioned in Paris in 1775. According to the memoirs of the court painter and future director of the Bavarian galleries, Christian von Mannlich, Duke Karl August, who ruled Zweibrücken from 1775 to 1795, decided on his own initiative to start a new collection: 'One morning, as I was sitting in my office bent over my accounts, I heard footsteps in my drawing-room. I ignored them. Eventually the door burst open; it was the Duke and his minister, who had been looking at my small collection of paintings in the drawing-room. As he entered, the Duke said: "You have some very fine paintings here, and I really must admit that they are very pleasing to look at. Let me inform you that I too should like to own some paintings, and should like to start my collection off with yours." Although I had grown used to these pictures and no longer took much notice of them, I was very attached to them, for they were very fine and brought back memories of Rome, Florence and Parma. I stammered that all my belongings were entirely at the Duke's disposal. "In that case," he replied joyfully, "I shall take them today. I am impatient to have them. I will not ask you about the price," he added, "I have already given Esebeck instructions to pay you whatever you ask. Leave your accounts and come to Karlsberg tomorrow to help me set the paintings out in my new reception-room next to my chamber. In the meantime, I will take with me in my carriage two small paintings which I particularly like." We went into my drawing-room, Esebeck took down the two paintings and His Most Gracious Highness carefully counted all the others, suspecting that I might try to keep one or two for myself.'

Some time later, the Duke acquired the collection of the architect of the Palatine court, Nicolas de Pigage, who in 1779 edited the famous catalogue of the Düsseldorf collection. To this were added over 500 paintings from the bequest of Duke Clemens of Bavaria. So many paintings were bought that, some twenty years later, the collection numbered 2,000 items. Half of these were hung in the gallery specially built at Karlsberg Palace in 1785. They included Martin Schongauer's *Nativity*, a triptych by Memling and a portrait by Frans Floris. The Flemish school was represented by Brouwer, Teniers, Joos de Momper, Siberechts and Pieter Boel. The largest proportion of works were by Dutch painters: e.g. Rembrandt's *Portrait of an Oriental*, Honthorst's *Prodigal Son*, two forest landscapes by Jacob van Ruisdael, Gabriel Metsu's *Cook*, an *Inn Parlour* by Sweerts, peasant scenes and *genre* paintings by Adriaen van Ostade, Esaies van de Velde, Duyster, Steen, Benjamin Cuyp, Philips Wouwerman, still-life paintings by Pieter Claesz and Willem Claesz Heda, landscapes by Salomon van Ruysdael, Wynants, Adriaen van de Velde and Berchem. French paintings included Claude Lorraine's two large paintings of *Hagar and Ishmael*, Le Moine's *Hunting Group*, Chardin's *Girl peeling Vegetables*, a portrait by Tocque, and finally Boucher's *Nude on a Sofa*.

When, during the revolutionary wars in 1793, Zweibrücken was occupied by the French, the Prussians and the Austrians in succession, the paintings were rescued at the last minute just before the French set fire to Karlsberg Palace. They were first sent to Kaiserslautern and then to Mannheim, where they were hung in the rooms made vacant by the transfer of the Mannheim gallery to Munich. When Karl August was succeeded on his death in 1795 by Maximilian IV (Joseph), the new Elector considered selling the collection to improve his financial situation. Mannlich, now appointed Director General of the Arts, was asked to draw up a catalogue. By the time this catalogue was completed in 1799, Maximilian IV had inherited Bavaria, and the sale was no longer necessary. The Zweibrücken paintings had yet again to be hidden from the French in Mannheim, where they were stored in cellars and bourgeois homes. In 1799 they finally arrived safely at Munich. But even Munich was not to be their final resting-place, as we shall see.

THE AMALGAMATION OF THE GALLERIES UNDER MAXIMILIAN I, KING OF BAVARIA

Not even in Munich did the galleries find a respite from war and revolution. Fortunately, the post of Gallery Inspector had since 1790 been filled by a man who was both conscientious and extremely knowledgeable, Georg von Dillis. Dillis was a secular priest and a painter, who relinquished his pastoral duties in order to dedicate himself wholly to art. When in 1796 Munich was threatened by French troops under General Moreau, Dillis was instructed to pack up 615 paintings and transport them on ten rafts to Linz and from there to Straubing. The paintings stayed there for over a year, to return to Munich after the Treaty of Campo Formio. But more was to come. In 1799, just when Mannlich had hung the contents of the Zweibrücken gallery in the Hofgartengalerie and at Schleissheim, they all had to be packed up yet again. Part of the collection was loaded on to thirty-six carriages and sent to safety in Ansbach, in neutral territory. For the second time Dillis went with the paintings, while Mannlich, back in Munich, tried to hide as many others as possible. In Schloss Schleissheim, paintings were buried under the floorboards. These precautions proved to be vital. When in the spring of 1800 French troops entered Munich, General Lecourbe went straight to the Residenz to take his pick of the booty, quickly followed by the French government commissioner for the arts and sciences, François-Marie Neveu. Paris was to become the world centre of progress and knowledge. According to the commissioner, what he selected was to be made part of an exchange, to be replaced by the central administration of French museums. Mannlich remarks: 'No one had any false illusions when seventy-two paintings were eventually despatched to Paris. Bonaparte kept for himself Altdorfer's *Battle of Alexander*, which he hung in his bathroom at Saint-Cloud.'

After much negotiation, twenty-seven paintings were recovered after Napoleon's fall from power. These included the *Battle of Alexander*, Burgkmair's *St Constantine* and *St Sebastian*, Titian's *Crowning with Thorns*, Rubens' *Battle of Martin d'Eglise, Meleager and Atalanta*, and *Hippopotamus Hunt*, Abraham Janssen's *Olympus*, and Pieter Lastman's *Ulysses and Nausicaa*. Attempts to recover other paintings from French provincial museums were abandoned on Dillis' advice, since the trouble and expense of transporting them would be too great. This decision seems strange, when among these works were Rubens' *Adoration of the Magi* (at Lyons), his *Wild-Boar Hunt* (at Marseilles) and his *Tiger and Leopard Hunt* (later lost in a fire at Bordeaux); Paul de Vos' *Wild-Boar Hunt* (in the Louvre); Tintoretto's *Virgin with Saints* (at Lille); not to mention other works by Rubens and Van Dyck.

Shortly after the collections had been amalgamated into one central gallery, there was a considerable influx of new treasures with the dispossession of the Church in Bavaria in 1803, and the annexing of the imperial towns and the Franconian Marks and monasteries. The Tyrol also had to enforce the dispossession of the Church when it came under Bavarian rule from 1805 to 1814. The commissioners received the following instructions: 'By a decree of 17 February of this year of 1803, His Highness the Elector has seen fit to ordain the dissolution of monasteries and convents, and has ordered the examination by experts of all collections of paintings, engravings, and other such objects in all monasteries and convents, so that those items of value may be sorted out from among the rest.' He designated Mannlich and Dillis for this task, giving them precise instructions for the accomplishment of their mission.

Mannlich gives an account of what happened in practice: 'So I visited all the monasteries and convents of Bavaria, and succeeded in reaping a good harvest of works of art, which I packed up and transported to Munich. Everywhere I went, I came up against commissioners who treated the abbeys harshly, apart from helping themselves to all the goods and furniture. On my return from this trip, I made out a detailed report on all that I had seen and encountered. I must have carried out my task successfully, because my departure for the great raid on Swabia and Franconia kept being postponed on various pretexts. People – not the monks or abbots, on whom too close a watch was kept – took advantage of this delay to sell, hide or dispose of all they could, thus robbing the state of incalculable treasures. When the Elector read in a newspaper one day that the paintings of the Bishopric of Kempten were to be auctioned, he despatched an emissary to get the sale postponed, so that I was able to select some articles for our gallery. So categorical were his demands that they had to obey, like it or not. The Elector's words to me were: "To prevent further complications, leave first thing tomorrow morning. Here are sixty gold coins; I shall give orders for additional expenses to be paid to you. If you come across anything of outstanding value, inform me personally. That is all, my dear Mannlich – I know you too well to have to remind you to treat the abbots and priests with courtesy and consideration. They have suffered enough already with the losses they have endured, and it would not be fair to insult them into the bargain."'

The dissolution of the monasteries brought approximately 1,500 new paintings to the Munich collections. The section of early German painters was enriched by Hans Holbein the Elder's *Kaisheim Altarpiece*, two scenes of the Passion by Wolf Huber, Dürer's *Mater Dolorosa*, the wings of Michael Pacher's *St Lawrence Altarpiece* and his *Altarpiece of the Church Fathers*, two altarpieces by Marx Reichlich, Grünewald's *St Erasmus and St Maurice* and *Mocking of Christ*, Cranach's *Crucifixion*, Altdorfer's *Virgin*, Hans Baldung Grien's *Portrait of the Count Palatine Philipp* and *Nativity*, and a *Crucifixion* by Pleydenwurff. All this without mentioning Rubens' *Woman of the Apocalypse* from Freising Cathedral, Tintoretto's *Christ in the House of Martha and Mary* and his huge *Crucifixion*, Tiepolo's *Adoration*, Pieter Bruegel the Elder's *Peasant Woman*, and Carel Fabritius' *Self-Portrait*.

As the ever-increasing number of paintings could not all be displayed at Munich, it was decided to set up subsidiary galleries in other important towns – some of these are still in existence today. The collection of Aschaffenburg Palace was allowed to remain there; the palace of the Margrave von Ansbach was left almost intact; the collections of the episcopal palaces of Bamberg and Seehof were enlarged with paintings from the Zweibrücken gallery; the episcopal collection of Würzburg was similarly allowed to remain there, since Würzburg had been designated as the residence of Crown Prince Ludwig; the imperial cities of Nuremberg and Augsburg in fact gained more paintings than they lost; and a gallery was set up at Innsbruck. All these collections were – and still are – administered from Munich.

Despite these substantial additions due to the dispossession of the Church, considerable sums were still set apart for important acquisitions. Paintings bought by King Maximilian I included Dürer's *Self-Portrait*, Hans Baldung Grien's *Cristoph von Baden*, Holbein the Elder's *St Sebastian Altarpiece*, Altdorfer's *Birth of the Virgin*, Cranach's *Adam and Eve* and *Virgin with Grapes*, Gerard David's *Adoration of the Kings*, landscapes by Jacob van Ruisdael, and Champaigne's *Portrait of the Vicomte de Turenne*.

Dillis was several times sent on expeditions to buy paintings. He was, for example, sent to Rome, by a royal order of 6 July 1818: 'Having been informed from various sources that many valuable paintings are at the moment on the market in Rome, we have decided to allocate 25,000 florins for such purchases, and we intrust our court banker A. Seeligmann to open an account for this sum at the exchange-bank in Rome so that our ambassador can draw on it according to his needs. To avoid the unnecessary purchase of copies or mediocre works instead of originals and masterpieces, we have decided to entrust this task of purchasing paintings to our gallery inspector Dillis, in whose diligence and expert knowledge we have complete confidence. He is therefore to hasten to Rome, where our ambassador will instruct him further. . . . It goes without saying that, if there should be a chance of a good purchase in a town other than Rome, he should go ahead all the same, provided he selects the works carefully and buys them at a relatively low price.'

LUDWIG I

It was Crown Prince Ludwig who had been behind Dillis' expeditions. As Ludwig I, he was King of Bavaria from 1825 to 1848. Ever since the day in 1804, when, at the age of 18, he first saw Canova's *Hebe* in Venice, Ludwig had been fired by the Wittelsbachs' traditional passion for the arts. Ludwig described this traumatic event in his own words: 'I was overcome with awe... everyone else had left the room, but I stayed there as though transfixed.... This was not desire or sensual pleasure that I was experiencing, but the power of art.' Henceforth, he devoted himself to art with a boundless ardour, energy and perseverance. His collecting was not just a matter of pure personal satisfaction, any more than had been that of his predecessors, but was intended to create a collection that would show the historical development of painting. It was not enough for a painting to be good; for Ludwig to acquire it, it had also to be significant from the point of view of the history of art. Ludwig said himself: 'As a child I took no pleasure in learning, except for history, which I always liked – the past has always attracted me.'

Ludwig's favourite adviser and confidant for all artistic questions was Dillis. The two men had become friends in Paris in 1806, and Dillis accompanied the Prince on his visit to the south of France. The voluminous correspondence between the two, which continued until Dillis' death in 1841, dates from the time of this visit, and gives a good picture of Ludwig I's collecting activities. Dillis was in some way connected with all his acquisitions. His first trip to Italy on the orders of King Maximilian I saw the beginning of an affair that was to occupy Dillis and the Crown Prince for several decades. On 20 August 1808, Dillis wrote from Rome:

Florence contains the jewels of classical painting – I have yet to see so many treasures hidden away in any other town. Most of the families have now lost their fortunes and are forced to sell off the works of art in their possession so as to be able to maintain their status. Lucien Bonaparte has already acquired a considerable number of works from the Riccardi Palace.

I introduced myself as a Swiss painter and art-dealer. All doors opened before me, unknown and insignificant as I am. I have in five days seen over 6,000 paintings in private houses. Here even the most simple household has a collection. I am amazed by the wealth of paintings that have managed to survive here all this time.

The following two paintings are of outstanding value. A self-portrait of Raphael as a young man, which is the counterpart to the Fornarina (in the Tribune) – this is in the Altoviti Palace. It is well known through Raphael Morghen's engraving of it. It has been preserved secretly and is in perfect condition – one of Raphael's best works, and his best portrait, better even than the one in the Tribune. The price is 5,000 sequins. A Madonna cradling the Child Jesus, a work of Raphael's best period – this is in the Marchese Tempi palace. I am sending Mannlich a print of it.

These two paintings are worthy of the greatest collection in the world. If I had a mandate or a letter of credit for Florence, they would probably both be in my hands now. I may perhaps be able to purchase them on my return, though. There is no time to lose and you must move all heaven and earth to get me a special credit for Florence, where these paintings are. I beg of you, speak with your father about this excellent opportunity. I can effect the purchase from here, as I have an anonymous friend there on whom I can count. If I receive the money in time, I am certain of success.

This news must have greatly excited the Prince. Not only was he himself particularly fond of the Italian classical painters, but the Munich collection needed works of this quality if it was to fulfil its educational and cultural role.

Although Ludwig was very careful with his money, almost to the point of miserliness, he never hesitated for a moment when it came to parting with enormous sums. He wrote to Dillis in September, enclosing a bill of exchange for 24,000 florins for him to buy the Raphael self-portrait. Eight weeks later the purchase was concluded and Dillis, delirious with joy, wrote in his diary: 'I have here in my hands, in German hands, the most wonderful painting in the world. Long live the Prince, champion of the arts. I am the happiest man alive who ever saw his wishes come true.'

The Crown Prince never let enthusiasm run away with him. He wrote to Dillis: 'Be cautious in your purchases, my dear Dillis, or you will lose my confidence. You know well enough that people here will be all too ready to criticize you.' Criticism was indeed violent in Munich, and doubts were raised about the authenticity of the Raphael portrait. The whole court united in condemning the acquisition. We now know that in fact the portrait depicts Bindo Altoviti and is not a Raphael (unfortunately, it was exchanged in 1958, and now hangs in the National Gallery, Washington). Dillis was greatly upset by this episode and for ever after remained extremely sensitive to other people's criticisms. Ludwig told him: 'A prince must consult the opinion of several authorities on all matters, on principle; and I find your reactions strange. Even the greatest philosophers or scientists – or art connoisseurs – sometimes disagree. You know how favourably disposed I am towards you, and I think I have given you sufficient demonstration of my confidence in you. So no more of this worrying in the future!'

The rapidly concluded acquisition of the supposed Raphael self-portrait incited the Crown Prince to open negotiations for the *Tempi Madonna* straight away. He secured as his agent in Florence the trusty, honest engraver Johann Metzger. Fearing that, with the postal services lacking any kind of security, his letters might be opened in transit, Ludwig corresponded with his agents in a code to which we still have no key. The Altoviti portrait was called 'cock-pigeon', the *Tempi Madonna* 'hen-pigeon', and Barberini's *Faun* 'sleep'.

The *Tempi Madonna* proved recalcitrant. In June 1809 'the hen-pigeon with the little boy could not be obtained unless some miracle were to happen' and Metzger wanted to know 'how much energy he could expend to bring this miracle about'. Ludwig replied: 'Energy expended on securing the hen-pigeon with the little boy can go up to 20,000 florins, but preferably less – it can rise to a few thousands more if absolutely necessary.' No headway was made. The Prince kept repeating: 'I already possess the cock-pigeon, and cannot allow Metzger to let the hen-pigeon escape my grasp'; 'the cock-pigeon now in Germany is pining for its hen-pigeon to come and join it'. Things seemed hopeless when Metzger announced on 19 April 1811: 'The day before yesterday I received an absolute refusal by way of the Casa Tempi doorkeeper, stating that his master had made up his mind not to sell his treasure at any price, so I could spare myself all future trouble.... The doorkeeper was sorry because he will not now get the good tip I promised him.' Ludwig chose to ignore this setback, and instructed Metzger to persevere.

Nothing would have come of the negotiations had not Metzger waited on in Florence many years. It was not until 12 February 1828 that he was able to announce to Ludwig (now king) that he had finally obtained the painting for 15,000 Tuscan crowns. 'I shall never forget this last week; I cannot believe that it is really true. I have just enough strength to inform you that I have secured victory, and the devil with the past!'

Patience and perseverance were the qualities most needed by a prospective buyer of good paintings in Italy at that time, if he wished to be successful. Metzger had to negotiate for five years to get the Ghirlandaio altarpiece from the high altar of Santa Maria Novella in Florence. But thanks to his patience, he succeeded in acquiring fifty paintings for Ludwig over the course of several years. These included Albertinelli's *Annunciation*, Fra Angelico's *Man of Sorrows*, Beccafumi's *Holy Family*, a Botticelli *Lamentation of Christ* and another by Raffaellino del Garbo, Fra Filippo Lippi's *Annunciation*, two works of Filippino Lippi, and Perugino's *Vision of St Bernard*.

Meanwhile, at Rome the painter Martin von Wagner was acting as the Crown Prince's agent. He too had to wait for years, often with no result, as in the case of the Camuccini collection. Competition from English, French and Russian buyers was keen – from the important collection of Cardinal Fesch, Wagner succeeded in acquiring only Le Sueur's *Christ in the House of Martha and Mary*. The Crown Prince took care to try to get the state to finance his acquisitions, since it was understood that his personal collection would eventually pass to the state galleries. But Dillis' words were all too true: 'Mannlich will have difficulty in purchasing a Le Sueur without funds. One cannot get anything out of the State Treasury without going through committee after committee. That leaves only the King's private treasury, and that is not always available for the acquisition of works of art, particularly if the money is to go abroad.'

In summer 1814 Ludwig spent eight weeks in London, and wrote to Dillis: 'If you want to see Italian works of art – that is, ones that could possibly be transported to Germany – go to the museums of Paris and England. This side of the Alps, I have rarely seen collections containing so many works I should like to acquire for our gallery as I have here. I did not expect this of London.' The Raphael *Madonna della Tenda* which he saw in the collection of Sir Thomas Baring made an indelible impression on him. When he was offered this work in 1818 by the London art-dealer William Buchanan, on a visit to Munich, his decision was a foregone conclusion. Four months later, this tiny jewel was on its way from the Escorial to Munich.

Dillis acquired another painting from the Escorial – Titian's *Virgin and Child in an Evening Landscape* – on his trip to France in 1815 to recover the paintings stolen by the Napoleonic army. This painting was owned by General Sebastiani, who had led the French troops against the rebel Spaniards. Thanks to Dillis, another work from the general's collection was acquired for Munich: Murillo's *St Thomas of Villanueva distributing Alms*. The favourable political climate allowed Dillis to purchase other works for Ludwig in France, such as Cima da Conegliano's *Virgin and Child* and Francesco Francia's *Madonna in the Rose-Garden*, both from the collection of the Empress Josephine.

On his way back from Paris, Dillis stopped off at Heidelberg to look at the Boisserée brothers' collection there. Ludwig had also been to see this collection shortly before. In December 1815, Sulpiz Boisserée wrote to Goethe: 'The second visitor was the Gallery Inspector, Dillis, on his way home from Paris with the recovered treasures. We had heard for some time of this remarkable man and his expert knowledge of art, but he surpassed even our expectations ... He was surprised by our early Flemish paintings.'

Sulpiz and Melchior Boisserée, who came from a merchant family, had decided, together with their friend Johann Baptist Bertram, to start a collection of early Flemish painting in Paris in 1802, on the suggestion of Friedrich Schlegel. Their return to Cologne coincided with the dissolution of the monasteries, when the altarpieces were being removed from the churches in the town. Sulpiz Boisserée described in his own words how the collection began: 'In the months immediately after our return, we were taking a walk with Schlegel in the Neumarkt, the largest square in Cologne, when we saw a stretcher loaded with all sorts of objects. Among these objects was an old painting, with gold haloes glittering in the distance... I was the first to notice it. I enquired after the owner, who lived nearby. Not knowing what to do with this large painting, he was only too happy to rid himself of it for a modest price. Now we had to find a home for it. So as not to be laughed at for looking ridiculous, we decided to take this dusty old object into our family home through the back door. Just as we arrived, our old grandmother happened to come out of the door. After staring at the painting for some time, she said to its somewhat embarrassed new owner: "That is a touching picture you have there. You have done well to buy it." This was the inaugural blessing on a collection that was to have a great future.'

The final collection comprised 216 works by early Dutch, Flemish and German painters, including Rogier van der Weyden's *Three Kings Altarpiece*, Dieric Bouts the Elder's *Resurrection of Christ* and *St John the Evangelist*, Dieric Bouts the Younger's *Pearl of Brabant*, Memling's *Seven Joys of the Virgin*, a large winged altarpiece by Joos van Cleve, Isenbrandt's *Rest on the Flight into Egypt*, two works by Bernard van Orley, and Engelbrechtsen's *Lamentation of Christ*. The Cologne school of early painting was widely represented. Other works in the collection included the wings of Dürer's *Jabach Altarpiece* and his *Lamentation of Christ*, Altdorfer's *St George*, and paintings by Cranach, Strigel and Conrad Faber von Kreuznach.

Berlin and Frankfurt were serious rivals for the acquisition of this collection. Sulpiz Boisserée gave an account of Ludwig's approaches in a letter of 1816: 'The very year we were due to go to Berlin, the Crown Prince came all alone to see me early one morning to advise us not to move to the north. Why not make your home in Munich, he added, and stay among the Catholics? You will find that much more pleasant than living among the Protestants.' In 1826 Ludwig, now king, approached the Boisserée brothers again, and on 12 February 1827 the sale was formally concluded. The price was 240,000 florins.

'What a collection I have now!' cried Ludwig in an audience with his brothers. 'Just wait until it is all set out together! My only wish is that there should be no mention of this in the newspapers, and especially that no one should get to know the price I paid for it. People nod their heads approvingly when you lose your money gambling or spend it on horses, but if you use it to acquire works of art they start talking of extravagance.'

In 1826 Sulpiz Boisserée wrote to King Ludwig I: 'If my collection – which is universally accepted as the most complete and representative collection of early North German paintings – were to be amalgamated with the Bavarian royal collection of early South German works the result would be an unparalleled collection, unique of its kind in Europe, not only as a testimony to German culture but as a testimony to the whole history of art. Bavaria possesses, thanks to the generosity of her present ruler, the finest works of Greek sculpture and of Italian painting, and the addition of these new masterpieces to the schools of painting already represented completes what will from now on be the fullest and most instructive collection of the world's art ever seen.' The acquisition in 1828 of Prince Wallerstein's collection, which Ludwig had first heard of in 1823, brought him one step nearer to this goal. Dillis had said of this collection at the time: 'The collection of paintings in Wallerstein Palace includes many important works of great historical significance.' With this collection, 219 paintings were acquired for the sum of 80,000 florins, which the King again paid out of his private treasury. The paintings were chiefly of Swabian, Franconian and Rhenish artists, and included Dürer's *Portrait of Oswolt Krel* and Altdorfer's *Danube Landscape* – the first true German landscape painting.

By the time Ludwig I abdicated in 1848, not only had he greatly enriched the Munich collections, but his foresight and catholicity of taste had played a large part in making the Alte Pinakothek into what it is today: one of the greatest galleries in the world. In the remaining twenty years of his life, Ludwig bought paintings for the Alte Pinakothek only rarely – modern art and the foundation and expansion of the Neue Pinakothek now consumed all his energies.

THE LAST HUNDRED YEARS

Georg von Dillis died in 1841, and King Ludwig I abdicated in 1848. The building of the new gallery was not completed, and the great age of the Pinakothek was already drawing to a close. No suitably qualified successor could be found to take Dillis' place. The post of Gallery Inspector dwindled in importance, till it became a haven of refuge for old, out-of-work professors. The historical painter Robert Lange filled the post till 1846, when he was succeeded until 1865 by Clemens Zimmermann. He was responsible for the auctioning of some works to pay for the completion of a set of portraits of the Wittelsbach family at Schloss Schleissheim.

Dürer's *Portrait of Anna Selbdritt* – today in the Metropolitan Museum of Art, New York – went for a mere thirty florins. When other museums were building up new collections which now enjoy a worldwide reputation, Munich thought that with the establishment of the Alte Pinakothek she had done all that was required of her. To make matters worse, the academicians had nothing but scorn for the works of the early German painters. The same attitudes persisted under the directorship of the historical painter Philipp Foltz, who did not improve the situation by badly damaging several paintings in the process of having them restored.

Things improved somewhat in 1875, with the appointment of Franz von Reber, Professor of Art History at the Technische Hochschule, to the post of Gallery Director. Now for the first time the Pinakothek found a director who was both a technical expert and an excellent administrator. Reber remained at the Pinakothek for thirty-four years. His main achievement was the reorganization of the gallery, which was made possible by the appropriation of rooms previously used for other purposes. The first scientifically compiled catalogue was published, with the collaboration of Adolf Bayersdorfer, in 1884. New annexes were set up, and a catalogue compiled for each one. The new Director's task was greatly hindered by the Association of Munich Artists, which kept pressing for the relegation of the early Italians and Germans to 'lumber-rooms', as well as the setting up of separate rooms, hung with appropriate draperies, which were to be reserved for certain paintings of Titian, Rubens and Rembrandt. In the end, Reber's tenacity won through against all opposition, and in 1888 he even succeeded in obtaining an annual allocation from the state budget of 20,000 marks for the completion of the Bavarian state art collections. By 1900 the sum was increased to 30,000 marks for the Alte Pinakothek alone. Although insufficient to finance important acquisitions, some valuable works did enter the gallery during these years. Leonardo da Vinci's *Virgin* was purchased in 1889 from Dr Haug in Günzburg at the price of 800 marks and the Knight's Cross of the Order of St Michael. Two paintings from Wilhelm IV's historical series, expropriated in 1632, were bought back from private Swedish owners.

In 1909, Reber was succeeded by Hugo von Tschudi, who had been forced to leave Berlin for having bought some works of the French impressionists for the museum. His two years as Director of the Pinakothek brought some fundamental changes. One-third of the 1,433 paintings on display in the Pinakothek when he took up his post were taken down. All the important works from the annexes were brought together at Munich – particularly the altarpieces whose different panels had previously been scattered among various galleries, such as Pacher's *Altarpiece of the Church Fathers*, now displayed complete for the first time. Tschudi's reorganization and re-arrangement of the paintings form the basis of the gallery as it is today. His most important acquisitions included El Greco's *Disrobing of Christ*, Goya's *Plucked Turkey*, and Guardi's *Venetian Gala Concert*. Tschudi also instructed Adolf von Hildebrand to draw up plans for extensions and a new complementary building but these plans were as impractical then as they are today.

On Tschudi's death, his colleague Heinz Braune took over the direction of the gallery, without official sanction. There could be no question of appointment as Tschudi's successor, despite his capabilities, because he was only thirty-one. The painter Toni Stadler was nominated as his superior. The nomination of a non-specialist, however talented he might be, brought out all the narrow-minded hostility of the cliques which had dominated Munich artistic life for the preceding thirty years.

In 1914, Friedrich Dörnhöffer was summoned from Vienna to Munich, where he remained as Gallery Director until 1933. The First World War caused no damage to the Pinakothek, although all the most important paintings were taken down in 1916 and replaced by less valuable works as a precaution. The Treaty of Versailles, however, demanded that the two wings of Dieric Bouts' *Louvain Altarpiece*, from the Boisserée collection, be surrendered to Belgium. Further enrichment of the collection was hampered by the country's difficult economic situation, and the works bought were acquired only by selling expendable paintings from the reserve stock. The acquisitions of this time consisted chiefly of works of the early Germans, although some other important purchases were made. Two new annexes were set up – one at Bayreuth and one at Füssen.

When Dörnhöffer's pupil, Ernst Buchner, took over the direction of the state collections in 1933, the activity of the gallery became increasingly subordinated to political developments. Buchner, too, was a distinguished specialist in the early German painters, several of whose works were purchased in the period before 1945. Since all the art galleries belonging to the Bavarian state were, and still are, centrally administered from Munich, the meagre budget allocated for acquisitions had, and still has, to cover the needs of both the old and modern collections. The modern sections have had to be given preference in order to keep them going at all – a strong backlash against modern art being, of course, created by the Nazi 'Degenerate Art' campaign.

Buchner's greatest contribution to the Pinakothek was his action in closing the gallery in 1939, the day after war was declared. The fact that the Alte Pinakothek collection suffered no serious losses in the Second World War is wholly due to his action. The building, however, was bombed and severely damaged.

LORENZ MAAS *A Room in the Alte Pinakothek*

In 1945 Eberhard Hanfstaengl was put in charge of the extremely difficult task of bringing the paintings back to Munich and storing them to preserve them from further damage. Provisional space was made available for exhibitions in the Haus der Kunst, and in January 1946 some of the masterpieces unseen for seven years were once again on display. The gallery's budget was, of course, tighter than ever, and so Hanfstaengl organized touring exhibitions of the chief masterpieces of the Pinakothek in several European capitals. These fund-raising activities enabled a few acquisitions to be made, such as Rembrandt's *Self-Portrait as a Young Man*. Ernst Buchner again became Director

General from 1953 to 1957, devoting all his energies to the reconstruction of the Alte Pinakothek. The necessary room for expansion was made available by moving the administrative offices, store-rooms and the collection of ancient *objets d'art* to another building, leaving the ground-floor vacant for exhibition halls. In 1957 Buchner was able to open the upper floor of the gallery. Museum experts were engaged in the reconstruction of the building, which emerged as a modern, streamlined gallery – still held up as a model of modern planning.

Buchner's successor, Kurt Martin, conscientiously carried on his work. By 1964 the whole gallery was open to the public. Under Martin's direction the Pinakothek was fortunate in acquiring several important works. A panel by Hans Schöpfer from Wilhelm IV's historical series returned to Munich together with Cranach's *Golden Age*, both of which are mentioned in Fickler's catalogue of 1598. Great stress was put on the reconstruction of the annexes – eleven of these have now been inaugurated and others will be opened in the course of the next few years. The principle of exhibiting a systematic selection of works covering the whole history of painting, as in the Alte Pinakothek, was abandoned in the annexes, whose paintings are now arranged in geographical and historical groupings.

In 1964 Halldor Soehner succeeded Kurt Martin, only to die unexpectedly four years later. As had been the case under his predecessor, it was considered increasingly urgent to direct all financial efforts towards building up the modern art collection. No budget could have kept up with the incredible spiralling of prices in these years. In order to prevent the Pinakothek from becoming totally stagnant, the collaboration of the Bayrische Hypotheken- und Wechsel-Bank (Bavarian Mortgage and Exchange Bank) was successfully secured – the bank buying the works required by the Pinakothek and giving them to the gallery on permanent loan in the form of an endowment. This arrangement enabled the eighteenth-century painting section, still rather thin, to be expanded.

The Bavarian state collections today include approximately 15,000 paintings, assembled over a period of 400 years. The most valuable of these paintings are in the Alte Pinakothek. The destinies and the history of this gallery reflect the destinies and the history of Europe and of Bavaria. It was surely this that King Ludwig I had in mind when he founded the Pinakothek: 'Long after the works of statesmen have passed away, the works of artists will continue to gladden the hearts of men.'

The Alte Pinakothek after bombardment

The Alte Pinakothek after bombardment →

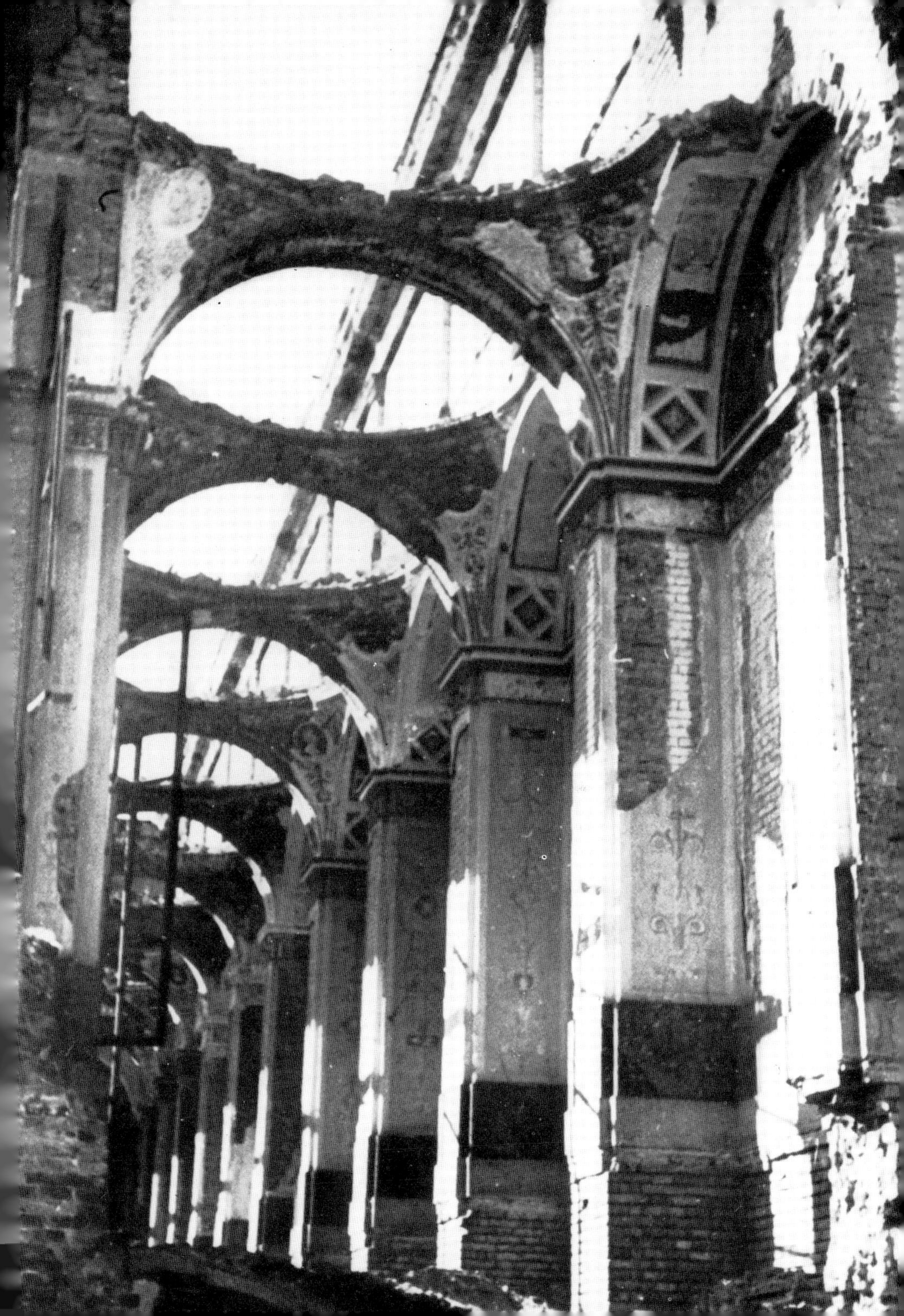

First floor

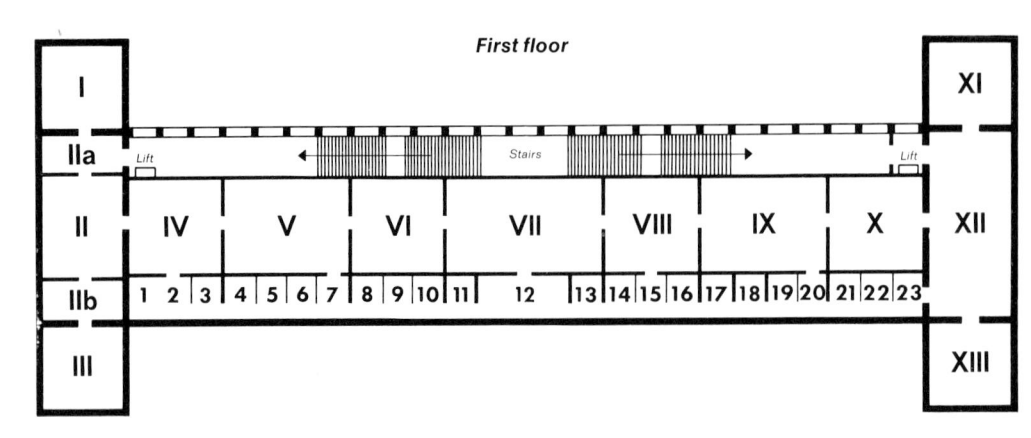

Room	I–III	Early German school	VIII	Van Dyck
	IV	Early Flemish school	IX	17–18th century Italian school
	V	Dutch school	X	Renaissance Italian school
	VI	Flemish school	XI	Spanish school
	VII	Rubens	XII	Venetian school
			XIII	French school

Cabinet	1–2	Early Flemish school
	3–10	Dutch school
	11	Brouwer
	12–14	Rubens
	15	Spanish school
	16–17	French school
	18–23	Early Italian school

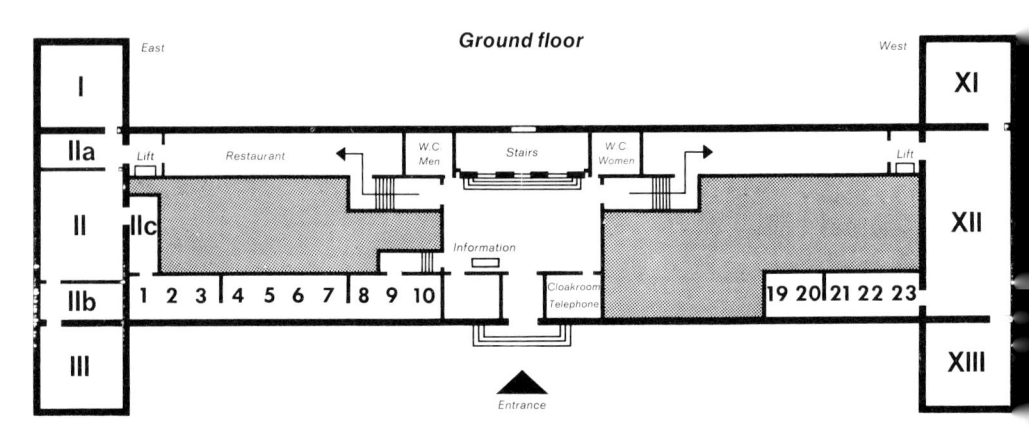

Ground floor

West — Early German school
East — German and Flemish Renaissance and Baroque painting

Rooms in the present Pinakothek

THE PLATES

GERMAN SCHOOL

MASTER OF ST VERONICA, active 1400–20
St Veronica with the Holy Kerchief
Pine: 30 11/16″ × 18 7/8″ (78 × 48 cm.) Catalogue No. 11866

This painting depicts the face of Christ with the crown of thorns. According to tradition, on the ascent to Calvary Veronica wiped Christ's face with a white cloth, which became imprinted with the marks of the Saviour's features. The Middle Ages ceaselessly copied and imitated this first and authentic portrait of Christ, although the manner of its depiction changed over the centuries. Towards the end of the Middle Ages, an expression of suffering starts to appear on the sublime, hieratic face, and a crown of thorns and a halo are placed around the head – originally bare. Veronica was often included in these paintings holding the kerchief, and here she displays it to us, retiring behind it. The central theme of the painting is the face of Christ, which explains why the saint's head is so small, her eyes lowered and her body hidden from view. Similarly, the eyes of the little angels in the corners are timidly raised towards the face of Christ.

The unknown artist takes his name from this painting, which bears the inscription *Sancta Veronica* on the saint's halo. It was probably painted around 1400, while the artist was a pupil of the famous master, Wilhelm of Cologne, possibly intended as the door of a reliquary.

The painting was originally in the Church of St Severin in Cologne. It was lost at the time of the dispossession of the Church, and rediscovered by the Boisserée brothers who purchased it in 1811–12. Ever since this time the *St Veronica* has been considered the most important work of the Cologne school. It was acquired for the Alte Pinakothek by King Ludwig I of Bavaria in 1827.

Goethe visited the Boisserée brothers' collection in 1814 and 1815, and in 1816 published an article on it. He thought this painting the most outstanding in the whole collection: 'Its power over the spectator is quite remarkable.'

Elegance and charm, soft colours and precious gold all combine to convey a mystical, religious force.

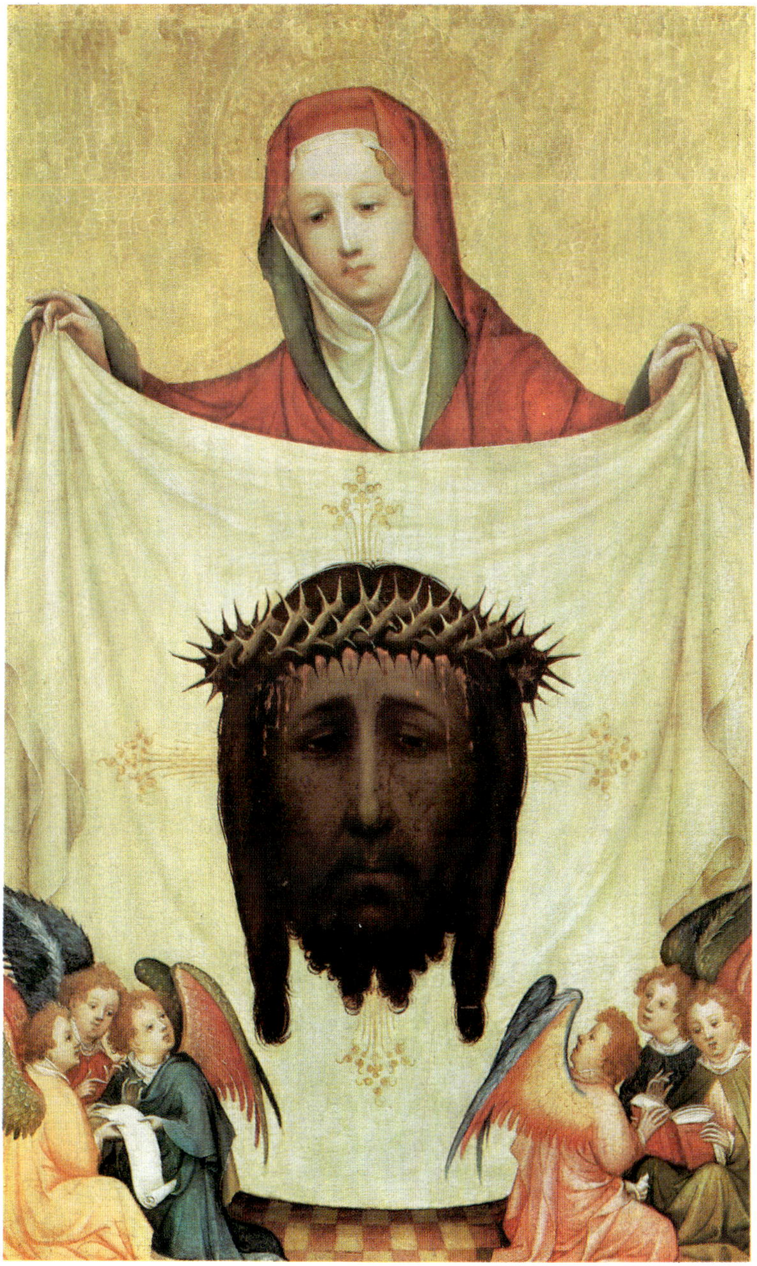

STEPHAN LOCHNER, c. 1410–51
Adoration of the Child
Wood: 14 3/16" × 10 1/16" (36 × 23 cm.) Catalogue No. 13169

The Alte Pinakothek has four panels by Lochner, including an early work, the *Virgin and Child before a Bank of Grass*, and the later *Adoration of the Child* of 1445 (also painted on the reverse with a Christ on the Cross between Mary and St John, against a red background). A wooden panel of identical measurements has now been discovered at Lisbon, also painted on both sides: on one, the *Presentation in the Temple*, and on the other, the *Stigmatization of St Francis*. Both these panels may have formed part of a small private altar. In medieval Cologne – known as 'Holy Cologne' because of its many churches – important bourgeois families often had their own small chapel, one of which was perhaps illumined by the blue and gold of this delicate devotional work. The painting has great intimacy: all alone, without even St Joseph, the shepherds or the three kings, Mary worships her Child, while He gives her His blessing, just as the man at prayer alone in his private chapel would have worshipped before this tranquil image of the Nativity, with its tender Virgin.

Of all the artists of the Cologne school, Stephan Lochner is the one whose life and works are known in most detail. His contemporaries studied and copied this painting, as well as his most famous work in Cologne Cathedral. Albrecht Dürer, on his way to the Low Countries in October 1520, stopped off at Cologne to admire 'the panels of Master Stephan'. This painting was later mentioned as being in the possession of the Duchess of Saxe-Meiningen, from whom it passed to the Princess of Saxe-Altenburg, and in 1919 to the Von der Heydt collection in Godesberg. It was transferred to the Alte Pinakothek from the state collection in 1961.

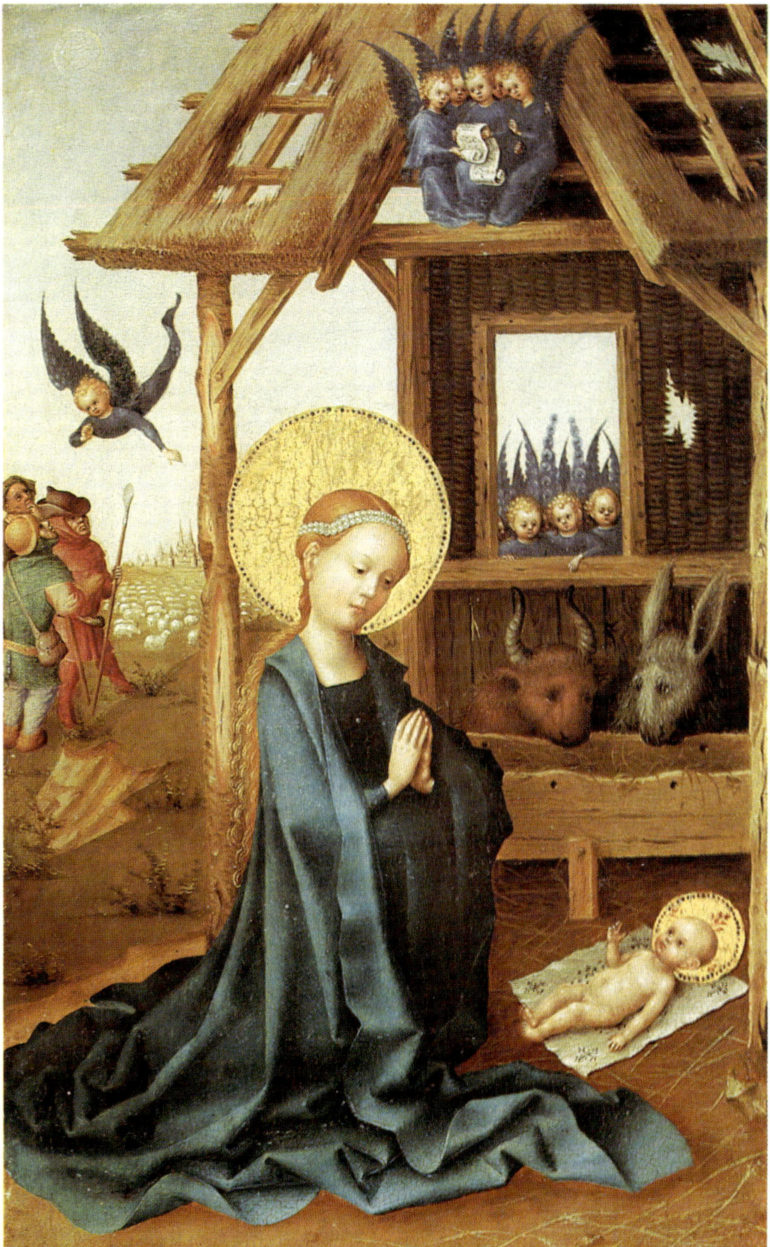

STEPHAN LOCHNER
St Anthony the Hermit, Pope St Cornelius, St Mary Magdalene and a Donor

These two panels are from the *Last Judgment* altarpiece, formerly in the old parish church of St Lawrence at Cologne. The centre panel is still in Cologne. According to popular tradition, these followers of Christ were considered to be influential intercessors.

STEPHAN LOCHNER
St Catherine, St Hubert, St Quirinus and a Donor

76

MASTER OF THE LIFE OF THE VIRGIN
Presentation in the Temple

MASTER OF THE LIFE OF THE VIRGIN
Annunciation

MASTER OF THE LIFE OF THE VIRGIN
Coronation of the Virgin

MASTER OF THE LIFE OF THE VIRGIN, active at Cologne 1463–80
Birth of the Virgin
Oak: $33\frac{3}{8}'' \times 42\frac{15}{16}''$ (85 × 109 cm.) Catalogue Nos. WAF 618–624
(Reproduction p. 78)

The painter of this work takes his name from the great altarpiece depicting scenes from the Life of the Virgin, seven panels from which are in the Alte Pinakothek, some of them painted on both sides. The obvious delight the painter has taken in 'narrating' the details of his story is strangely moving. In style and composition this painting belongs to the Cologne school of Lochner, but it also shows strong Flemish influence. The artist was clearly acquainted with Rogier van der Weyden's *Three Kings Altarpiece* (now in the Alte

Pinakothek, see p. 115), and probably knew the work of Dieric Bouts. But unlike these two Flemish painters with their clear, simple landscapes, the Cologne painter preferred to retain the splendour of a gold background: his 'landscape' is a golden sky. The donor of this altarpiece was the father of the Mayor, Dr Johann von Hirtz, known as Eberhard, who died some time before 1481. He is depicted in the foreground of the *Visitation* panel, on the left, holding on a chain the medal of the Order of the Holy Ghost and kneeling beside his coat of arms, which recurs on the back of several panels. Towards 1470 he bequeathed this altarpiece to the Church of St Ursula in Cologne, to be placed in the south aisle. This must mean that St Ursula had several other altarpieces – indeed it is hard for us today to imagine the wealth of altarpieces which the churches of Cologne must have possessed in the period 1450–1550. The Alte Pinakothek alone has altars by the following Cologne artists of the time: Master of the Aix-la-Chapelle Altar, Master of the Munich Crucifixion Altar, Master of the Holy Family, Master of Liesborn, Master of St Severin, Master of the Lyversberg Passion. Among them the Master of the St Bartholomew Altarpiece deserves special mention.

MASTER OF THE ST BARTHOLOMEW ALTARPIECE, c. 1450–after 1510
St Bartholomew Altarpiece
Oak: centre panel $50\frac{13}{16}'' \times 63\frac{3}{8}''$ (129 × 161 cm.); each wing $50\frac{13}{16}'' \times 29\frac{1}{8}''$ (129 × 74 cm.) Catalogue No. 11863

The delicate shades of the vividly portrayed donor and his coat of arms, the sumptuous brocades and the magnificent, elegant garments bear witness to the splendour of the rich Hanseatic town of Cologne. The proportions and stature of the figures in the foreground show Renaissance influence, superbly assimilated by the artist without any loss of his native Rhineland qualities of elegance, gentleness and grace.

This altarpiece was purchased by Melchior Boisserée in 1809 from the Church of St Columba in Cologne. Three years later the Boisserée brothers also acquired the altar of the Master of the Life of the Virgin. In fact, the conservation of the great majority of these Cologne altarpieces is due to the patriotism of these two rich citizens of Cologne, whose romantic inclinations and profound Catholic piety led them to give up their respectable cloth-trading business, the firm of Nicolaus Tongres, so as to be able to dedicate their lives solely to art and the satisfaction of their passion for collecting. When King Ludwig I of Bavaria – another passionate collector – bought their collection in 1827, it included over 200 early paintings.

MICHAEL PACHER
Altarpiece of the Church Fathers:
The Devil presenting
the Missal to St Wolfgang

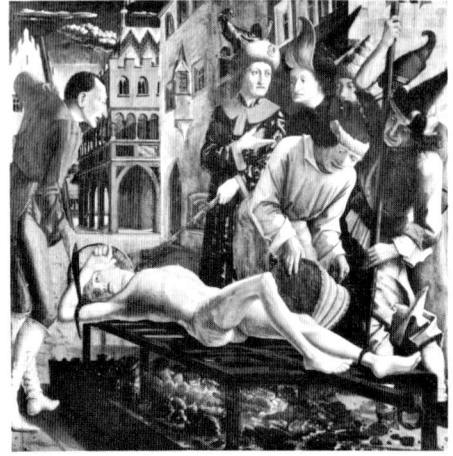

MICHAEL PACHER
St Lawrence Altarpiece:
Martyrdom of St Lawrence

MICHAEL PACHER, c. 1435-98
Altarpiece of the Church Fathers: St Augustine and St Gregory
Pine: centre panel $83\frac{7}{16}'' \times 78\frac{3}{4}''$ (212 × 200 cm.); each wing $85\frac{1}{16}'' \times 35\frac{13}{16}''$ (216 × 91 cm.) Catalogue Nos. 2579-2600
(Reproduction p. 82)

The *Altarpiece of the Church Fathers* consists of a square centre panel depicting St Augustine and St Gregory, and two wings with St Jerome on the left and St Ambrose on the right. The reverse sides of these wings, each painted with two scenes, were removed in the nineteenth century and are now exhibited as four separate panels. They illustrate scenes from the life of St Wolfgang. This altarpiece was commissioned during the years when Leonhard Pacher, probably a relation of the artist, was Prior at Neustift near Brixen in the South Tyrol, and was completed in 1480. Neustift was an important and wealthy foundation of the Augustinian order, hence the subject of the altarpiece and the prominence given to St Augustine, a mere bishop, over the Pope St Gregory. Each of the four Church Fathers is seated alone on a raised seat in a sort of recess under a great canopy, with a pulpit in front of him. Beside each saint's face hovers a dove—symbol of the Holy Ghost and of divine inspiration. The gestures of the figures indicate that they are communicating with a man, animal or text respectively, thus symbolizing their role as teachers, for the Middle Ages their most important function. The lower part of each panel depicts a different scene: St Augustine is shown gazing at a young boy who is trying to empty the sea with a spoon, an image of the parable of the unfathomable mystery of the Holy Trinity. Pope Gregory is depicted saving the Roman Emperor Trajan, although a pagan, a good man, from the fire of purification. St Jerome, dressed in red and wearing his cardinal's mitre, is extracting the thorn from the lion's paw with his knife. In front of St Ambrose, dressed in bright green, is a child asleep in a cradle—according to legend, the crying of a young child was the decisive factor in his election as Bishop of Milan.

The altarpiece has the form of a Gothic wooden carved altar. With great skill the artist has succeeded in differentiating the wonderfully alive figures of the Church Fathers and the lifeless, wooden abstractions of the carved saints on the pillars. Certain elements in these figures anticipate the new type of individualized portrait which was to appear in Dürer's *Four Apostles* (see p. 98). The austerity, sharp gestures and harsh light-effects of this work contrast with the usual style of Cologne painting of the time, reflecting the difference in character of the Tyrolese from the Rhinelander. This stylistic variation is also due to the influence of the Mantuan artist, Andrea Mantegna. Mantegna's clear outlines, and his technique of lighting his figures, modelling towns in perspective, and painting clouds are evident in the panels of Pacher in the parish church of St Lawrence, near Bruneck in the South Tyrol.

This altarpiece is an early work, which we know was paid for in 1462–3. Pacher also carved the figures in wood. He painted many works for his native town of Pacherhof near Bruneck, but also received commissions from Salzburg, where he died. Works by him can still be seen today in Salzburg (in the Franciscan Church of St Wolfgang am Abersee), together with other works which show his influence.

The district of Brixen was annexed by Bavaria in 1806, under whose rule it remained for ten years. With the dispossession of the Church in 1812, all the above-mentioned works of Pacher together with his *Coronation of the Virgin* – at that time all in Neustift – were appropriated for the Bavarian State collections at Schleissheim. The Alte Pinakothek acquired works of Pacher only at the end of the nineteenth century, with the four *Church Fathers*, followed in 1910 by the panels of the *St Lawrence Altarpiece* and the *Coronation of the Virgin*.

MARTIN SCHONGAUER, c. 1435–91
Holy Family
Lime wood: $10\frac{1}{4}'' \times 6\frac{11}{16}''$ (26 × 17 cm.) Catalogue No. 1132
(Reproduction p. 84)

This small, delicate panel of around 1480 is a devotional picture. The Virgin, dressed all in red, sits on a grassy bank, with a mountain landscape in the background. Inside the dilapidated stable are the ox and the ass, while in front of them Joseph is picking up his stick. There are no subsidiary scenes whatsoever. The Virgin has, with her delicate, finely-drawn fingers, plucked a flower from the chicory plant on the left among the strawberries covered with flowers and fruit, and dangles it in front of the child like a toy. Chicory, which grows in wasteland areas and is virtually a weed, has a flower which withers almost instantly when picked. Why, then, has the Virgin chosen such a mean flower for her Son? Folklore attributed to chicory the power of warding off evil. In the late fifteenth century, scenes from the life of the Virgin were depicted with great imagination, particularly in the small details. The stick and the flower are presumably meant to indicate the departure on the flight into Egypt.

The precise draughtsmanship of the figures and of minor details remind us that the artist was also a well-known engraver, much admired by the young Dürer. Schongauer lived in Colmar and Brisach, on the left bank of the upper Rhine.

This work remained on the left bank of the Rhine when it entered the Wittelsbach collection at Zweibrücken, where it is listed in a catalogue of 1800. It was transferred to the Pinakothek with the rest of the Zweibrücken gallery.

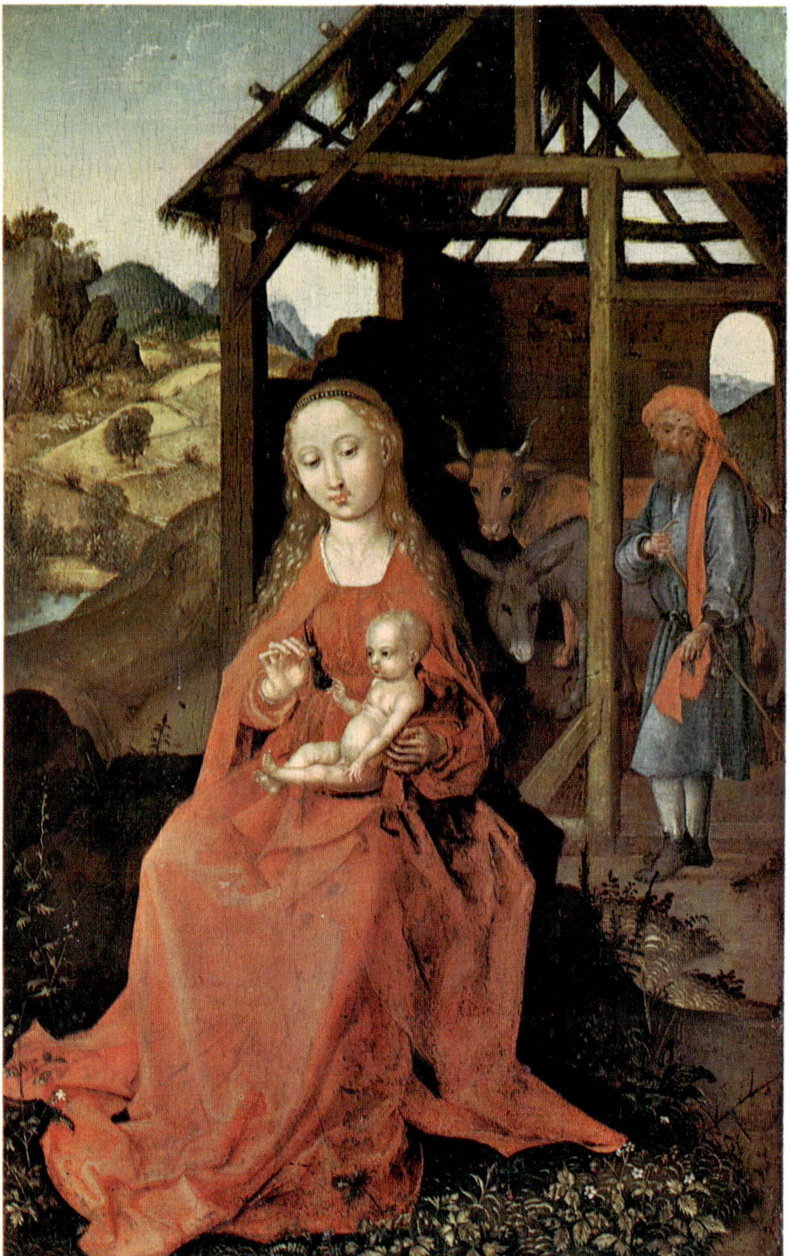

Hans Holbein the Elder, c. 1465-1524
Presentation of the Virgin, wing of the *Kaisheim Altarpiece*
Pine: $70\frac{7}{16}'' \times 32\frac{1}{4}''$ (179 × 82 cm.) Catalogue Nos. 721-736

The Cistercian monastery of Kaisheim lies to the north of Donauwörth in Swabia. In 1531 a chronicler of the monastery recounted: 'In 1502, the Abbot George had a magnificent altarpiece painted for the choir. For this the three finest masters in Augsburg were engaged: the cabinet-maker Adolf Kastner, the sculptor Gregori and the painter Hans Holbein. This painting cost a great deal of money.' The wooden carvings have been lost. Gregor Erhart's 216 cm. tall Virgin, probably the main figure, was in the Deutsches Museum, Berlin, but was destroyed in 1945 during the war. The only fragments of this altarpiece remaining today are the panels in the Alte Pinakothek. They were brought from Kaisheim to Munich on 3 February 1803, the eight panels, painted on both sides, having some time after 1715 been sawn in half to make 16 separately framed panels. It is extremely difficult to say how the different panels were originally assembled, but we do know that the insides of what used to be the wings depicted eight scenes from the life of the Virgin, with the *Presentation of the Virgin* on the top left, followed, from left to right, by the *Annunciation*, the *Visitation* and the *Nativity* with, on the lower row, the *Circumcision*, the *Adoration of the Kings*, the *Presentation in the Temple* and the *Death*. In each scene the Virgin wears the same bright blue garment, while differences in age are indicated by her features, appearance and posture. In the *Presentation*, the Virgin's small figure shyly climbs the temple steps, while the high priest descends from the altar to meet her. At the foot of the steps are Mary's aged parents, Anna and Joachim, whose strongly-defined faces gaze intently at one another. Three young women stand behind Anna outside the building, at the foot of the statue of Moses holding the tablets of the Ten Commandments. In the background is a rocky landscape with a river.

The expressive hands and restrained gestures are characteristic of Holbein, as are the portrait-like studies of the main characters. His use of rich, deep colours brought him many commissions for stained-glass windows.

The outside panels of the altarpiece depict scenes from the Passion: the *Agony in the Garden*, the *Betrayal*, *Christ before Pontius Pilate*, the *Flagellation*, the *Crowning with Thorns*, the *Ecce Homo*, the *Crucifixion* and the *Resurrection*.

ALBRECHT ALTDORFER, c. 1480–1538
Victory of Alexander the Great over Darius, King of the Persians, at the Battle of Issus (detail)
Wood: $62\frac{3}{16}'' \times 47\frac{1}{4}''$ (158·4 × 120·2 cm.), trimmed on all sides. Catalogue No. 688. Signed and dated on the scroll 'Albrecht Altdorfer zu Regensburg fecit', and bottom left: 'AA 1529'

The soldiers having broken camp before dawn, the battle rages before a fortress at the foot of a range of mountains. The Greek cavalry and infantry, well arrayed and superbly armed, follow their king's lead. Alexander the Great, on horseback in the middle of the battlefield, pursues the fleeing Darius with a long spear. The latter stands in a chariot drawn by three horses, while in the left foreground another chariot bears Darius' wives in distress. The battle over, the sun is setting and casts its last rays over the sea and the mountains which stretch into the distance. In the sky a crescent moon pierces the clouds. Heaven and earth stand witness to the momentous action of the day.

This work is one of a series of historical paintings, depicting scenes from the lives of heroes and heroines of antiquity, commissioned by Duke Wilhelm IV of Bavaria to decorate his 'pleasure palace'. In the oldest catalogue of the Munich collections – that of 1598 – the *Battle of Alexander* is listed as no. 3195. The court account-books record the restoration of this painting by Johann de Pey in 1658. In 1800, Napoleon carried it off with him to France to hang in his private apartments at Saint-Cloud. Friedrich Schlegel saw it at Paris while it was being restored, and it was his enthusiasm for this work which led him and the whole Romantic circle round him to focus their attention on Munich as an art centre. The painting returned to Munich after 1815.

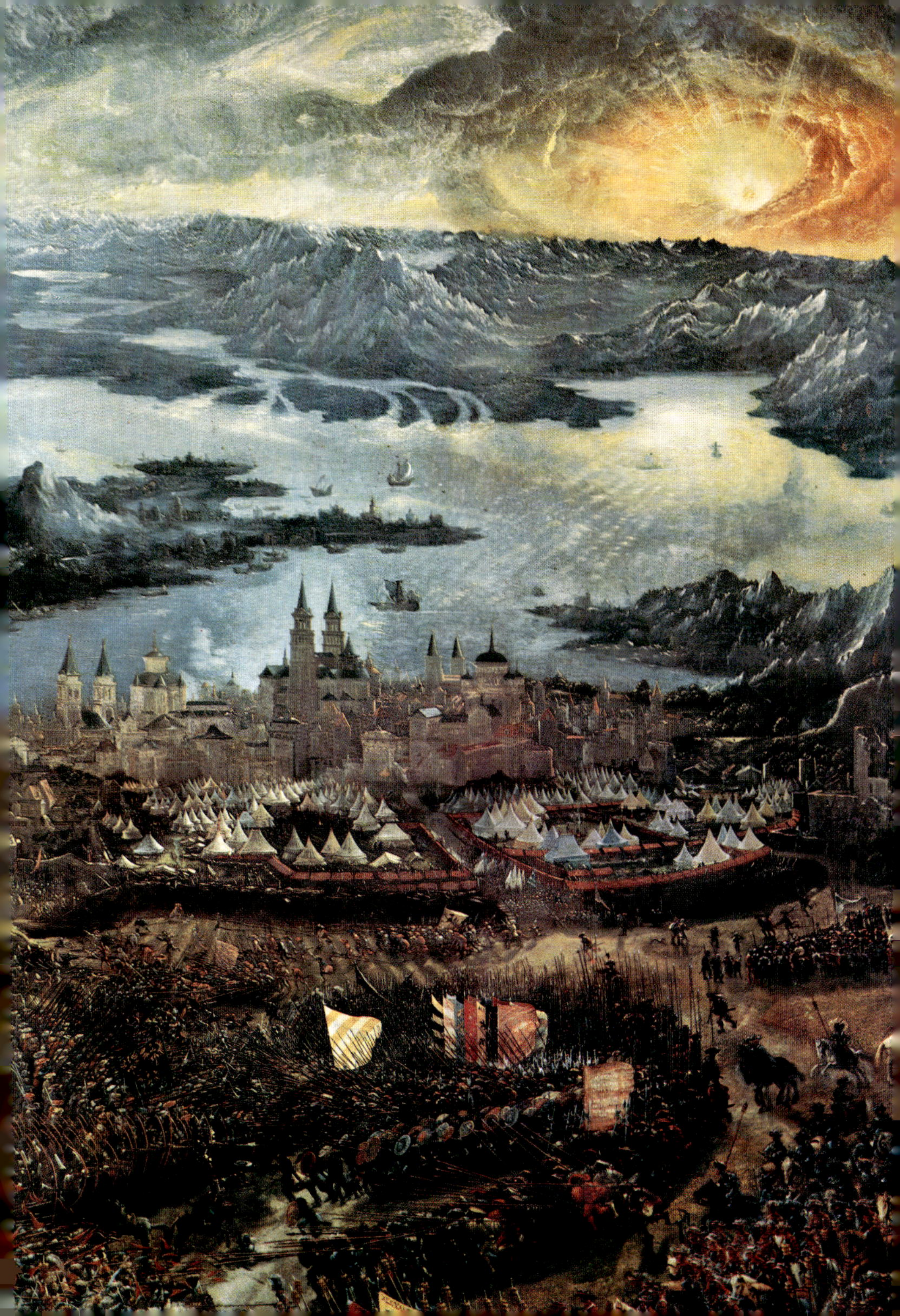

ALBRECHT ALTDORFER
Birth of the Virgin
This panel, painted around 1520-25, probably came from Regensburg. It was acquired at Salzburg in 1816, and was transferred from Schleissheim to Augsburg around 1834. It has been in the Alte Pinakothek since 1911.

ALBRECHT ALTDORFER
Susanna bathing and the Punishment of the false Accusers
This work, painted in 1526, was one of the first acquisitions of the Munich collections. It is listed with a detailed description in the catalogue of 1598. The pen drawing of the same subject is in the Düsseldorf Academy. This painting has been in the Alte Pinakothek since 1836.

ALBRECHT ALTDORFER
St George and the Dragon in a Wood
It is odd that Andromeda, daughter of the king of Ethiopia – the cause of the fight with the dragon – should not figure in this painting. The date and the monogram are inscribed on the second tree trunk on the right. This work was in Regensburg until 1816, and was acquired by the Alte Pinakothek with the Boisserée collection.

ALBRECHT ALTDORFER *View of the Danube Valley near Regensburg*
This work of around 1522 is the first pure landscape in the history of German painting. It was acquired by the Pinakothek with the Wallerstein collection.

BERNHARD STRIGEL, 1460-1528
Conrad Rehlinger the Elder with his eight Children
Wood: Left panel $82\frac{5}{16}'' \times 39\frac{3}{4}''$ (209 × 101 cm.), right panel $82\frac{5}{16}'' \times 38\frac{9}{16}''$ (209 × 98 cm.) Catalogue Nos. WAF 1064/5

The Augsburg patrician, Conrad Rehlinger (1470-1553), had been a widower for two years when he had this portrait of himself with his children painted. The artist commissioned for this work was Strigel, a member of the council of his native town of Memmingen, a wealthy trading centre in Swabia. Strigel had a great reputation as a portrait painter, having been in the service of the Emperor Maximilian in Vienna. The result of the meeting of these two successful men, Rehlinger and Strigel, was these two panels – the first full-length and the first life-size portraits to be painted in Europe. In the fifteenth century, donors were portrayed as small figures at the foot of some religious scene. Strigel retained the division into two panels of these religious works, but the Virgin and Child surrounded by angels no longer form the focal point of the painting; they are now reduced to small figures in the background, in the sky above the landscape visible through the small window.

The father and some of the children have their hands joined in prayer. The inscriptions above their heads are presumably the words of their prayers – the father's reads: 'Oh Lord, in Thy infinite goodness, guard my children and myself from sin', while above the eldest son is written: 'Oh Holy Virgin, be our Mother, we pray Thee'. With these two panels Strigel created a new *genre* that was to have a great future. This new type of portrait gradually developed until it reached its peak in seventeenth-century Dutch painting with Rembrandt's *Ironmasters* and Frans Hals' portraits of archers.

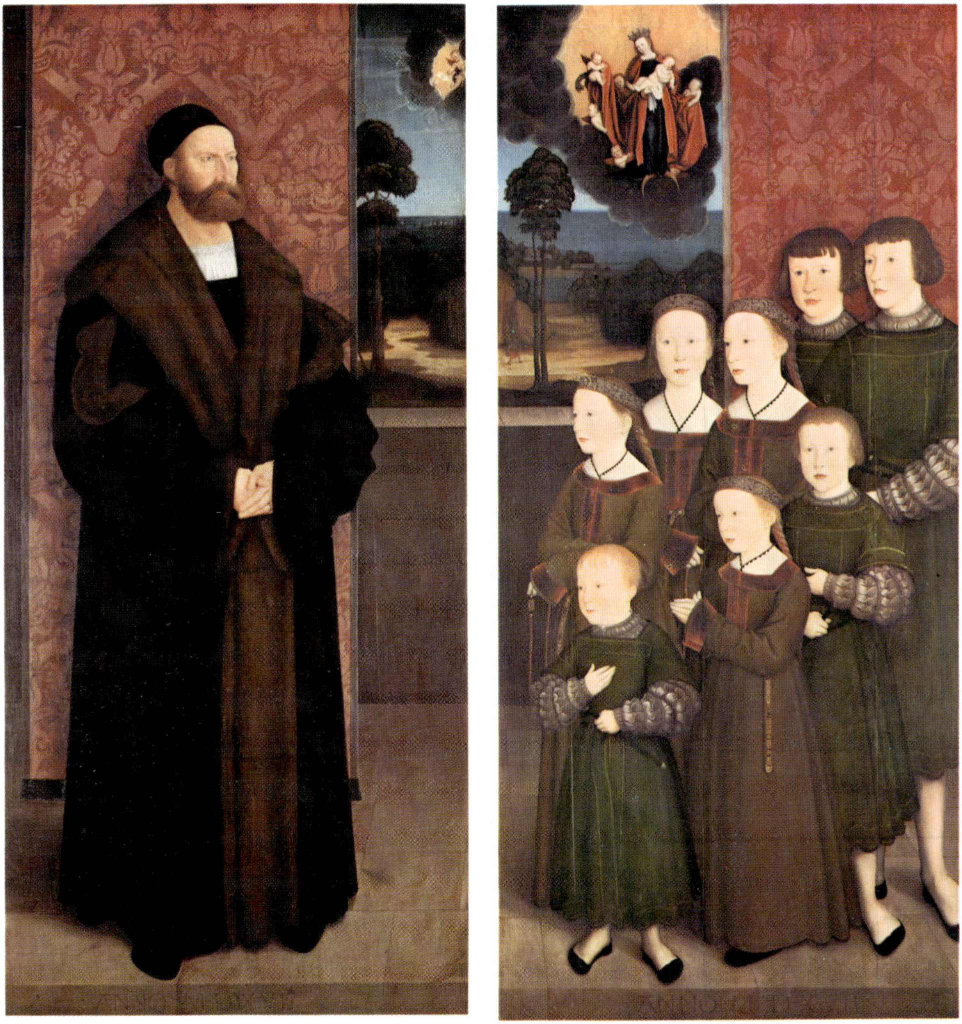

ALBRECHT DÜRER
Death of Lucretia
This panel, painted in 1518, was acquired for the Munich collections some time before 1550 – the first of Dürer's works to be acquired by the Wittelsbachs. Additions to the drapery around the hips were made around 1600.

ALBRECHT DÜRER *Oswolt Krel*
Oswolt Krel was an important figure in the Company of Merchants of Regensburg, who lived in Nuremberg until 1502. From 1511 to 1534 he was mayor of Lindau. This work of 1499 was acquired for the Pinakothek with the Wallerstein collection.

ALBRECHT DÜRER *Paumgartner Altarpiece:* centre panel and wings
The figures of St George and St Eustace on the two wings represent the donors Stephan and Lukas Paumgartner respectively. It is not known whom the figures in the centre panel represent. This altarpiece was finished in 1504 and hung in the Church of St Catherine in Nuremberg in memory of Martin and Barbara Paumgartner. It was acquired by Duke Maximilian I in 1613.

ALBRECHT DÜRER *Portrait of a Young Man*
This portrait, painted in 1500, probably depicts one of Dürer's three brothers. It was acquired by Crown Prince Ludwig of Bavaria in 1809.

1500
AD
Albertus Durerus Noricus
ipsum me proprijs sic effin-
gebam coloribus aetatis.
anno XXVIII.

ALBRECHT DÜRER, 1471–1528
Self-portrait in a Fur Coat
Lime wood: $26\frac{3}{8}'' \times 19\frac{5}{16}''$ (67 × 49 cm.) Catalogue No. 537
Signed and dated top left: AD 1500; inscription top right: ALBERTUS DURERUS NORICUS/IPSUM ME PROPRIIS SIC EFFIN/GEBAM COLORIBUS AETATIS/ANNO XXVIII

Dürer painted several self-portraits, but this is the most famous. Why? It is a plain full-face portrait, constructed geometrically: the nose and hand form a central axis, the bust and arms a right angle, and the head with the hair coming down to the shoulders a triangle. In both line and technique, the quality and beauty of this painting are quite outstanding. Despite the sensuality of the mouth, the expression is one of relentless severity, and the deep, questioning eyes have a hypnotic power. Austerity and self-discipline govern this tense, troubled, passionate figure. In the sixteenth century this portrait was thought to represent the face of Christ. The Bremen Kunsthalle possesses a drawing by Dürer, signed and dated 1522, titled: *Self-portrait as the Man of Sorrows*, showing the artist in half-profile, seated, unclad, holding in his hands the instruments of the Passion, his face twisted in agony, his mouth open, his hair dishevelled. In his writings Dürer expressed a desire 'to live according to the Lord'. This notion of the 'Imitation of Christ' is in keeping with the ideas of the Middle Ages – the basic Old Testament 'Thou shalt be as God' interpreted in the light of the New Testament doctrine of grace: 'Thou shalt strive to be more like God'.

It is of this that Dürer was thinking when he painted this portrait. It is an almost mystical vision of personal sublimation, avoiding the banal through its austerity. The drawing in which Dürer tried to express his suffering, that of body and soul reliving the Passion of Christ, must be interpreted in the same way. Dürer declared on several occasions that the sole end of art was to portray and illuminate the Life and Passion of Christ.

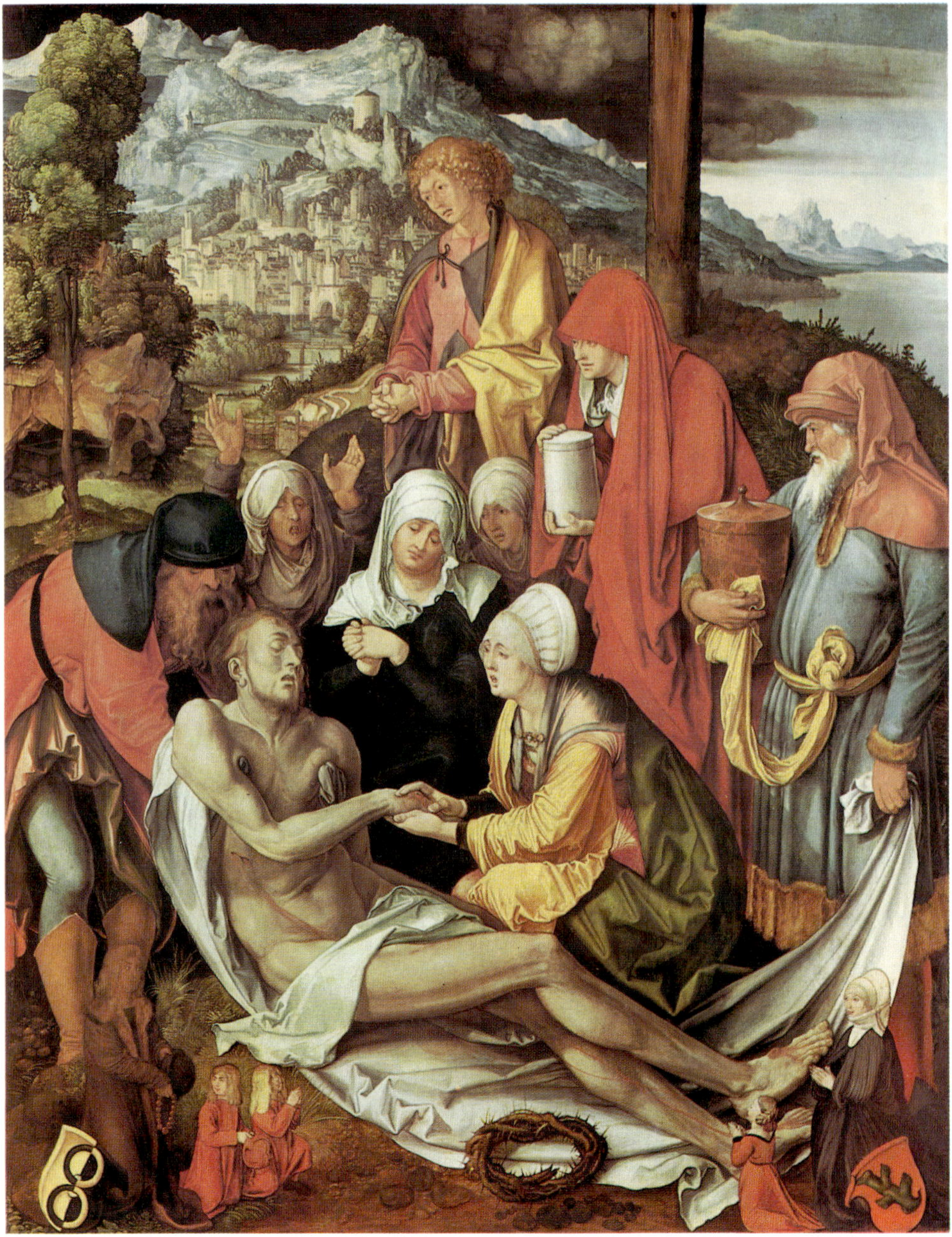

ALBRECHT DÜRER, 1471-1528
Lamentation of Christ
Pine: $59\frac{7}{16}'' \times 47\frac{5}{8}''$ (151 × 121 cm.) Catalogue No. 704

A horizontal format was almost always used to depict the theme of the Lamentation, presenting the body of Christ stretched out on the ground with weeping women bending over him (see Botticelli's and Poussin's paintings in the Alte Pinakothek). Dürer, however, has chosen an upright format. The body of Christ is raised into a sitting position. His mother kneels beside his head, in the exact centre of the painting, while behind her the tall figure of St John the Apostle towers above the other figures, his head forming the apex of the triangle which contains the characters. Behind him is a town, perched on a hill, with tall mountains in the background and black clouds above, spreading towards the river. The colours of the garments are wonderfully bright. The treatment of skin colour is still that of the fifteenth century, but the structure and composition of the figures anticipate later styles. Most paintings of scenes from the Passion distinguish between two different episodes: the Deposition and the Entombment – here Dürer has combined the two. Only the foot of the Cross can be seen on the right, but the crown of thorns is symbolically displayed in the foreground. Joseph of Arimathaea, who provided the tomb, stands by, taking hold of the shroud, ready to embalm and bury the Saviour.

In a book of 1546, Johann Neudörffer, the Nuremberg historian, tells us that Dürer painted this work for the goldsmith Glimm (an old acquaintance, probably through Dürer's goldsmith father). Albrecht Glimm is represented in the painting, if in a somewhat diminutive form. He kneels with his two sons beside his coat of arms on the bottom left, opposite his first wife, Margareth Holtzmann, with one of her daughters. The same source says that this 'fine painting' used to hang beside the pulpit of the Dominican Church at Nuremberg. Some time around 1500, some fifty years after its completion, it was acquired by Hans Ebner, from whom it passed to the Imhoff family in Nuremberg. It was offered to the Emperor Rudolf in Prague in 1588, along with other works from the Imhoff collection, but was eventually acquired by the Elector Maximilian of Bavaria shortly after 1600. It bears number 704 in Maximilian's catalogue. Although this painting changed hands no more, it did change in appearance – the figures of the donors were twice painted over and mutilated. In 1924 the Glimm family finally emerged from behind the layers of paint hiding them from view.

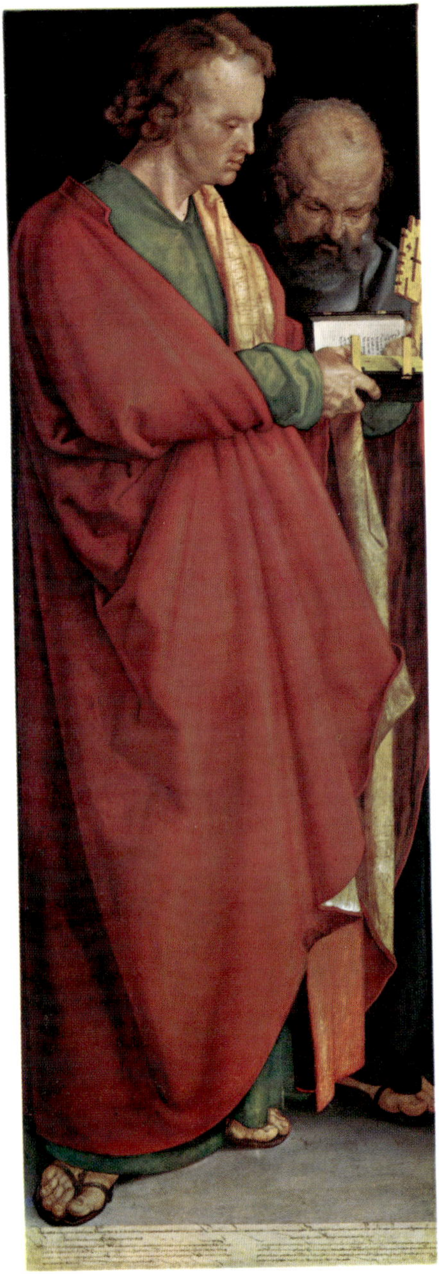

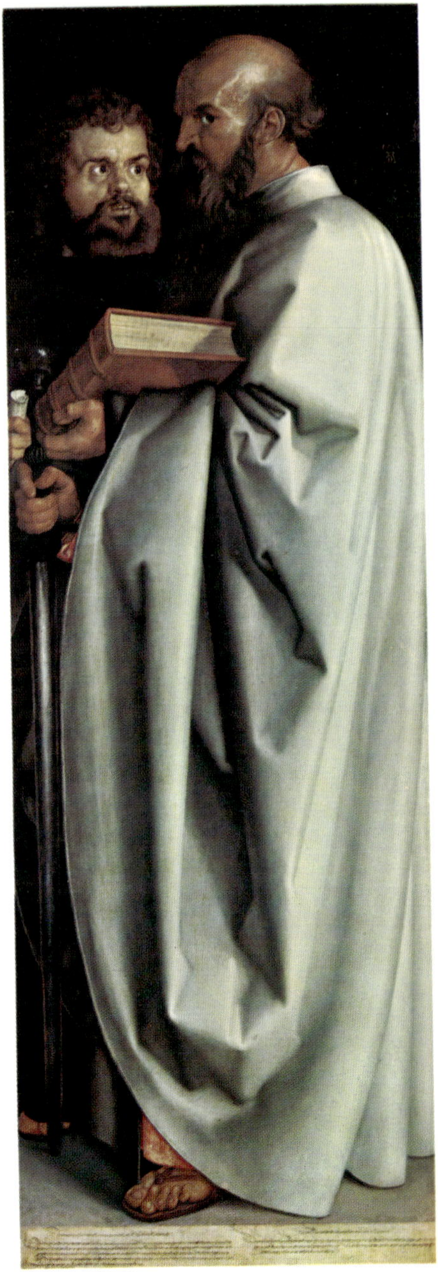

ALBRECHT DÜRER, 1471-1528
The Four Apostles
Two panels: left-hand panel, St John the Evangelist and St Peter; right-hand panel, St Mark and St Paul.
Lime wood: each panel $84\frac{5}{8}'' \times 29\frac{15}{16}''$ (215 × 76 cm.) Catalogue Nos. 545, 540
Signed and dated top left: AD 1526

It took Dürer two years to paint these panels, as is shown by the many preliminary sketches and studies which are today scattered throughout the museums of the world. The basic artistic conceptions developed here can be discerned in earlier paintings, some of which may, to a certain extent, be seen as preparatory works. Not without reason has this late work been considered the culmination of Dürer's long career. His donation of these panels to the town council of Nuremberg, as a source of inspiration to them in times of difficulty, is of only secondary importance; what does matter are his personal and artistic intentions. The inscriptions beneath the apostles sum these up perfectly. The upper line at the bottom left is a gloss on the Book of Revelation, XXII, 18: 'In these perilous times the mighty of this world must beware of mistaking the reasonings of man for the Word of God.' So reads the warning to the four saints: Peter, John, Paul and Mark. Beneath the figure of St John is a quotation from the Second Epistle of St Peter, II, 1: 'But there were false prophets among the people, even as there shall be false teachers among you.' Below this are verses 1-3 of ch. IV of the Gospel according to St John.

It was through contemporary copies that these two paintings first became known, but ever since then their fame has continued to grow. They represent the summit of artistic achievement – the beauty of simplicity and purity in form and colour. Dürer has for the first time succeeded in conveying the full force and power of the human personality, at a time when man was standing on the threshold of a new era, an era in which for four centuries the individual was to be the determining factor. These panels symbolize the triumph of painting over the other arts; from a flat surface the artist, with pen and brush as his only tools, has managed to erect a veritable monument.

These two panels were acquired from the town council of Nuremberg by the Elector Maximilian I of Bavaria in 1627.

MATHIS GOTHARDT-NEITHARDT, called GRÜNEWALD, c. 1475–1528
St Erasmus and St Maurice
Lime wood: 89" × 69$\frac{5}{16}$" (226 × 176 cm.) Catalogue No. 1044

On the left the Bishop St Erasmus stands proudly erect in his sumptuous robes of office. In his right hand he holds the symbol of his martyrdom: a spindle, wound about with his torn-out intestines. St Maurice, in a silver breastplate, addresses him with his white-gloved right hand. St Maurice was commander-in-chief of the so-called Theban Legion, the first Roman legion of Christian soldiers formed at Thebes in Egypt, and massacred in the Rhône Valley for their faith. Behind St Erasmus stands an old scholar-priest, probably the bishop's counsellor, while behind St Maurice are his trusty soldiers. In posture, bearing, movement, dress, features and colouring, the four figures strikingly represent the four estates of the medieval social hierarchy. The great European primate receives the great African soldier in a politico-religious confrontation played out, as it were, on the world stage, a testimony to the power and magnificence of the Catholic Church of two continents.

In reality, however, St Maurice is a portrait of the donor of this altarpiece, Albrecht von Brandenburg, well known through several contemporary portraits. He was appointed Bishop of Mainz and Magdeburg in 1514, Bishop of Halberstadt in 1518, and later a cardinal and chancellor of the Empire. A fanatical opponent of the Reformation, he founded the monastery of St Maurice at Halle-an-der-Saale. It was for the chapel of this monastery that Grünewald, court painter at Aschaffenburg since 1516, painted this work. Shortly after the altarpiece, painted between 1518 and 1520, had been installed, the monastery was closed down, and the painting was moved by Albrecht to the collegiate church of Aschaffenburg in 1541.

This rich and brilliantly coloured work has been in the Alte Pinakothek ever since its opening in 1836.

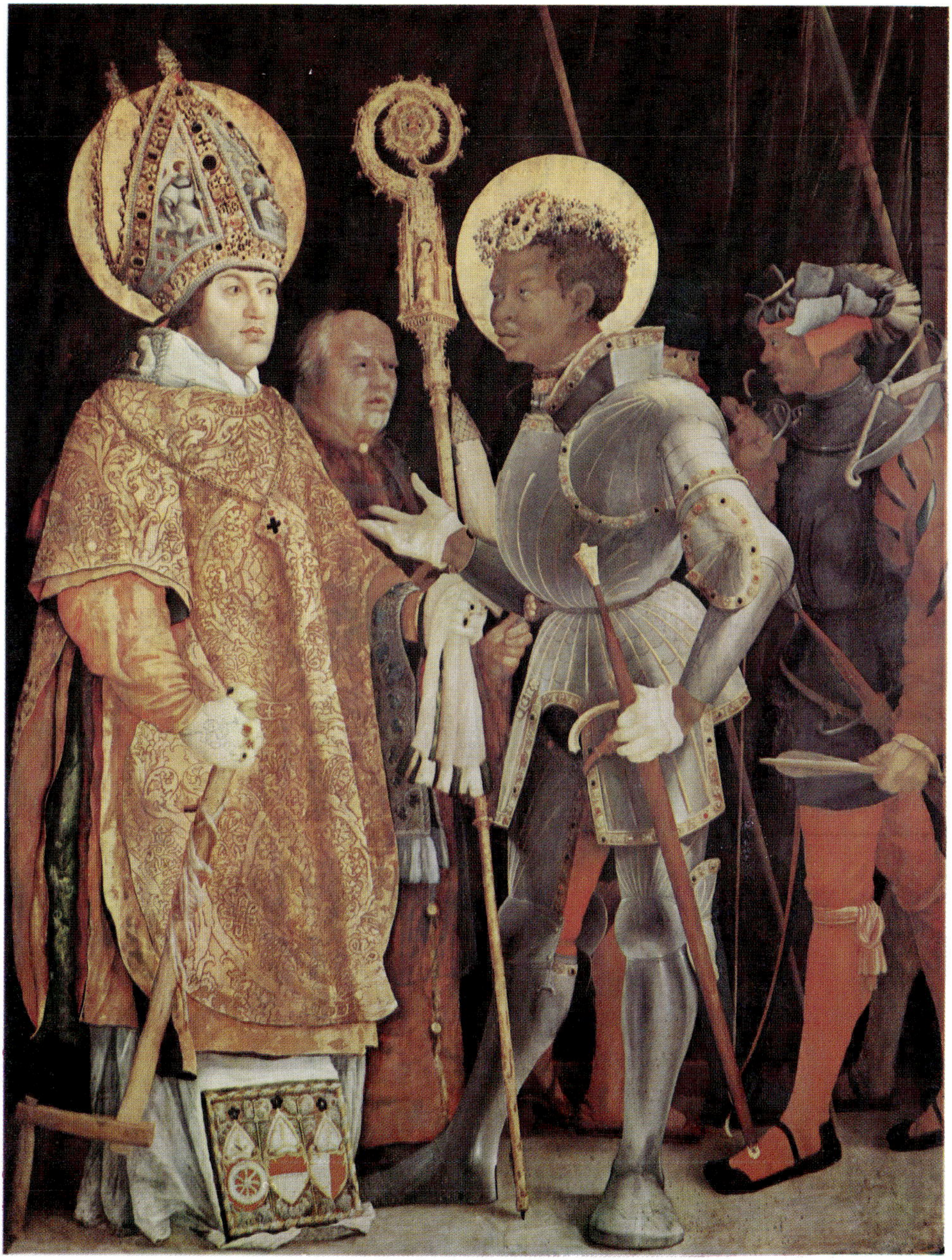

MATHIS GRÜNEWALD
Mocking of Christ
This work, painted in 1503, was probably one of a series of panels depicting the Passion of Christ. Originally in the Carmelite church in Frankfurt, it was transferred to the Carmelite monastery in Munich, and in 1803 to the Munich collections. It was identified as a Grünewald in 1910.

HANS BALDUNG GRIEN
The Margrave Christoph von Baden
This portrait was painted in 1515, the year in which the Margrave abdicated and divided his possessions among his sons. It was purchased from the Franciscans at Munich in 1802.

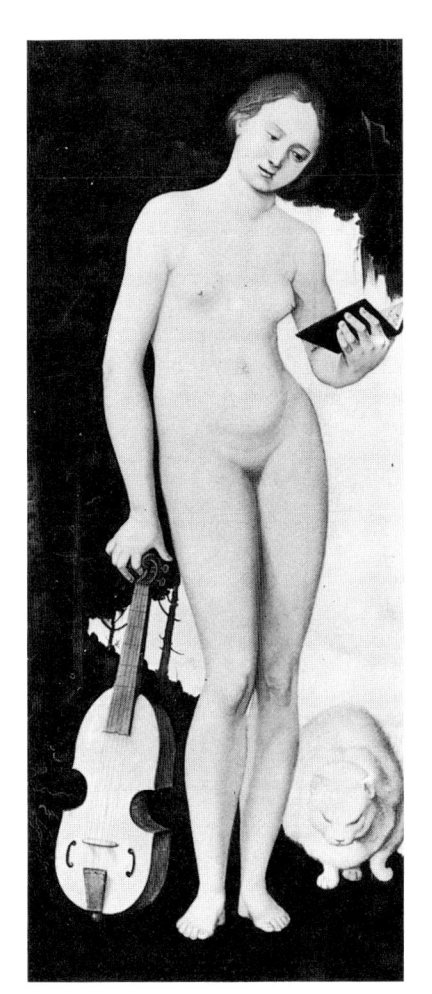

HANS BALDUNG GRIEN
Allegorical female Figure
This panel has also been called *Allegory of Music* because of the viol and song-book. It was originally in the collection of the Electors of Bavaria.

HANS BALDUNG GRIEN
Allegorical female Figure
This panel of 1529 forms a pair with the *Allegory of Music*, possibly symbolizing prudence. It was originally in the collection of the Electors of Bavaria.

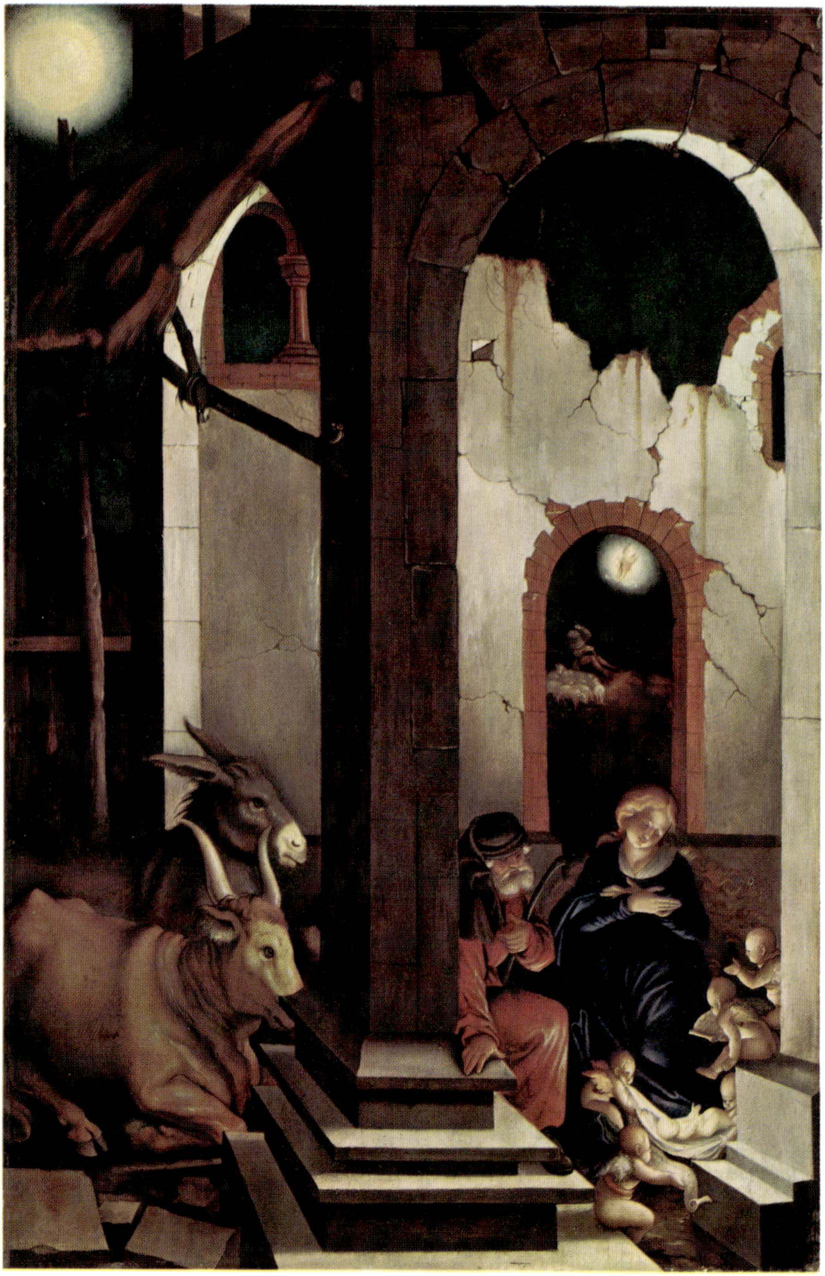

HANS BALDUNG GRIEN, 1484–1545
Nativity
Wood: $41\frac{5}{16}'' \times 27\frac{9}{16}''$ (105·5 × 70·4 cm.) Catalogue No. 6280
Signed and dated: HBG 1520

Three things stand out especially in this painting: first, the large dark Renaissance-style pillar in the foreground, cutting the gilded picture in half. Then, the darkness of the night outside. Only three points are spotlighted in the whole painting: the full moon top left; the angel announcing the Child's birth to the shepherds, partially visible in the background through the doorway; and, in the right foreground, the Child Jesus himself. Light emanates from him as though his bed were a hearth around which men and animals gather. The Virgin, the light playing on her face from below, is full of charm. The third striking aspect is the stable – the enormous wall looming dimly in the background, and shot through with sinister cracks, seems to have a life of its own. It recalls ruins of the last war, even some twentieth-century painting.

Baldung worked in the same district as Grünewald, and this painting and Grünewald's *St Erasmus and St Maurice* have stayed together on all their travels, from Halle-an-der-Saale to Aschaffenburg in 1541, and in 1814 from Aschaffenburg to the Bavarian State collections in Munich.

HANS BALDUNG GRIEN
The Count Palatine Philipp

HANS BALDUNG GRIEN
A Strasbourg Knight of St John

LUCAS CRANACH THE ELDER, 1472–1553
Crucifixion
54$\frac{11}{16}$″ × 38$\frac{13}{16}$″ (138 × 99 cm.) Catalogue No. 1416
Dated bottom left: 1503

One has only to think of any one of the countless crucifixions painted in the fifteenth century to appreciate the originality of Cranach's treatment of the subject. Completely new is the triangular arrangement of the three crosses, with the Virgin and St John together in the centre and the crosses surrounding them. In earlier paintings, Christ is always shown between the Virgin and St John. The inherently passive presentation of these earlier paintings of the Crucifixion is dynamically transformed by Cranach. The Virgin and St John are engaged in conversation (see Grünewald's *St Erasmus and St Maurice*, p. 101). It is through the attitude and gaze of these two figures that we are first made aware of the figure on the Cross. The Virgin also seems to be conversing with Christ. This theme of dialogue was a new one at the time; it betrays the influence of the Viennese humanists whom we know Cranach frequented when he was living in the imperial capital in 1503. Large-scale crucifixions normally included a number of secondary figures whose function was to illuminate and, by their simplicity, throw into relief the majesty of Christ. Here, however, the drama is played out by five characters alone on a stage stretching from the foot of the Cross away into the dynamic, highly individualistic and original landscape in the distance. The decorative motifs of the thick clouds gathering over Christ's head and the enormous loincloth take on a life of their own. This intensity of expression is found only in Cranach's early works.

This painting was acquired in 1804 on the dissolution of the monasteries.

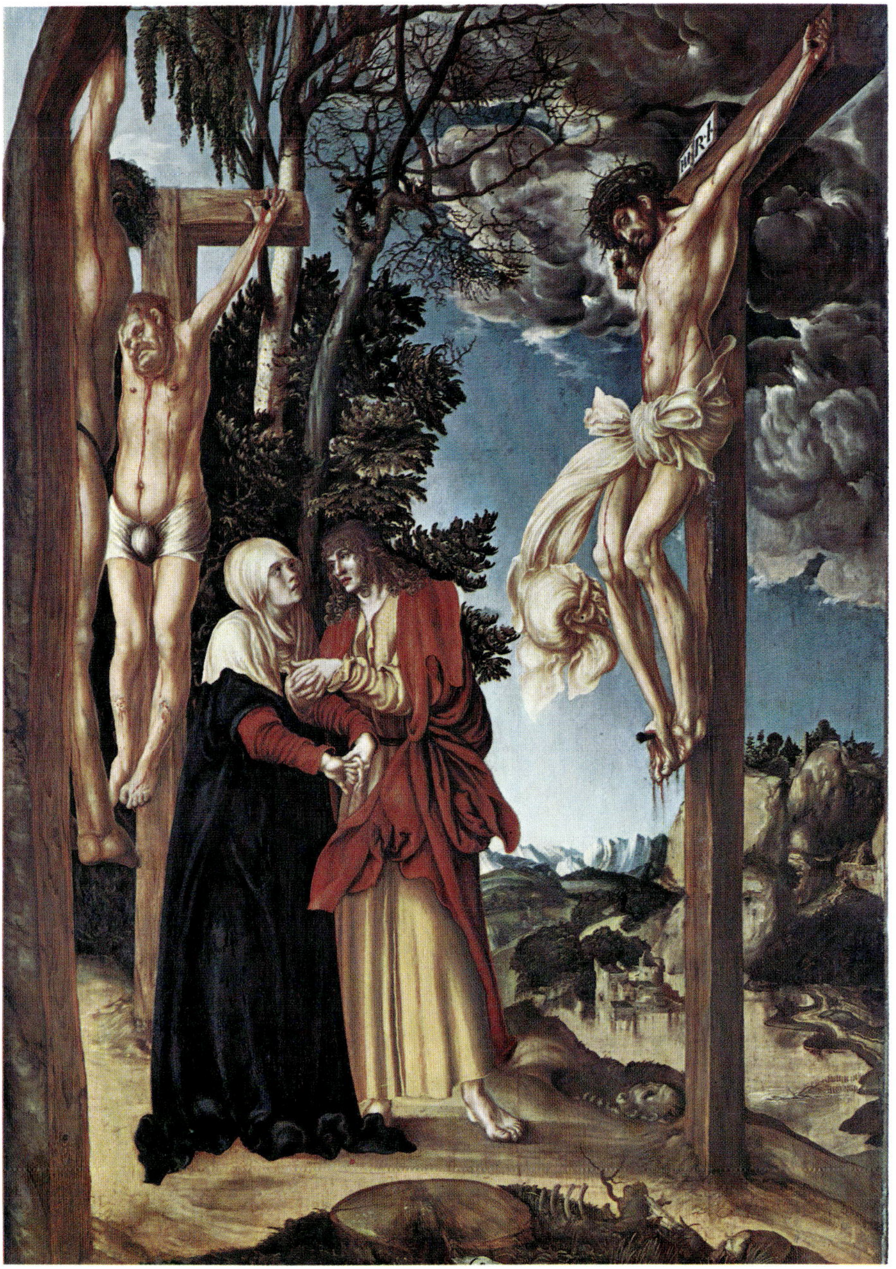

LUCAS CRANACH THE ELDER
Johannes Geiler von Kayserberg

LUCAS CRANACH THE ELDER
Virgin and Child

LUCAS CRANACH THE ELDER *The Golden Age*

Lucas Cranach the Younger
Venus and Cupid
This work was transferred from Bayreuth Castle to Nuremberg in 1812. It entered the collection at Schleissheim in 1864, and has been in the Pinakothek since 1910.

Lucas Cranach the Elder
Lucretia
This work of around 1524 was probably acquired by Duke Maximilian I of Bavaria in 1608.

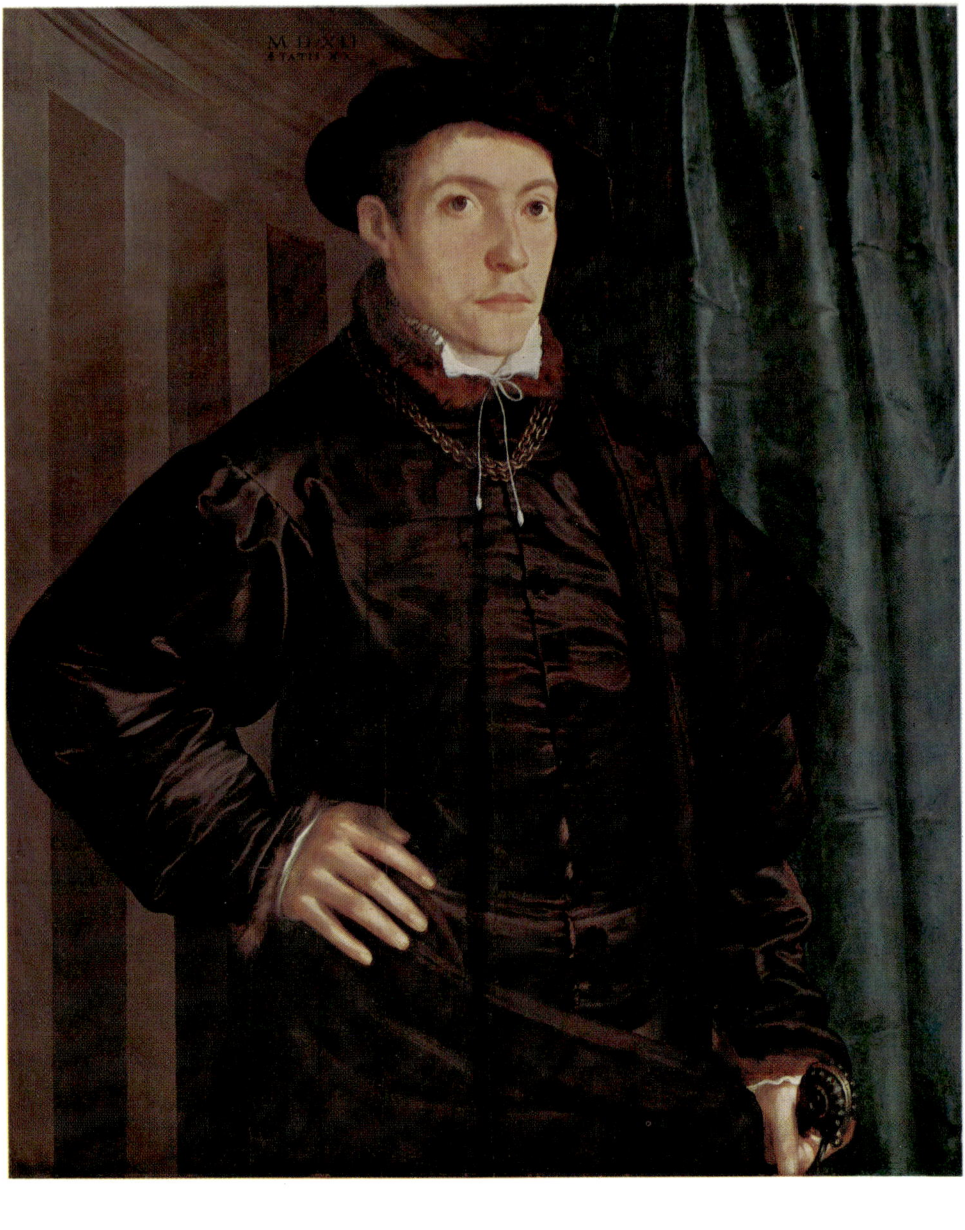

CHRISTOPH AMBERGER, c. 1505–62
Portrait of Christoph Fugger
Wood: $38\frac{7}{16}'' \times 31\frac{1}{2}''$ (97·5 × 80 cm.) Catalogue No. 9409
Dated top right: 1541 AETATIS XX

The figure seen here in half-profile is incorporated into this almost square painting in such a way that the head is at the very top of the canvas and the arms, both at an angle, lend the figure added breadth. He stands in front of a grey Renaissance interior, on the right concealed by a vivid green silk curtain. The young man is dressed in black silk. The only light areas are the young face, light pink in colour, and the two hands whose positioning indicates a slight tilt of the hips.

Portrait painting first reached its peak in the German Renaissance. Dürer, Cranach, Baldung, Kulmbach, Schaffner, Beham, Strigel, Holbein all have magnificent portraits in the Alte Pinakothek. But these are all on a much smaller scale, and still make use of bright colours. Both these qualities disappear with Amberger, not just because of the new Spanish vogue for black dress, but also due to Italian influence – particularly the works of Pontormo, Bronzino and their school. The portrait-painters of this generation put new emphasis on the proportions and movements of their models, thus giving birth to the realistic portrait.

A native of Augsburg, Amberger lived there all his life. Another of Augsburg's many talented sons, Hans Holbein the Younger, was only eight years his senior. When Holbein left Augsburg at an early age, Amberger was left with plenty of opportunity to make his own name as a specialist portrait-painter.

This portrait depicts a member of the Augsburg family of the Fuggers, whose international trading house had for a generation brought them wealth, power and a world-wide reputation. Christoph Fugger, son of Raimund Fugger, was born in 1520, and died a bachelor in 1579. The fortune he left on his death went to finance the foundation of a Jesuit college in Augsburg.

The Pinakothek purchased this painting in 1927 from the surviving descendants of this family, the Princes Fugger-Babenhausen.

ADAM ELSHEIMER, 1578–1610
The Flight into Egypt
Copper: 12$\frac{3}{16}$″ × 16$\frac{1}{8}$″ (31 × 41 cm.) Catalogue No. 216
Marked on the reverse: Adam Elsheimer fecit Romae 1609

The hurried visitor will pass this painting by without noticing it, it is so small and its colours so unattractive. But the visitor who is observant will be quick to see what a fine painting it is; and if he is prepared to give it more of his time, he will find it hard to drag himself away. Looking at this painting is like trying to see at night: it takes time for one's eyes to get used to the darkness. The first thing to emerge is the magnificent sky, with the Milky Way and myriad stars, the brightest of which is the full moon reflected in the still water on the right, silhouetting the enormous cluster of trees in the foreground which provide a dark backcloth to the Holy Family group. The three

ADAM ELSHEIMER
The Burning of Troy

figures are at the very bottom of the painting, so that the spectator, like them, looks up at the trees and sky stretching out above. Joseph's torch gives only a faint light, but the shepherds' camp-fire is bright and strong. Darkness invades the whole picture, emphasizing the secrecy of the flight, the cheerlessness of the fire, the silence of the forest, and the mysterious, mirror-like quality of the water. The landscape compels one to look deeper into it, holding one's breath to catch every sound in the silence. Elsheimer has given this painting a feeling of space and of living nature.

The connoisseur will return to this work again and again, remembering that Rubens, who befriended Elsheimer during his stay in Rome, recognized his extraordinary talent and sang his praises on many occasions. It is recognized that Elsheimer influenced Rembrandt and the Dutch landscape-painters, as well as the great French masters Claude Lorraine and Nicolas Poussin, who like Elsheimer spent most of their life in Rome. Elsheimer's life abroad prevented him from becoming well-known in Germany, although he enjoyed a great reputation in other countries where he was, and still is, regarded as a typically German painter – perhaps the greatest after Dürer.

The original owner of the *Flight into Egypt* was Elsheimer's pupil and friend Hendrik Goudt, who made an engraving of it in 1613, four years after it had been finished – this engraving helped to spread the painting's fame throughout Europe. It was copied, imitated and engravings were made after it until as late as the eighteenth century. This tiny masterpiece was acquired by the Elector Maximilian I for his Munich Residenz in 1628.

EARLY FLEMISH SCHOOL

DIERIC BOUTS THE ELDER
The Betrayal

HANS MEMLING *St John the Baptist*

HUGO VAN DER GOES
*Virgin and Child, with Angel
holding the Instruments of the Passion*

GERARD DAVID
Virgin and Child

GERARD DAVID
Christ's Farewell to the Virgin

HIERONYMUS BOSCH *Last Judgment:* Fragment

ROGIER VAN DER WEYDEN, 1397–1464
Adoration of the Kings (St Colomba) Altarpiece
Oak: centre panel $54\frac{5}{16}'' \times 60\frac{1}{4}''$ (138 × 153 cm.), wings $54\frac{5}{16}'' \times 27\frac{9}{16}''$ (138 × 70 cm.) Catalogue Nos. 1189–91

The colours of this painting are extraordinarily compelling – even on the horizon their brilliance and clarity are undimmed by dust or shadow. Each individual colour is vivid and intense: the pure lapis-lazuli of the Virgin's garment, repeated in each of the three panels, the sumptuous yellow of the first king's sleeve, the equally sumptuous blends of red in Joseph's modest habit, the velvet hat in the middle and the rich brocade of the king on the right. The olive-green and violet of the dress of the woman offering the doves in the Presentation in the Temple are of great subtlety. The precision of draughtsmanship of every detail is quite outstanding, particularly in the robes of the kings, which reflect all the elegance of the Burgundian court where the artist worked. Despite this meticulous realism and display of worldly pomp, the whole remains subordinated to the painting's overall theme. This religious theme is logically developed by means of abstractions. The stable before which the Virgin sits is merely an attribute – the only reality being the Virgin sitting enthroned full-face in the centre of the picture. Although her delicate face is bent over the Child, it remains majestic and austere. A crucifix hangs above

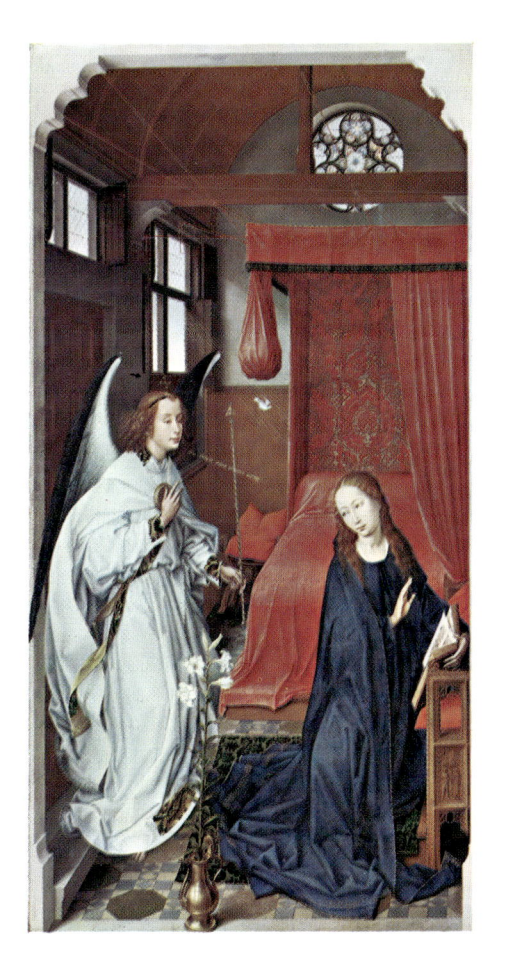

DIERIC BOUTS THE YOUNGER (?), c. 1448/50–91
Small Adoration of the Kings Altarpiece, known as the *Pearl of Brabant*
Oak: centre panel 24$\frac{13}{16}$″ × 24$\frac{3}{8}$″ (63 × 62 cm.), wings 24$\frac{13}{16}$″ × 11″ (63 × 28 cm.)
Catalogue Nos. WAF 76–78

In 1390 the Duchy of Brabant became part of Burgundy. Already with a long cultural tradition, it experienced a great artistic flowering in the sixteenth and seventeenth centuries under the Habsburgs. Its largest, most important towns were Brussels, Louvain and Nivelles. This small altarpiece, long considered one of the Duchy's finest paintings, acquired the name of *Pearl of Brabant* because of its wonderful enamelled colours, so beautiful and flawless that they looked like precious stones. This jewel-like quality is in keeping with the theme: the kings offer precious gifts, so precious that in the middle of the painting we see a table specially set up to bear them, while Joseph stands behind it formally receiving the offerings. The Virgin cradles the Child on her lap, while on the right panel St Christopher carries him on his shoulders, and on the left John the Baptist presents the Lamb, symbol of the Child – three interpretations of a single divine concept. The figure standing on the left, with her withered right hand resting on top of the wall, is the legendary Salome. It is said that she acted as midwife to Mary and expressed doubts about her virginity; when she tried to find out for herself her hand withered up; she prayed to God, faith was granted her and she was later cured by touching the Child Jesus.

The idea of depicting a particular time of day is something new; the sun stands low on the horizon, lighting up the river and the bright, clear, gently rippled water in the steep gorge through which St Christopher is wading. The wings are painted on the reverse with *grisailles*: St Catherine on the left wing, and St Barbara on the right. The artist of these supernatural landscapes is unfortunately unknown, but he is thought today, probably rightly, to have been the eldest son, and pupil, of Dieric Bouts.

This work, originally in the private chapel of the Snoy family of Malines, was acquired in 1813 by the Boisserée brothers.

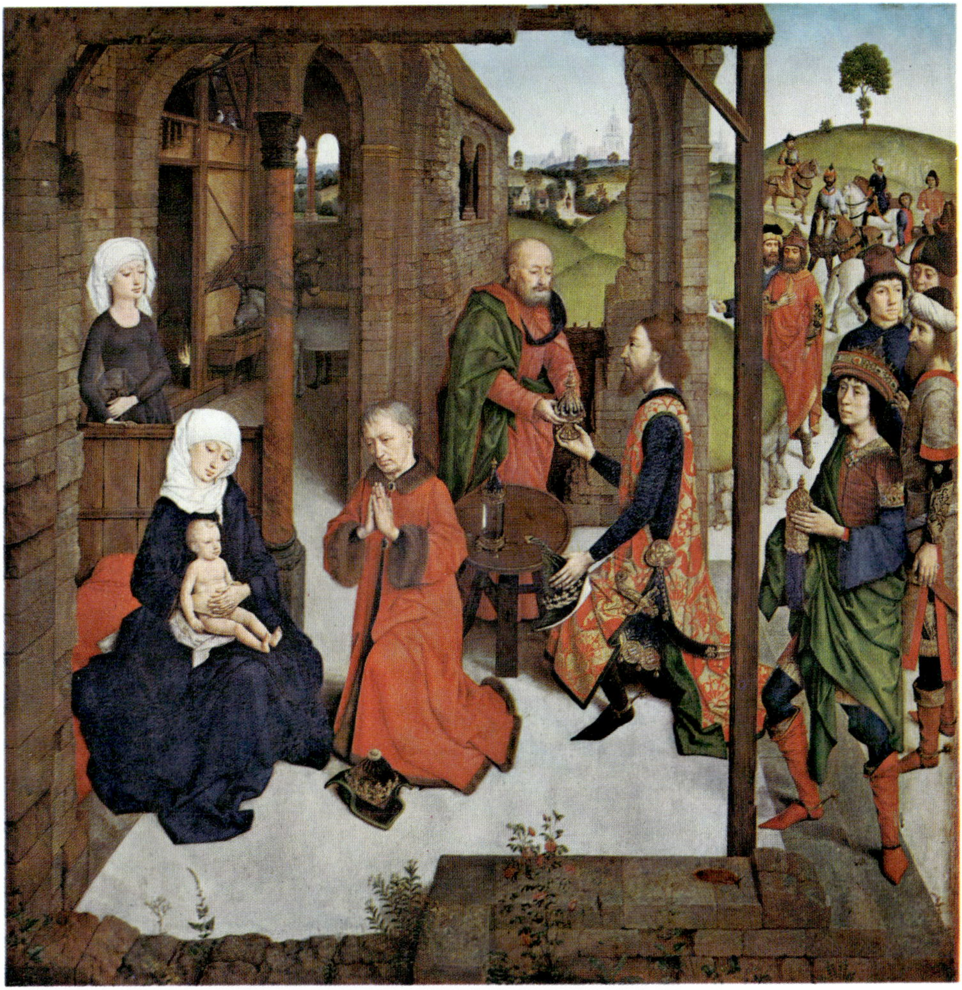

JAN GOSSAERT, called MABUSE, *c.* 1478–1532
Danaë
Oak: $44\frac{1}{2}'' \times 37\frac{3}{8}''$ (113·5 × 95 cm.) Catalogue No. 38. Signed and dated on the bottom step: IOANNES MALBODIVS PINGEBAT 1527

According to Greek mythology, Acrisios, king of Argos, was told by the Delphic Oracle that he would be killed by one of the sons of his daughter Danaë. He therefore shut her up in a room made of bronze. But Zeus, king of the gods, fell in love with Danaë and, eager for adventure, entered the tower where she was held prisoner in the form of golden rain. From this union she bore a son Perseus. The angry Acrisios had mother and child locked in a chest and floated out to sea. This story was a popular one, illustrated by Correggio, Titian and Rembrandt: these portrayals are all later, however. Mabuse's *Danaë* is the earliest painting on this theme. We are therefore forced to ask what led him to treat this theme in this particular way. In Northern Europe representations of Danaë were unknown, but in Italy the legend was taken up by Renaissance literature, often illustrated with miniatures or small woodcuts (Venice 1499).

Mabuse has rightly been called the first student of Romance languages in the Netherlands, for he was very well acquainted with Italian literature. From 1515 onwards he signed his works with the latinized form of his name, as here. He was also familiar with Italian architecture, as is shown by the magnificent round alcove in this painting, with its gleaming columns with their delicately carved capitals, used to produce interesting light-effects. This alcove does not have windows, but columns with spaces between, like a Mediterranean temple. Through these spaces can be seen an Italian-style building with a loggia and flat roof edged with balustrades and another tall domed building, while on the right is a church in Flemish late Gothic style and on the far left an ordinary north European bourgeois brick house. Despite, or perhaps because of, the accumulation of buildings in the background to the total exclusion of landscape or vegetation, the artist succeeds in conveying the sense of Danaë's total isolation, thus setting the scene for the intimate event that is about to take place. Danaë, a bewitchingly pretty young girl, raises her bright blue eyes towards the ceiling as she holds out her blue cloak to catch the golden rain. Her garments fall aside enticingly to reveal her breasts which, together with the position of her legs, give the painting a certain erotic character, all the more so since the walls which surround Danaë on three sides thrust her towards the spectator. This eroticism is countered by the coldness of the columns.

The success of this painting lies in its colours. They are deliberately and with originality restricted to grey-blue, contrasting wonderfully with the golden rain, and the dull red, finely differentiated according to substance, of the cushion and sections of the marble.

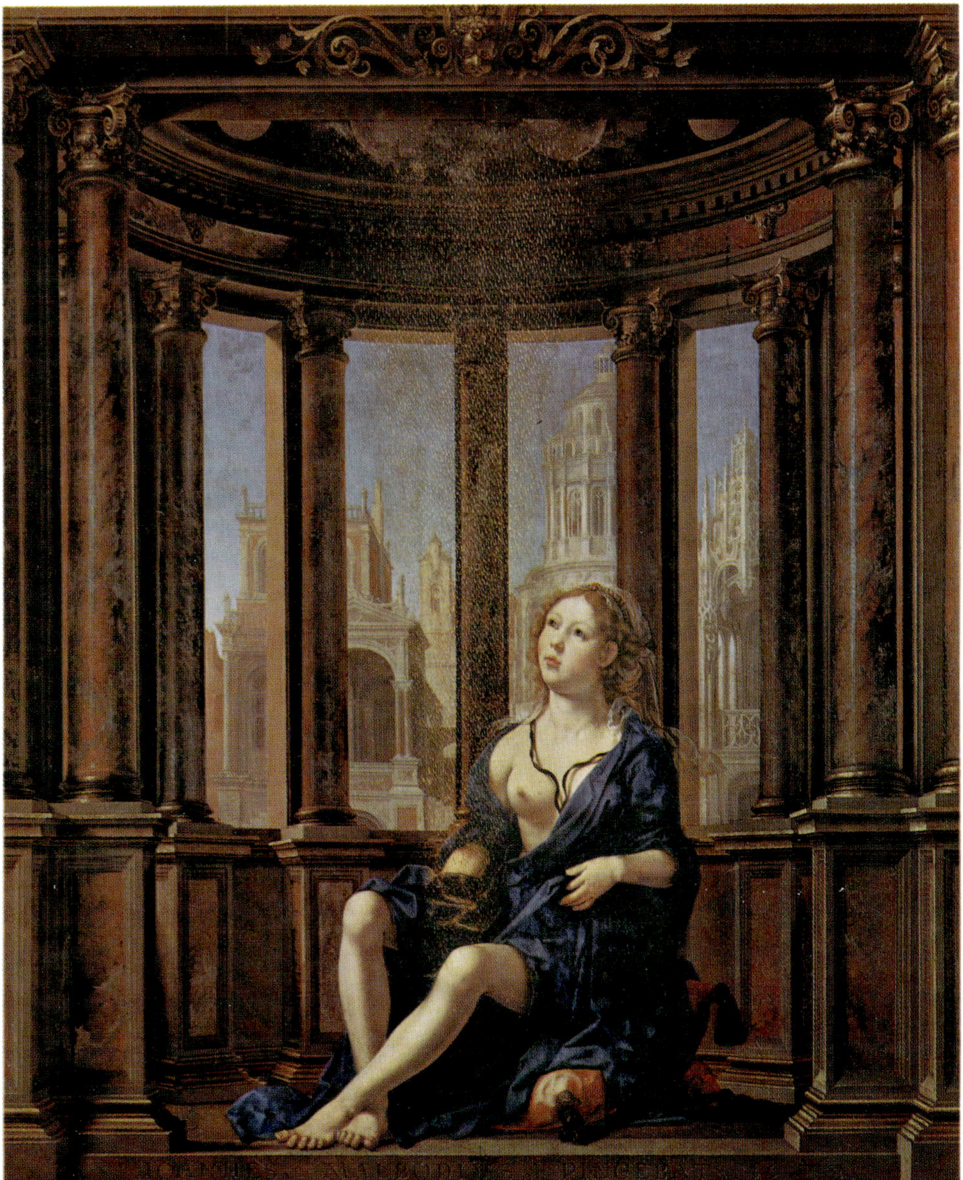

Mabuse was court painter to Philip of Burgundy (1465–1523), youngest illegitimate son of Duke Philip the Good. Philip of Burgundy was an admiral, and in this capacity was sent on several diplomatic missions. In 1508 he was dispatched to Rome, whither Mabuse accompanied him charged with the task of making copies of ancient buildings and sculptures. In 1517 Philip, a great humanist, became bishop of Utrecht. The post of admiral fell to his nephew, Adolph of Burgundy, whom Mabuse went to serve on Philip's death. Mabuse also worked in the service of Margaret of Austria, aunt of the Emperor and governor of the Low Countries, as well as that of Charles V's sisters, Eleanor and Isabel. His patrons would certainly have had some say in his choice and treatment of themes.

The catalogue compiled in December 1621 for the collection of Prague castle, as a kind of bequest of the Emperor Rudolf II, mentions an original Danaë by Mabuse as its entry for no. 1015 – this is probably the painting we have here.

This work was transferred from the Electors' gallery at Munich to the Hofgartengalerie in 1781, and entered the Alte Pinakothek in 1836.

MABUSE *Virgin and Child*
There is a replica of this painting in the Kunsthistorisches Museum, Vienna, and an engraving was made of it by Crispin de Passe. It was acquired with the Boisserée collection.

HANS MEMLING *Diptych: Madonna in the Rose-bower, with St George and a Donor*

HANS MEMLING, *c.* 1433–94
The Seven Joys of the Virgin
Oak: 31$\frac{15}{16}$″ × 73$\frac{3}{8}$″ (81 × 189 cm.) Catalogue No. WAF 668
(Reproduction pp. 126–7)

Stretching out before our eyes is a composite landscape of valleys and rounded hills, cottages and houses with domes and towers, sugar-loaf mountains and a sea with ships in the background. Curiously, the landscape is composed of beiges and browns rather than greens, delicately applied so that the little figures dotted all over the painting stand out clearly in their reds and blues. We are made to wonder what all these people are doing here, whether they are setting off on some journey. They are, in fact, the three kings who have come on horseback from the distant Orient to worship the Saviour; the Adoration of the Kings, the most important and beautiful scene in the picture, is

125

depicted in the centre. The kings had previously encountered King Herod, who had shown them the way from his palace through the narrow valleys. The kings go happily on their way, oblivious of the Massacre of the Innocents taking place simultaneously on the other side of the painting. The title of the painting is in fact inaccurate. Twenty religious scenes are depicted: the Annunciation, the Nativity, the Annunciation to the Shepherds, the Appearance of the Star to the three Kings, their Visit to Herod, their Journey, the Adoration, the Massacre of the Innocents, the Flight into Egypt, the Temptation of Christ, the Resurrection, the Noli me Tangere, Christ at Emmaus, Peter on the Water, the Appearance of Christ to his Mother, the Ascension, Pentecost, the Death of the Virgin, and the Assumption. The arrangement of the scenes does not follow the logic of modern thematic conceptions, but artistically speaking the theme is treated originally within a harmonious composition. According to the inscription on the original frame, Memling painted this work in 1480. As the construction and coloration of the figures shows, he was a devoted pupil of Rogier van der Weyden. He does not possess the terse vigour or religious power of his master; his talent is rather for pleasing and evocative narration. His gentleness and grace betray his native Rhineland (he was born near Mainz) despite his total adoption of Flemish styles.

This painting was commissioned by Peter Buyltink and his wife for the tanners' chapel in the Frauenkirche at Bruges. The members of the guild offered it to the Austrian governor of Brabant about 1780. Later owners were the Beauharnais family, M. Biron at Laeken near Brussels, and in 1813 the Boisserée brothers. It was acquired for the Pinakothek by Ludwig I.

ITALIAN SCHOOL

Segna di Buonaventura *St Mary Magdalene*

Giotto *Crucifixion*

Fra Angelico *Entombment*

TADDEO GADDI
Death of Celano

FLORENTINE SCHOOL, c. 1360
Bishop Saint with Goldfinch

SIENESE SCHOOL, c. 1340
Assumption of the Virgin
Wood: 30¾" × 14³⁄₁₆" (78·5 × 36 cm.), including frame. Catalogue No. WAF 671 (Reproduction p. 130)

The chief characteristic of Sienese painting is a feeling for poetry and lyricism, as opposed to the Florentine preference for dramatic action. It is not surprising then, that Sienese painters were particularly fond of scenes from the life of the Virgin to which they gave an intimate charm which still moves us today.

This panel is traditionally titled the *Assumption*, although a more exact description would be the reception of the Virgin in heaven. The apostles have been left below on earth, out of sight; Mary is already on high, in the celestial regions, where the angels greet her joyfully. Mounting towards the firmament she sits with sublime calm, enthroned upon a cloud supported by two little angels in the background. Tympani, trumpets, drums, flutes, harps, violins, lutes, organs, guitars and cymbals join in harmony accompanying her

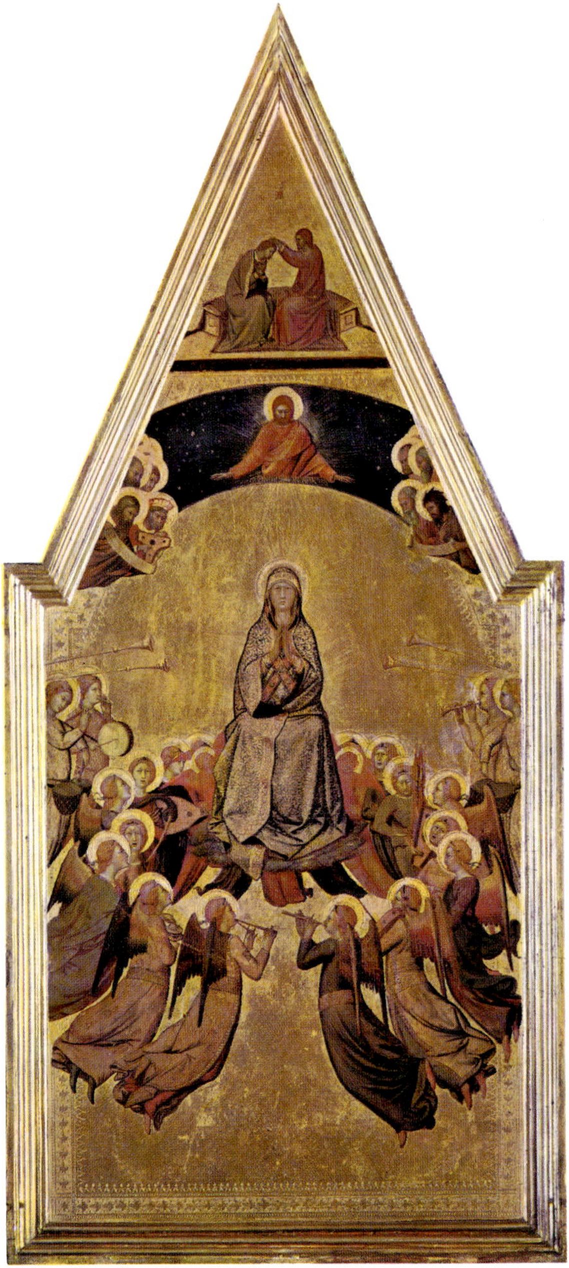

on her way to the heavens. There Christ awaits her with arms outstretched, while the host of the saints and prophets, including John the Baptist and David with his harp, impatiently await her arrival. Christ and the Virgin reappear together at the top of the painting, cut off from the main scene by a dark line. The Virgin's reception in heaven is here symbolized not by the traditional coronation, but by Christ laying his hands upon her head in blessing.

The rather heavy figure of Mary seems still weighed down with earthly cares, and contrasts sharply with the weightlessness of the other delicate celestial beings whose ring continues and completes the arc of the sky. The muted, blended colours of their robes are relieved with gold brocade motifs which serve to integrate the figures into the golden background, giving them a timeless, ethereal quality.

The style of this Assumption shows traces of the influence of Simone Martini, the famous Sienese master whose poignant *Annunciation* hangs in the Uffizi, Florence.

This work was acquired by Crown Prince Ludwig in 1825.

FRA GIOVANNI DA FIESOLE, called FRA ANGELICO, 1387–1455
St Cosmas and St Damian: the Incitement to Idolatry
Wood: $14\frac{15}{16}'' \times 18\frac{1}{8}''$ (37·8 × 46·6 cm.) Catalogue No. WAF 36
(Reproduction p. 132)

According to legend the Arabian twin brothers Cosmas and Damian, pious doctors practising their art for the love of God, were accused of witchcraft and brought, with their brothers, before the Proconsul Lysias. Their refusal to renounce their Christian faith and worship pagan gods brought them martyrdom. This painting is one of a series of small panels in which Fra Angelico tells the story of these two saints, with the profusion of detail characteristic of Florentine, early Renaissance painters. The scene is a square before Lysias' palace, covered with thick grass and flowers and bordered by a marble enclosure. In the centre of the composition the supreme judge sits on his throne decorated with carved lions. He points graphically to an idol, before which the five accused are invited to give evidence of their veneration. Counsellors and soldiers form a second group to Lysias' left. The strange headgear of the figures, otherwise dressed in contemporary clothes, gives the scene an exotic flavour, indicating that it takes place in some distant land. This fairy-tale quality is further emphasized by the brightly coloured garments, contrasting sharply with the delicate shading of the architecture and the dark green of the ground.

This painting originally formed part of the *predella* of the high altar painted around 1440 for the Dominican Church of San Marco in Florence. Together with two other small panels from the same group, it was purchased in 1822 from a Berlin art-dealer.

FRA FILIPPO LIPPI, c. 1406–69
Annunciation
Wood: $79\frac{15}{16}'' \times 72\frac{13}{16}''$ (203 × 185 cm.) Catalogue No. 1072

The joyful tranquillity of Italian art of the early Renaissance is exemplified in this painting. Cautiously and hesitantly, the artist advances along new and untrodden paths, still reluctant to leave behind altogether the traditional styles of the Middle Ages. The youthful modesty of this work bears witness to the vitality and untapped energy of a new beginning, like a bud bearing within itself the seeds of that splendid flowering that was to be the High Renaissance.

The scene is a magnificent room with marble-covered walls, divided by a partition rather like a rood-screen, an idealized interior such as that found in contemporary architecture. Through the three arched openings one can see from the narrow foreground through to a carefully tended garden cut off from the outside world by a high wall. The composition of the painting is strictly symmetrical with the central axis emphasized by the tall straight tree and the gabled garden gate. Intimacy, seclusion, silence dominate the scene, reflecting the Virgin's piety and purity. The touching fragility of her figure and the delicate lines of the architecture give an impression of ethereal spirituality. Standing with head humbly bowed, the Virgin listens to the Archangel's message, while the dove, symbol of the Holy Ghost, sent by God the Father glides towards her on a shaft of light. The mystery of the Immaculate Conception, the true theme of the painting, is thus delicately portrayed. The figure of the Archangel acting as intermediary remains at a distance from that of the Virgin – they are to some extent united by the common gesture of hand over heart (expressing greeting), but their eyes do not meet and between them stands the barrier of the *prie-dieu*.

The scene is accompanied by a number of symbols which have figured in scenes from the life of the Virgin ever since the Middle Ages: the dove (symbol of the Holy Ghost), the Tree of Jesse (also an allusion to the Tree of Knowledge in the Earthly Paradise), the closed door along the central axis, the walled garden, the glass vase, the roses and lilies carried by the angels (symbols of purity and virginity, and of the promised redemption). The triple arcade crowned by a larger arch can also be interpreted as an allusion to the Holy Trinity.

This painting was donated for the high altar of the Convento delle Murate Church in Florence in 1443, but was probably not completed until some years later. It was acquired by Ludwig I of Bavaria in 1812 at the time of the dissolution of the monasteries.

FRA FILIPPO LIPPI, *c.* 1406–69
Virgin and Child
Wood: 30" × 21½" (76·3 × 54·2 cm.) Catalogue No. 647

The light colours of the *Annunciation* are in this painting replaced by more sombre, austere shades, and the ethereal figures of the former by creatures of flesh and blood. The new understanding of the human body of the school of Masaccio and Donatello is clearly visible; the only remnants of the old style

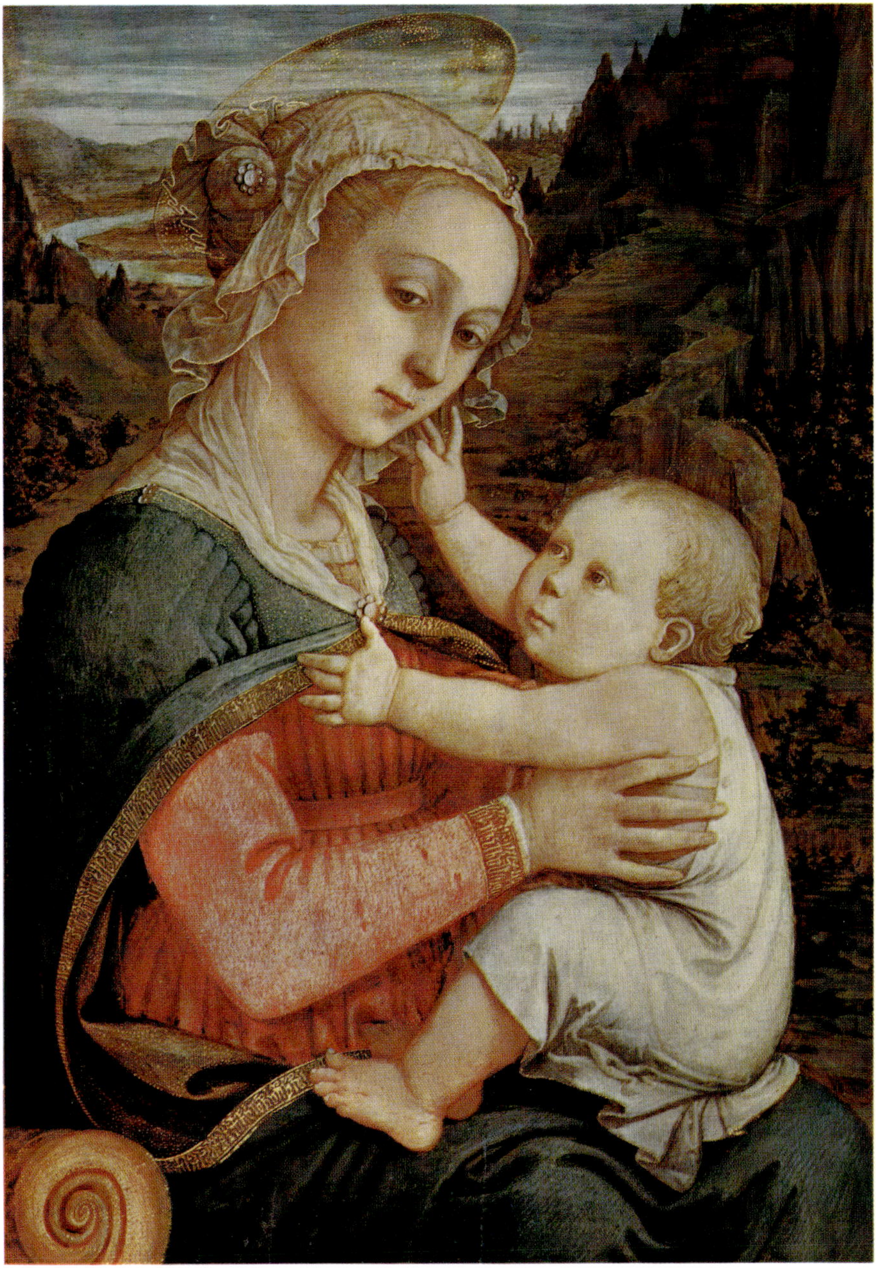

are the rocks in the right background. The intimacy of Mother and Child contrasts with the vast expanse of landscape encompassing mountain and valley, town and river, which the spectator looks down on from a height. The two figures are conceived in charming contrast: the Madonna is slender and delicate with regular features, composed in expression and gesture; the Child is awkward and heavy as he stretches his arms out towards his mother with childlike insistence. But as decorative motifs the two are gracefully united by the curve of the child's back mirrored by the billowing edge of the Virgin's cloak.

This painting is a mature work of around 1460. It was acquired in Florence in 1808 for Crown Prince Ludwig of Bavaria.

FILIPPINO LIPPI *Intercession of Christ and the Virgin*
This altarpiece of around 1495 originally belonged to the Grey Friars of Palco, near Prato. It was acquired by Crown Prince Ludwig of Bavaria in Florence between 1814 and 1816.

DOMENICO BECCAFUMI
Holy Family with the Infant St John

LUCA SIGNORELLI   *Virgin and Child*

ALBERTINELLI   *Annunciation*

FERRARESE MASTER, active c. 1480–90
Family Portrait
Canvas: $44\frac{1}{16}'' \times 35\frac{7}{16}''$ (112 × 90 cm.) Catalogue No. 8709
Later inscription added on the upper edge of the window: UBERTUS ET MARCHIO TOMAS DE SACRATO

The portraits of the early Renaissance depict remote, inaccessible, self-assured characters, whose personality is mostly limited to external indications of rank and status. Dress, jewels and accessories serve to conceal rather than emphasize individual personality. It is rare to find a painting in which several figures are depicted communicating with each other, except when they form part of a total scene. The figures' feelings for one another convince not through open suggestion, but through reticence and restraint. Similarly, the three static figures here do not look at each other, but Umberto de Sacrati, a Ferrara nobleman, has his hand on his wife's shoulder in a quiet gesture of conjugal love more touching than any open display of emotion. The close bond between mother and son is clearly indicated by a similarly delicate gesture. The father reflects the strength and security of the man; on his gloved hand rests a falcon, symbol of his nobility. His stance expresses the inflexible pride of the Italian nobleman of the Renaissance, while his wife, richly dressed and decked with jewels, maintains a virtuous reserve. In the boy's childlike face a certain obstinacy and insolence can be detected.

The background decorative elements clearly dispersed throughout the work – the two pieces of fruit, the folds in the drapery and the coral necklace – are strictly linked to its central axis, giving the supple composition of the group added firmness and balance. The austerity of design, bordering on ugliness, and the immobility of the figures suggest that this is a work of the Ferrara school. It has been attributed to Baldassare Estense, but is now thought more likely to be the work of Antonio da Crevalcare.

Originally in the Palazzo Sacrati-Strozzi at Ferrara, this painting was purchased for the Alte Pinakothek in 1913.

VBERTVS LEMARCHIO FILIO TOMAS DE SACRATO

PIERO DI COSIMO *Legend of Prometheus*

PACCHIA
Virgin and Child, with Angels

ANDREA DEL SARTO
*Holy Family, with St John the Baptist,
St Elizabeth and two Angels*

FRANCIABIGIO *Virgin and Child*

LIBERALE DA VERONA
Lamentation of Christ

BOTTICINI *The Young Tobias with three Archangels*

SANDRO FILIPEPI, called BOTTICELLI, 1444/5–1510
Pietà
Wood: $54\frac{3}{4}'' \times 81\frac{1}{2}''$ (139·5 × 207·3 cm.) Catalogue No. 1075

In this work, the immense grief which followed the death of the Saviour is expressed with all the melancholy solemnity of the music of a choral Passion. The faces and gestures of the figures grouped around the body of Christ reflect the infinite sorrow to which – not yet comprehending God's scheme of salvation – they thought they had been abandoned, as victims of some cruel fate. The loose blocks of stone threatening to crash down on them add to this sense of utter despair. Mary has fainted, overcome with grief. Her face has a waxen, deathly hue like that of the body of her son lying across her lap – a fine beardless young man, reminiscent of Dürer's notion that Christ must be portrayed as absolute perfection just as the ancients saw Apollo as the paragon of ideal beauty. Of all the onlookers only St John has maintained his presence of mind, as he tenderly and compassionately helps to support the Virgin. The three female saints are sunk in despair. Mary Magdalene raises Christ's feet, which she had once wiped with her hair, while another female saint ardently presses her face to that of Christ, as the third gazes in horror at the nails of the Cross which she holds in her hands, stifling her sobs with the flap of her cloak.

But the principal theme of this painting is not death or despair. That Christ's sacrifice consisted precisely in overcoming these is made clear by the secondary figures who, not participating directly in the action, might seem out of place here. Of these St Peter is the key figure. With right hand raised, he turns towards the spectator to instruct and guide him, fulfilling his role as leader and supreme head of the Church. On the left St Jerome, striking his breast with a stone, and St Paul, deep in silent prayer, turn believers from their sorrow to the path which leads through penitence and meditation to God.

This work, painted during the last decade of the fifteenth century, could be described as a 'sermon-painting', and it is not entirely fanciful to suggest, as many have done, that Botticelli was inspired by Savonarola's preaching on penitence. The contrast between the gloomy colours of Christ's body, the stones and the dark background on the one hand, and the gay brilliant colours of the garments on the other, is striking, again an allusion to the theme of the painting – the contrast between oppression and hope, death and life.

A true Florentine, Botticelli has chosen a dramatic, deeply tragic style, controlled in this case, however, by a strict symmetry. The preponderance of figures on the left-hand side is balanced by St Peter's isolated position on the right, at the same time emphasizing the importance of the latter to the understanding of the picture.

It is not known who commissioned this work, or where it was originally hung. In the early nineteenth century it belonged to the San Paolino monastery in Florence. It was purchased by Johannes Metzger on behalf of Crown Prince Ludwig in 1814.

Domenico di Tommaso Bigordi, called Ghirlandaio, 1449–94
Virgin in Majesty, venerated by four Saints
Wood: 87″ × 77$\frac{15}{16}$″ (221 × 198 cm.) Catalogue No. 1078
(Reproduction p. 144)

The late works of Domenico Ghirlandaio were almost all commissioned by the Florentine banker Giovanni Tornabuoni. Between 1484 and 1490 he painted for this patron a series of frescoes, in the choir of the Dominican Church of Santa Maria Novella in Florence, depicting the lives of the Virgin and St John the Baptist. It was probably shortly after this that Ghirlandaio received the commission for this altarpiece for the high altar of the same church, the *Virgin in Majesty* being the centre panel. The prescribed intention and destination of the painting demanded something that was easily comprehensible, clearly constructed and brightly coloured. Ghirlandaio, with his gift for clear, logical composition, fulfilled these requirements admirably.

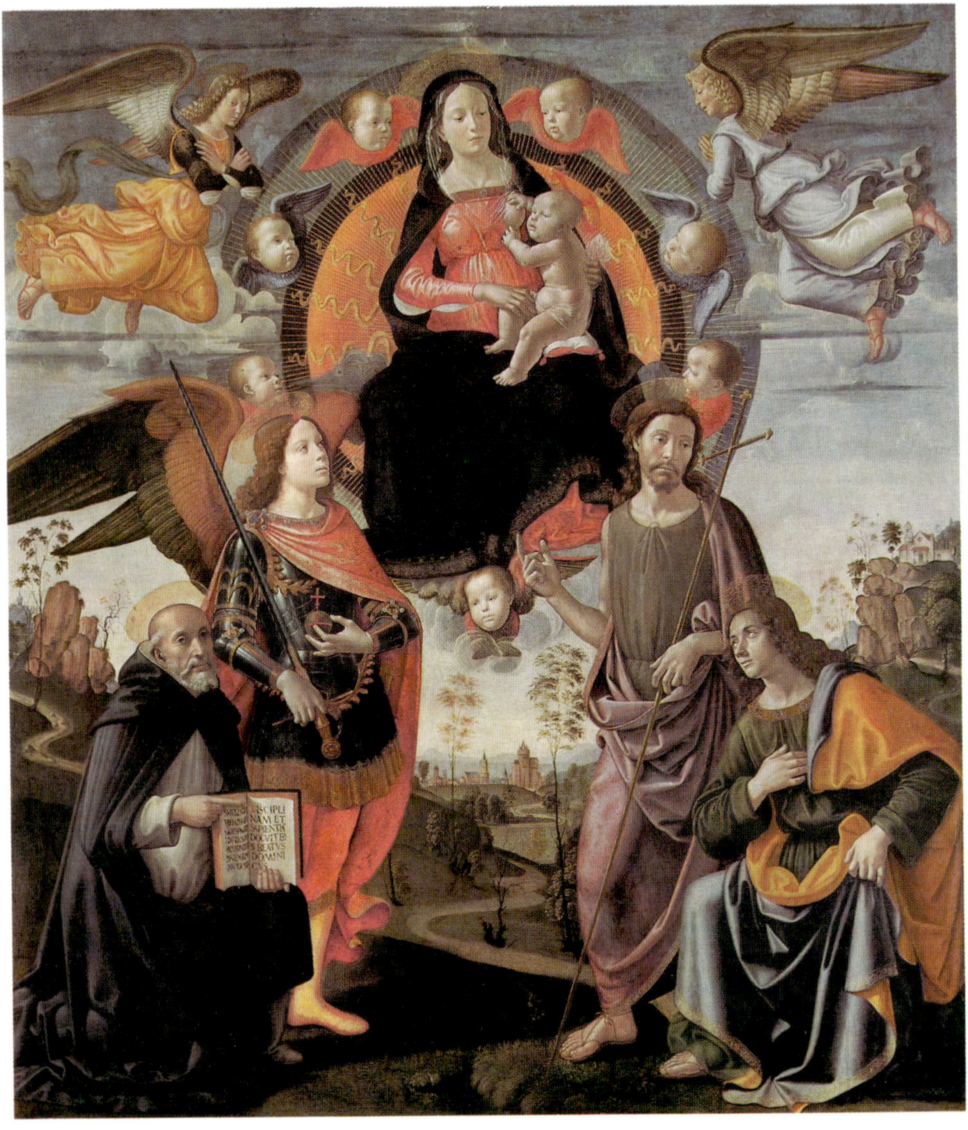
SCIPLI
NAM ET
SAPIENTI
DOCUIT E
S BEATUS
DOMINI

The group of figures is constructed in the form of a pyramid, with the two saints at the Virgin's feet standing sufficiently far apart for a whole landscape to be seen between them. St Dominic kneeling on the left looks and points at the spectator – as founder of the Dominican order, his inclusion in a high altar for a Dominican church was a matter of course. Next to him stands the Archangel Michael, one of the patron saints of Florence, with a globe in one hand and a drawn sword in the other, symbolizing his role as defender of the town. His distinctive, pale complexion suggests his celestial nature. The Virgin, Patron of the Church, sits enthroned with the Child, surrounded by angels and the centre of a nimbus composed of differently coloured circles, representing the different spheres of the Universe, all illumined with the light of the Mother of God. The two figures of Mother and Child combine intimacy and grandeur, symbolically portraying the unity of their twofold human and divine nature. In the right foreground St John the Baptist, the most illustrious of Florence's patron saints, stands with his raised right hand pointing to the Saviour; beside him kneels the young St John the Evangelist, included in this honourable assembly probably because he was patron saint of Giovanni Tornabuoni – his attitude of intercession would seem to confirm this.

The geometrical shapes which make up the strict linear construction of the composition are arranged so that the triangle formed by the group of figures interlocks with a second triangle enclosing the concentric circles of the nimbus. The base of this second triangle passes through the apex of the first, the other two sides being formed by St Michael's sword and St John the Baptist's cross.

Vasari tells us that, on Ghirlandaio's death, this painting was found still unfinished in his studio. It was completed by pupils who had worked for him previously. When the high altar was demolished in 1804, this work was acquired by the Medici, from whom it was acquired by Crown Prince Ludwig in 1816.

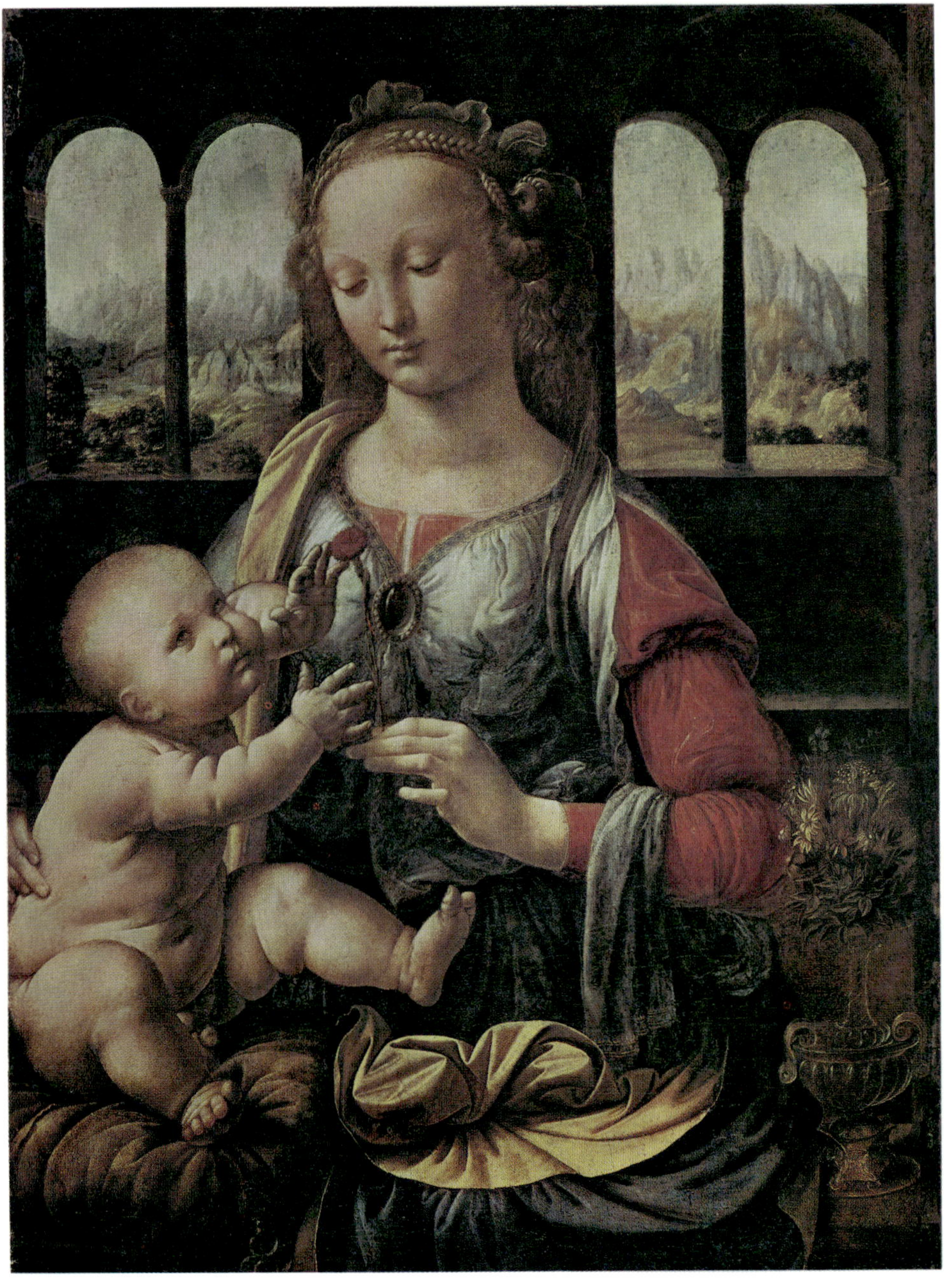

LEONARDO DA VINCI, 1452-1519
Virgin and Child
Wood: $24\frac{7}{16}''\times 18\frac{1}{8}''$ (62 × 46·5 cm.) Catalogue No. 7779

Raphael and Leonardo are the two artists who achieved a realization and synthesis of all the aspirations of the Renaissance. When we talk of the masterpieces of the High Renaissance, it is of their works we think. Both were inspired portrayers of the Virgin, but their interpretations of this theme were fundamentally different. For Raphael the Mother of God was primarily a creature of flesh and blood, personifying in an idealized form all the joys and sorrows of earthly life. The charm of Raphael's Madonnas is in the effect of bodily charms sublimated. But Leonardo saw the Virgin as a transfigured apparition of celestial beauty, whose spiritualized features glow with divine radiance. Her absolutely spotless character, her quintessential purity, are not of this world. This early work already shows Leonardo's conception of the theme. The delicately modelled face rises above the complex folds of the robe, which harmonizes in form and colour with the strange mountains in the background. No emotion clouds the perfect harmony of the Virgin's face; only the hint of a smile plays around her small mouth. Her slightly veiled features gives an impression of distance and remoteness, the beginnings of the *sfumato* technique that Leonardo was later to use with such mastery. A similar effect is produced by the waving and interlacing of the hair and the robe. Unlike this calm, severe Virgin, the Child Jesus is depicted in violent motion, quivering with excitement as he struggles to grasp the red carnation delicately held by his mother. His right leg pushes against the cushion and the other waves in the air as he leans forward and reaches upwards, as though trying to catch a butterfly in his clumsy hands. Like a precious stone, the Virgin is set in a region of darkness sheltering her in its calm and solitude from the harsh mountain landscape outside.

Leonardo painted this work around 1478 while he was still working in Verrocchio's studio. There are, in fact, certain similarities with Verrocchio, although the conception and execution already reveal the unmistakable hand of genius. This painting was purchased from a private collection in 1889.

PIETRO VANUCCI called PERUGINO, *c.* 1450–1523
Vision of St Bernard
Wood: $68\frac{1}{8}'' \times 66\frac{15}{16}''$ (173 × 170 cm.) Catalogue No. WAF 764

The subtle art of Perugino – who, as master of no less a painter than Raphael, counts as one of the greatest artists of the Umbrian school – is often misunderstood. The distinguishing features of his work are its tranquil harmony, realistic simplicity and profound spirituality.

This work, painted in the last decade of the fifteenth century, was commissioned by the Nasi brothers, Bernardo and Filippo, for the altar of their family chapel in the Church of Santa Maria dei Pazzi in Florence.

RAPHAEL (RAFFAELLO SANZIO), 1483–1520
Tempi Madonna
Wood: $29\frac{1}{2}'' \times 20\frac{1}{2}''$ (75 × 52 cm.) Catalogue No. WAF 796

This painting, with its reminiscences of the Umbrian school which so decisively influenced Raphael's years of apprenticeship, has a radiance of its own which emerges only gradually but leaves an indelible impression on the mind. Raphael reached artistic maturity at a very early age, painting this work when he was barely twenty-five, towards the end of his four-year stay in Florence shortly before his departure for Rome in 1508. None of his many other portrayals of the Virgin is more deeply felt or more poignant than this; in its delicate simplicity it creates an impression of grandeur and dignity. This effect is heightened by the vertical format tightly enclosing the figure, and by the gentle, harmonious curves. The simplicity of the painting is deceptive; all the mystery of the incarnation is here transformed into living reality, in a quite unique way.

It has rightly been observed that the Virgin is portrayed in motion. The veil streaming behind her shoulders and her cloak billowing out behind her indicate that she is advancing slowly to the right, carrying her Son over a vast, open landscape towards the world of men, represented by the town silhouetted in the background. This work is not a simple idyllic picture of maternal joy; the Virgin knows that she is leading the Child towards his calling, she senses the destiny which awaits him. Her face, which with

RAPHAEL
Madonna della Tenda
This work was painted by Raphael during his stay in Rome. It remained in the Escorial probably until the beginning of the nineteenth century. It was bought by Crown Prince Ludwig of Bavaria from Sir Thomas Baring in 1814.

half-closed eyes she rests tenderly against the Child's head while embracing and protecting his body with her arms, is imprinted with the humility of the 'handmaid of the Lord'. Her veiled, melancholy gaze reflects submission to the will of God, while the Child's wide-open eyes indicate that he too is ready for the sacrifice. The clear allusion to the 'Lamb of God' sometimes found in earlier paintings of the Virgin is here replaced by a penetrating psychological study.

King Ludwig I acquired this masterpiece from the collection of the Tempi family in Florence in 1829, after twenty years of negotiations.

RAPHAEL (RAFFAELLO SANZIO) 1483–1520
Canigiani Holy Family
Wood: $51\frac{9}{16}'' \times 42\frac{1}{8}''$ (131 × 107 cm.) Catalogue No. 476
Signed on the neckline of the Virgin's bodice: RAPHAEL. URBINAS
(Reproduction p. 152)

In the *Tempi Madonna* Raphael was primarily concerned with expressing the religious and human aspects of the scene, while what concerns him here is artistic problems. The strictly symmetrical triangular composition of the five figures – pyramidal, in fact – reflects the aspirations of the High Renaissance towards harmony and absolute beauty. The composition of the group at first sight appears forced and artificial, but each figure maintains its natural grace and pose. The Virgin is highlighted as the main figure by the richer colouring of her garments, while the colouring of the two children and St Elizabeth and St Joseph serves to link them in pairs.

The group is surrounded by an attractive landscape, emphasizing in its charming diversity the monumental, architectural effect of the work. Unfortunately, an important element in the balance of the composition has now been lost: there were originally symmetrically arranged groups of angels in the two top corners, but in the early eighteenth century they were painted over because they were badly damaged.

This work was painted in Florence shortly after the *Tempi Madonna*, although the latter in fact shows greater maturity. It was owned by Domenico Canigiani before passing to the Medici collection, and in 1691 was sent to Düsseldorf by Cosimo III as a gift to his son-in-law, the Elector Palatine Johann Wilhelm. It has been in Munich since 1806.

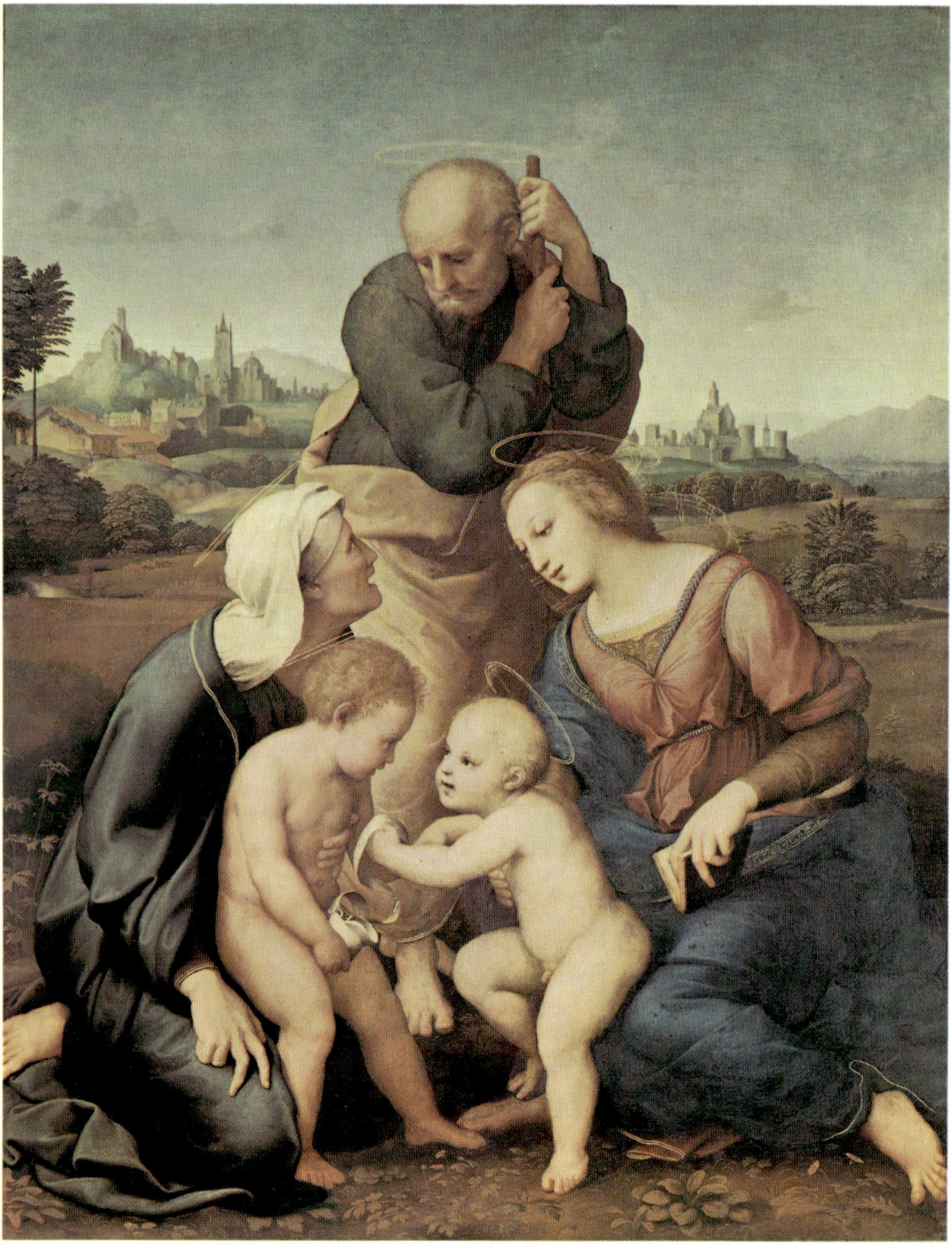

ANTONELLO DA MESSINA, *c.* 1430–79
Virgin of the Annunciation
Wood: $16\frac{1}{2}'' \times 13''$ (42·5 × 32·7 cm.) Catalogue No. 8054

The blue cloak quietly and majestically falls over the Virgin's fragile figure, emphasizing the seclusion and tranquillity of her existence, soon to be shattered by an external event. A trace of agitation is even now apparent in the inside curve of the oval framing the face with its one pointed end jarring with the soft, rounded forms of the outside curve. This agitation is evident also in the childlike face with its wide-open eyes and parted lips, in the rigid posture of the head and the tensed neck muscles, and particularly in the nervous contraction of the hands, crossed over her chest as a sign of submission.

Deeply troubled by the divine presence, the Virgin partly turns her head away from the messenger whom one imagines kneeling beside her, and frightened and bewildered looks at him out of the corner of her eye. But the resignation with which she accepts the inconceivable – 'Behold the handmaid of the Lord, be it unto me according to Thy Word' – lends her face great dignity.

This little devotional work, painted around 1474 probably for a private commission, derives its sense of solitude from its portrayal of the Virgin lost deep in thought. This was clearly not intended to form a pair with another painting depicting the angel of the Annunciation, but was meant as an individual, self-sufficient work.

This painting was purchased from a Munich art-dealer in 1897.

JACOPO DE' BARBARI, c. 1450–before 1515
Still-life
Wood: $19\frac{11}{16}'' \times 16\frac{9}{16}''$ (50 × 42·5 cm.) Catalogue No. 5066
Signed and dated: Jac. de barbarj P 1504

The depiction of several heterogeneous objects harmoniously arranged is almost as old as painting itself. But in earlier periods still-life was only an accessory, one element of an interior, serving only to adorn or symbolically reinforce the theme of the work. The Renaissance freed still-life painting from this subordinate position, making it the subject of individual paintings. In the seventeenth century, thanks to Dutch painting, the still-life came to acquire the same status as other *genres*. This work, however, is one of the earliest still-life paintings known.

On a light-coloured wall are hung from a nail a pair of iron gauntlets with wriststraps, and a dead partridge, pierced diagonally by the plumed bolt of a crossbow, objects all closely linked with the manly activities of hunting and war. Another important element in the composition is the folded note, which bears the artist's signature and the staff of Mercury which he frequently used to mark his graphic works. Each object has been studied with great care and love of detail, and its individual qualities translated on to the canvas with great precision – for example, the shading of the different materials even in the darkest areas of shadow, and the treatment of the worn condition of one of the gloves. But faithful depiction of detail is not sufficient to give a painting artistic value; only by the incorporation of detail into an ordered whole is a work of art created, as this painting shows.

The artist was born in Venice and moved to Germany around 1500. It was during his German period that this work was painted. In 1764 it entered the Elector's collection at Schloss Neuburg on the Danube, and moved to Munich in 1804.

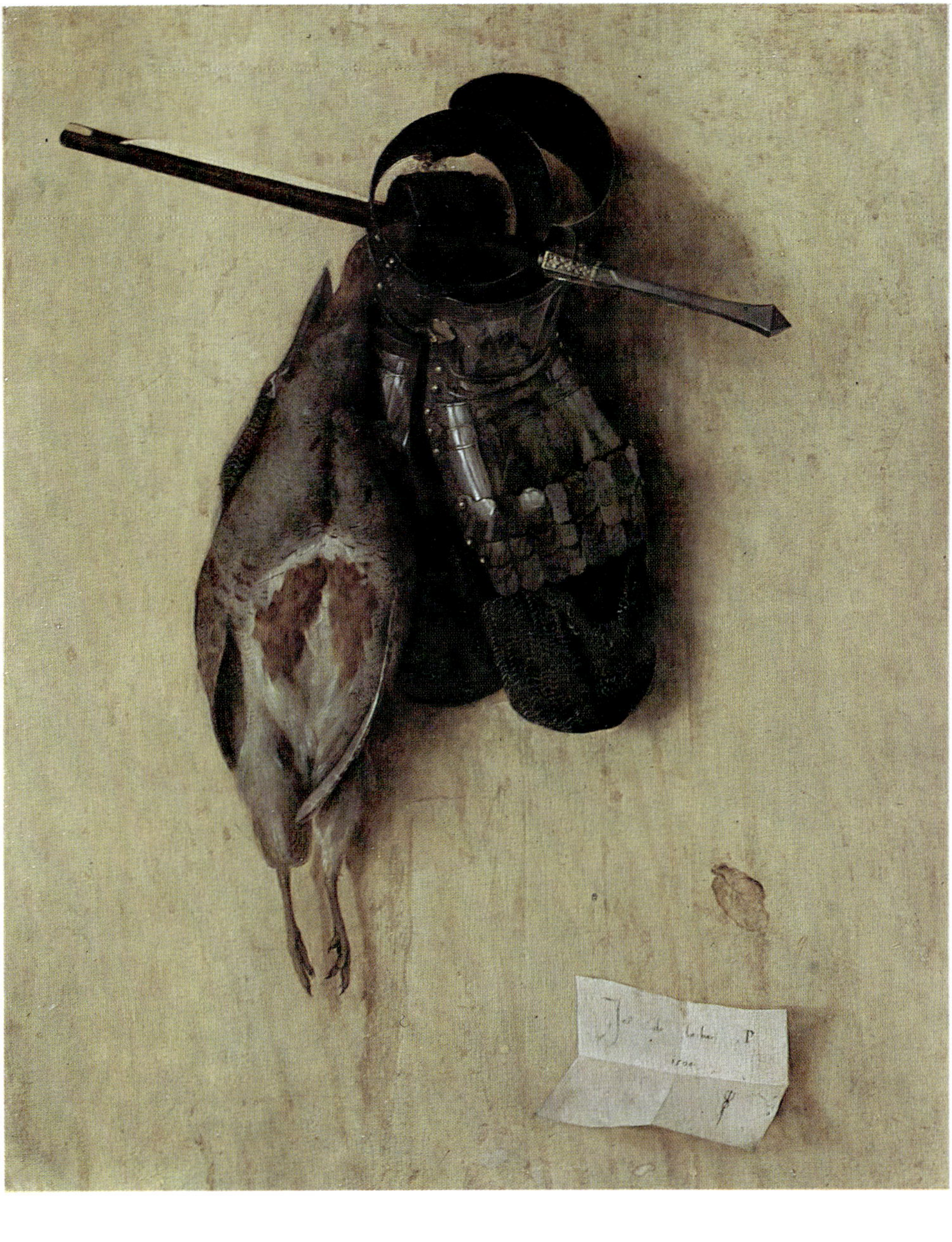

MORETTO *Portrait of an Ecclesiastic*

BAROCCIO *Noli me Tangere*

CRESPI *Massacre of the Innocents*

GUIDO RENI *Assumption*

LUCA GIORDANO
St Andrew's Descent from the Cross

MAGNASCO *Coast Scene*

GIOVANNI BATTISTA CIMA DA CONEGLIANO, 1459/60–1517/18
Virgin and Child with Mary Magdalene and St Jerome
Wood: 31½″ × 48 7/16″ (80 × 123 cm.) Catalogue No. 992
Signed: IOANNIS BAPTISTAE CONEGLANENSIS OPUS

The *sacra conversazione* is the most pure and perfect expression of that atmosphere of intimate contemplation which characterizes Venetian painting of the Renaissance. In the last quarter of the fifteenth century the altars of Venetian churches were adorned with portrayals of full-figure groups of saints standing calm and motionless, often around the Virgin. The same style of painting, but with half-figures, was adopted in the devotional works painted for the private palaces of the city of the Doges. Giovanni Bellini was the undisputed master in this field – without him the painting we have here would never have existed.

Four figures are linked in pairs by their gestures and the slight inclination of their bodies. Even this slight movement goes beyond the limits of the *sacra conversazione*, but its essential features of complete silence and inner repose are preserved. The movements of the figures are not conscious but more in the nature of reflexes indicating the object of their deep meditation. Only the Child Jesus, lifting the lid of Mary Magdalene's jar of ointment in childlike curiosity, acts in a manner that is natural, escaping the general immobility.

The two saints have a serious, knowing expression, while the Virgin's younger face, turned away from the Child, is filled with a touching melancholy. Her thoughts dwell on the vision of things to come, and are more in tune with St Jerome's instruments of penitence than with the playful joy of the Child. The simplicity of composition corresponds to the rather solemn sadness of the figures. The Virgin sits on a raised seat, above the standing saints whose heads are on the same level as that of the Child – this uniformity is, however, cleverly attenuated by the valley which cuts the background landscape in two, restoring visual equilibrium to the work by making St Jerome's head appear above the horizon, thus throwing him into greater relief. The Venetians gave little attention to the volume of their figures or to the laws of perspective; this is seen clearly in the landscape here which, although an important element in the composition, lacks any clear spatial definition. The figures are like actors on a stage hemmed in by the piece of painted scenery behind them and the strip of marble, equally lacking in perspective, in front. The colours suggest serenity, equilibrium and composure, each individual tone part of a network of multiple relationships and harmonies covering the whole picture, in which all violent contrast is avoided.

This work once belonged to the Empress Josephine's collection at Malmaison, and was bought in Paris by Crown Prince Ludwig in 1815.

Lorenzo Lotto, *c.* 1480–1556/7
Mystic Marriage of St Catherine
Wood: $27\frac{15}{16}'' \times 35\frac{13}{16}''$ (71 × 91 cm.) Catalogue No. 32
Signed along the edge: Laurent. Lotus F.

Lotto was a contemporary of Titian and, like him, a representative of the Venetian school. Titian's work is for us the culmination of sixteenth-century Venetian painting, the very personification of the spirit of the city of the lagoons. Lotto's works, however, defy any such classification. They are the work of a solitary genius who, despite his many links with the art of his native city, always opted for the personal solution. Even his contemporaries recognized his special position and unique talent, characterized as much by personality as by nationality. This may have limited his scope in Venice, but it opened up new opportunities in Trevira, Bergamo, Rome and Loretta, all of which mark decisive stages in his artistic career.

The *Mystic Marriage of St Catherine*, an early work, already has all the signs of Lotto's individual qualities. In composition and colour this work clashes with the Venetian mood of calm and comtemplation. The balance of the composition, with the central group enclosed in a strict triangle, is deliberately upset by the diagonal position of St Joseph, almost out of the painting, a position which bears no relation to the landscape on the opposite side. His backwards tilt corresponds neither to the static figure of the Virgin in the centre, nor to the moving Child, but if anything to the forwards inclination of the body of St Catherine; this, far from stabilizing the composition only serves to emphasize further the diagonal movement which seems to push him out of the painting. The complexity and violence of the linear composition are matched by the colouring. Vivid, brilliant, strong colours are daringly juxtaposed in a way very different from normal Venetian practice. The contrast between the colours is reinforced to produce a disequilibrium and disharmony not found in the works of Bellini, Giorgione or Titian. This technique creates colour effects of incomparable richness and beauty: the moss-green of the curtain contrasting with the intoxicating deep red, the blue and green in which the pale pink of the Child is set like a jewel, the exquisite harmony of the cream and pale blue of St Catherine's sleeves juxtaposed with the surrounding pale browns and brilliant reds.

This painting was transferred from the archiepiscopal palace of Würzburg to the Hofgartengalerie at Munich in 1804, from where it moved to the Alte Pinakothek.

TITIAN
Virgin and Child in an Evening Landscape

TITIAN *Portrait of a young Man*

TITIAN
Virgin and Child, with St John the Baptist and a Donor

TITIAN *Vanity*
This work was probably in the collection of the Emperor Rudolf II. It was at Schleissheim in 1748, in the Hofgartengalerie in 1781, and in 1836 was transferred to the Alte Pinakothek. It was attributed to Giorgione until 1884.

PALMA VECCHIO
Virgin and Child, with St Roch and St Mary Magdalene

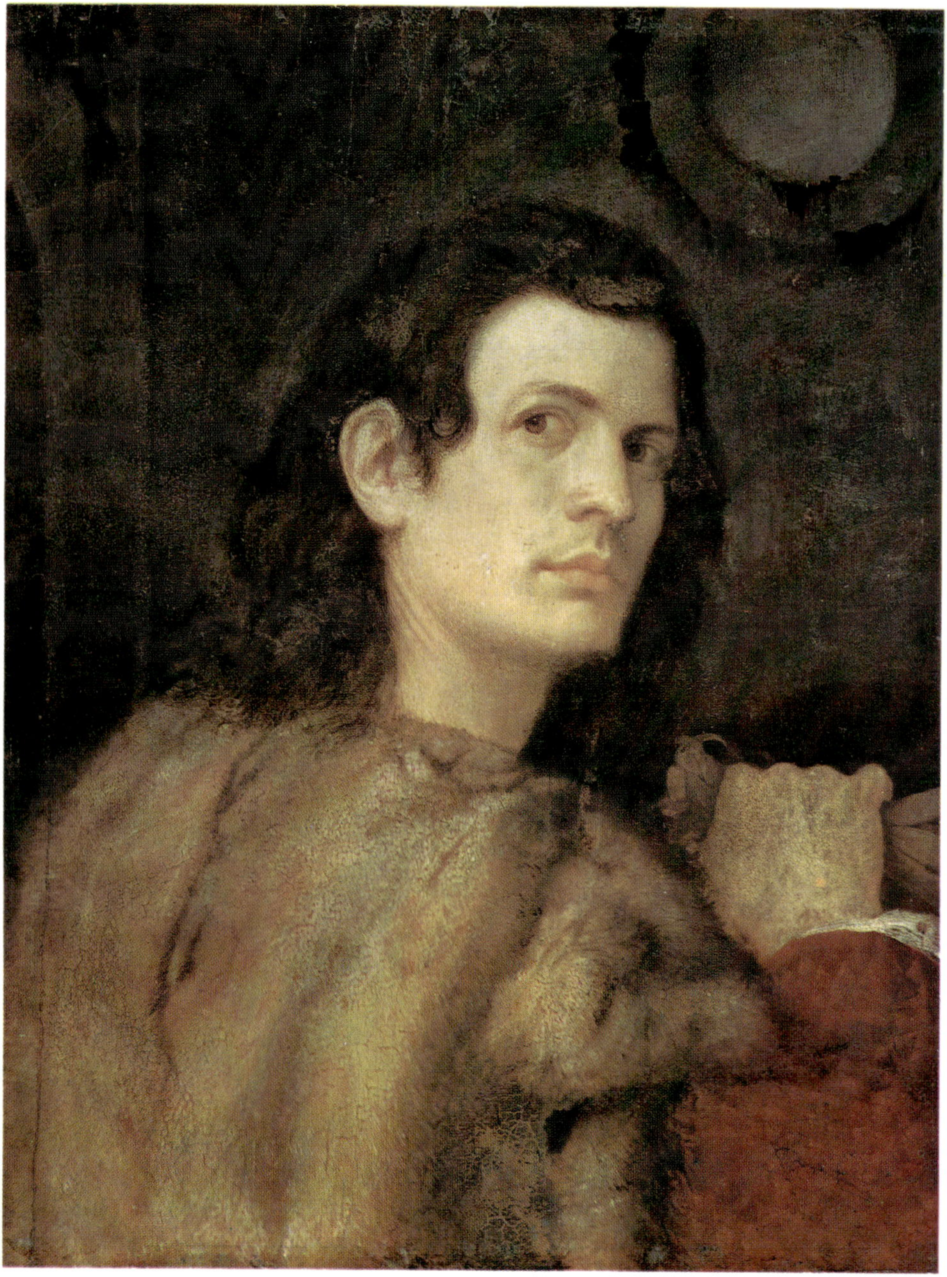

VENETIAN PAINTER OF THE SCHOOL OF GIORGIONE
Portrait of a young man
Wood: $27\frac{9}{16}''\times 21\frac{1}{4}''$ (70 × 54 cm.) Catalogue No. 524

For a hundred years this painting has been the object of violent controversy among experts. There is agreement about the place and date (Venice, early sixteenth century) and about the quality of the work. But the many attempts to attribute the painting to a specific artist have so far met with failure. Giorgione, Titian, Palma Vecchio, Cariani and Mancini have all been suggested, but there are just as many arguments against as for. All we can safely say is that the painting is closely related to the work of Giorgione, whose genius, in his five short years of activity, profoundly and permanently transformed Venetian painting. The gentle, romantic, indecisive character of this young man is reminiscent of Giorgione: intelligent and dreamy, apparently timid and lethargic, yet also capable of energetic action. It is a subtle, complex personality which cannot have been far removed from contemporary ideas of bodily and spiritual perfection.

This painting has belonged to the Electors of Bavaria since 1748.

TITIAN (TIZIANO VECELLIO), c. 1488–1576
The Emperor Charles V
Canvas: 80" × 48" (203·5 × 122 cm.) Catalogue No. 632
Signed and dated: Titianus F.; MDLVII

After his victory over the *Schmalkaldischen Bund* alliance of Protestant princes at Mühlberg, Charles V convened the Diet of Augsburg. As painter to the imperial court, Titian was invited together with all the most important religious and lay dignitaries. He stayed in Augsburg from the beginning of 1548 until October. Already highly thought of by his contemporaries, he painted a series of portraits during this stay, including that of Charles V himself.

The most powerful prince of the western world is here depicted without pomp or finery, like any distinguished merchant of his time except for the Order of the Golden Fleece on his chest, and his sword, which indicate that he must be a knight. But in this simple composition there is great dignity, emphasized by the structural elements which throw the figure into relief: the figure of the seated emperor (until this time the seated position in portraits had been reserved for popes) is inserted into a tall, narrow format with almost a quarter of the total surface area left empty above the Emperor's head. This area, together with the landscape, creates a great impression of space, grandeur and independence – symbolically expressed by the imperial emblem depicted on the column (an allusion to the emperor's motto). But these allusions are a minor detail: the prime focus of the painting is on the personality of his model.

Charles V, at the age of 48, appears prematurely aged, his pale face marked by the weight of his responsibilities. Titian did not, however, see him as the tired old man, the sick, weary monarch who we know was already thinking of abdicating. This bodily fragility is given little emphasis; it is offset by a spiritual superiority which has shaken off all ties with the things of this world. Beneath the slightly arched eyebrows, the two deeply set eyes question the unknown with sceptical disbelief. The vertical furrow in the centre of the brow and the thin lips suggest reflection, while a vague smile plays around the mouth.

In a second portrait painted at the same time (now in the Prado, Madrid), Titian depicted the emperor on horseback as the glorious conqueror of Mühlberg. The portrait here shows the other, ascetic, brooding, spiritual side of his character, bequeathing to posterity an eye-witness account of Charles V's greatness as a man. For a character study as penetrating as this, great mutual understanding must have existed between painter and model.

This portrait has been in the collections of the Electors of Bavaria since 1748.

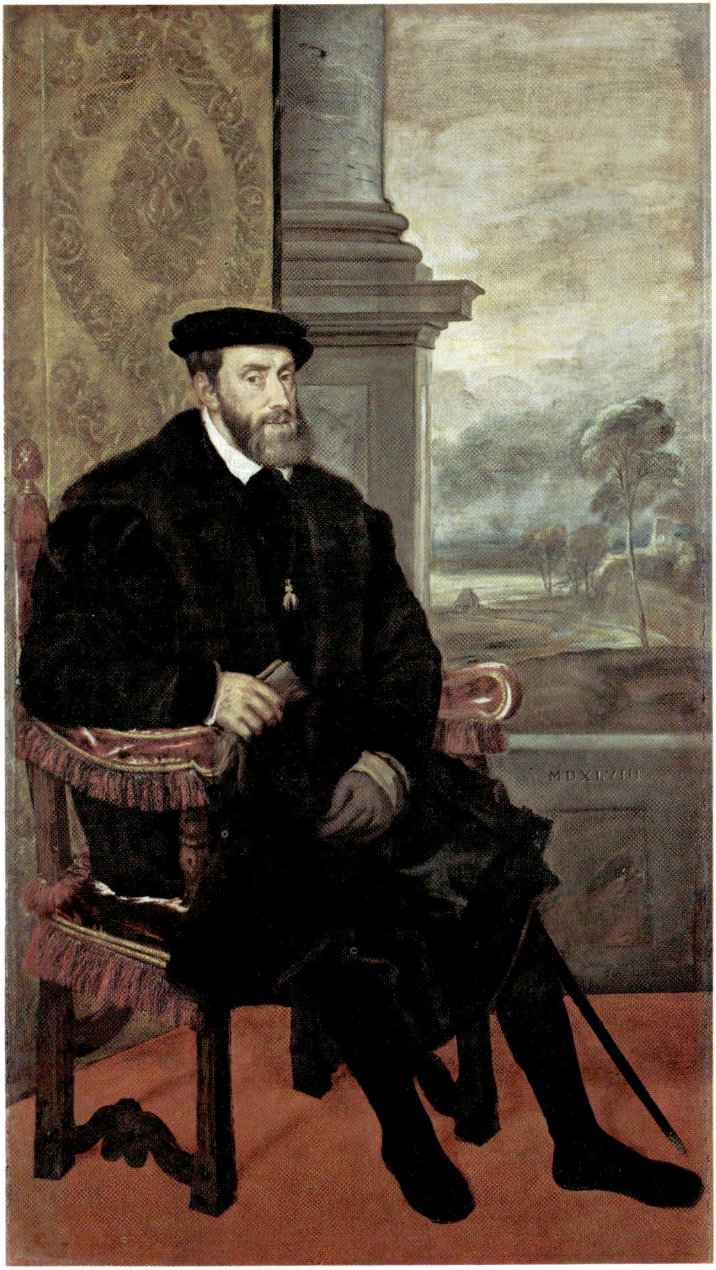
MDXLVIII

TITIAN (TIZIANO VECELLIO), c. 1488–1576
Crowning with Thorns
Canvas: $110\frac{1}{4}'' \times 71\frac{5}{8}''$ (280 × 182 cm.) Catalogue No. 2272

It is given to only a handful of great masters to complete their whole life's work with a creation eclipsing all that has gone before. Titian is such a one, as this painting shows. The theme of the Crowning with Thorns, used by many painters to form the basis of a violently dramatic painting, is transformed in Titian's hands into a quiet scene, almost a devotional work. The executioners perform their cruel task in silence, fixed in attitudes that are angular and unreal. Christ, eyes lowered, silently endures the tortures inflicted on him, leaning only slightly to one side, with his head forced back at an angle beneath the blows of the sticks beating the crown of thorns into his brow. The scene is animated only by the flickering, smoking flames whose light blurs the outlines of the figures, dimly revealing in the background a sort of prison building. Closer study reveals that underlying this seemingly spontaneous, natural composition is a conscious, ordered construction: the figures are spaced out at different levels along a diagonal going upwards from the bottom right, with Christ in an intermediate position between the two counterbalancing figures with their backs turned. A counterdiagonal, starting from the top right, links the candelabra to the central figure, continuing along the line of the executioner's bent leg. The empty space visible through the central archway beneath the crossed sticks depicts the original position of Christ's head before it was brutally knocked to one side; if we look long enough we can easily visualize this movement, which gives us some idea of the suffering voluntarily endured by Christ.

Titian had thirty years earlier painted another work on this theme (in the Louvre) which has many points in common with this one. But the resemblance is only superficial. The Louvre version moves us with its tragic depiction of the scene, but at the same time delights us by its harmony of line and richness of colour; here it is the deep spirituality of the whole which impresses us, rendering any superficial beauty superfluous.

This canvas, like the late works of Rembrandt and Michelangelo, transports us into a world beyond all calculation and reason.

The *Crowning with Thorns* probably belonged originally to Tintoretto, and was sold by his son Domenico to a Scandinavian. It has been in Munich since 1748.

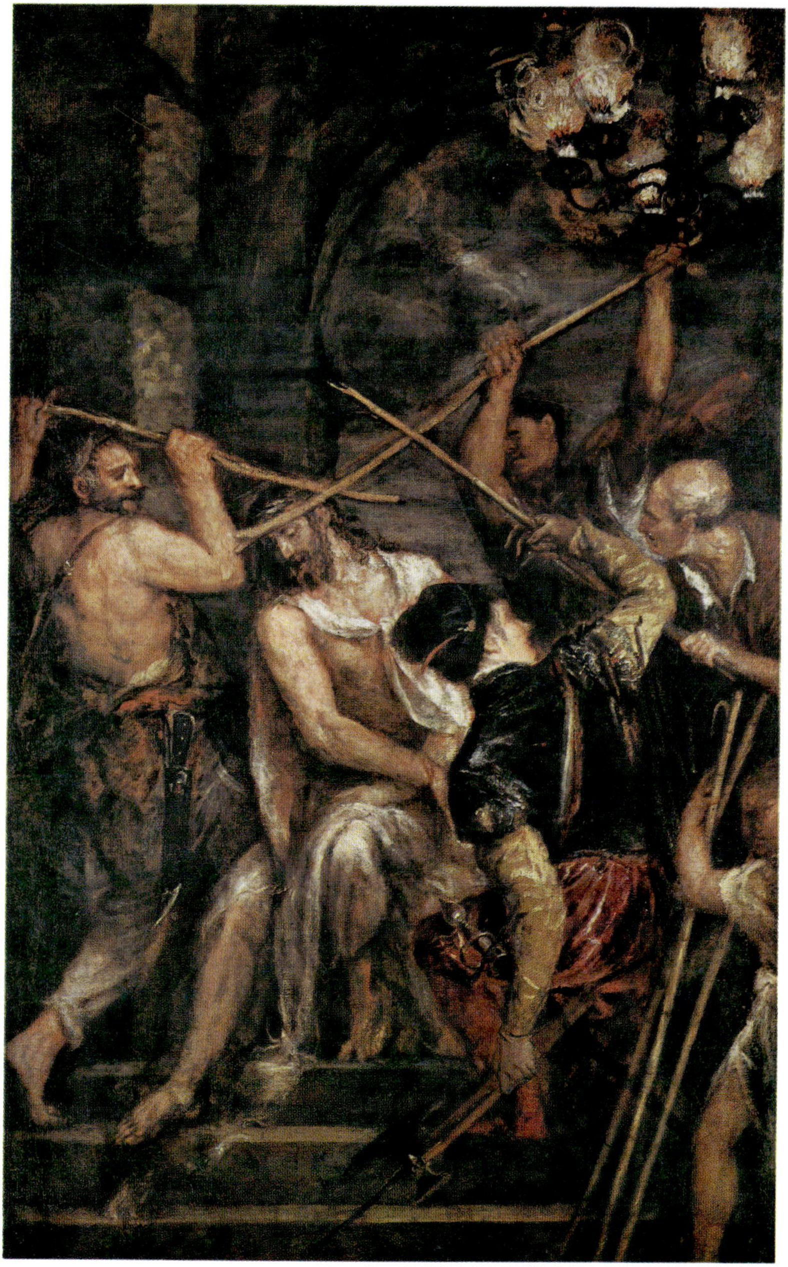

PAOLO CALIARI, called VERONESE, 1528–88
Portrait of a Venetian Noblewoman
Canvas: $46\frac{1}{16}'' \times 39\frac{3}{4}''$ (117 × 101 cm.) Catalogue No. 594

Portraits number among the finest creations of the Venetian school, particularly those of Titian. But other Venetian painters, such as Tintoretto, contributed to the development of this *genre*. Veronese's portraits, compared with the enormous volume of his total output, are relatively few in number, but in quality they equal the finest works of his contemporaries.

This work shows that, despite a long-standing general preconception, Veronese is not just a painter of exuberance and external display. The unknown noblewoman is portrayed without artifice or idealization, with a strict realism. Not exactly an ideal specimen of female beauty, nevertheless she has a strong personality, with great energy, self-assurance and independence of mind. Experience has destroyed all her illusions, has taught her to grow a hard protective shell, has made her down to earth and cynical. Her character is matched by her dress: wealthy because of her high rank, but neither extravagant nor ostentatious, she has no time for frivolity, and tittle-tattle. Veronese has shown great insight in penetrating and portraying the character of this woman. His economical use of colour, limited to browns shading off into reds, whites and yellows, corresponds to this character. She stares calmly at the spectator, the one sign of unrest being the bright white handkerchief in her hand and the ruffled curtain which saves the painting from monotony, forming a striking contrast with the imposing figure. The curtain is linked with the figure, otherwise unrelated to her surroundings, by a diagonal passing from the handkerchief in her hand up through her puffed sleeves.

This work was probably painted around 1570. It has been in the possession of the Electors of Bavaria since 1748.

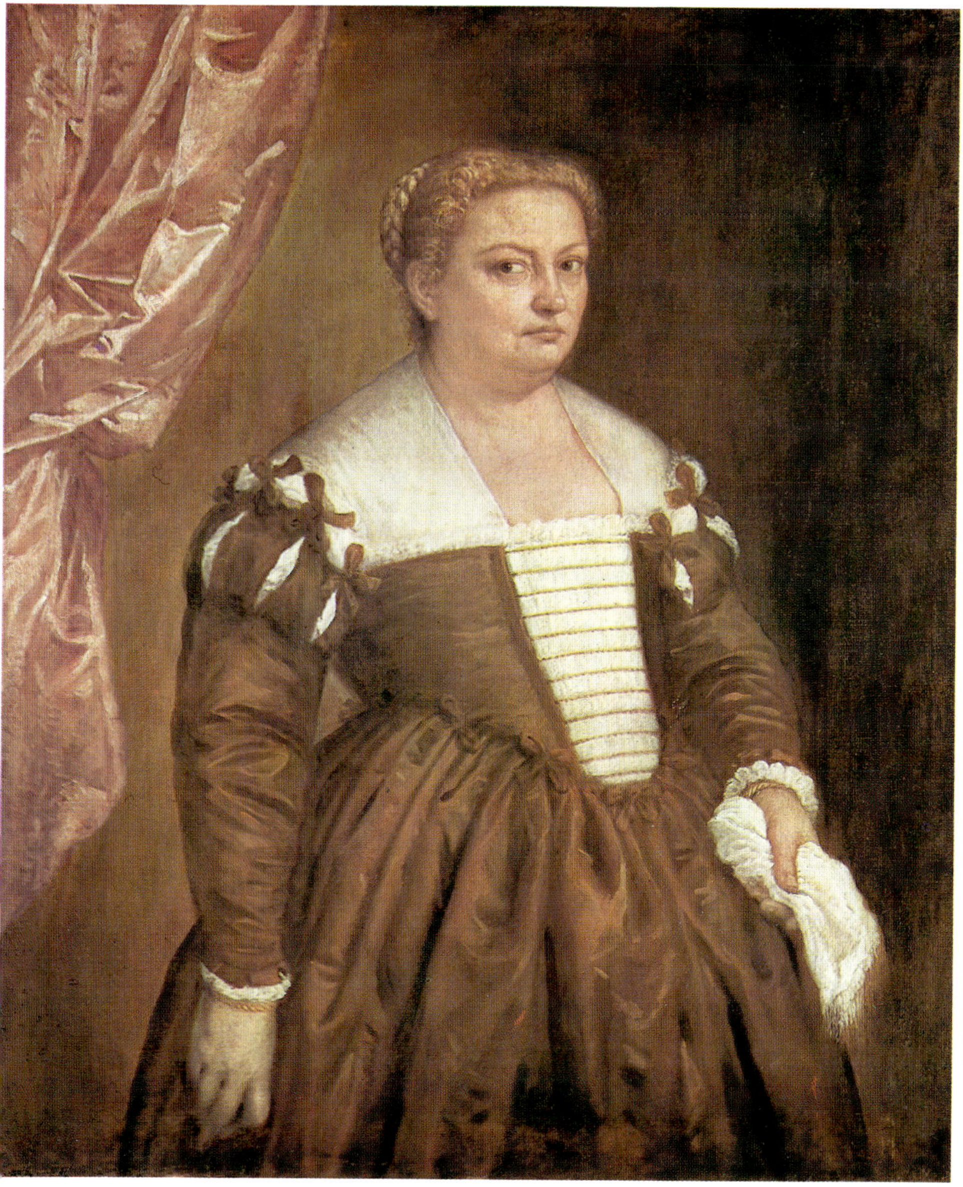

VERONESE
Virgin and Child with a Donor
During the eighteenth century this work, painted in 1560, was attributed to Carlo Caliari. It was originally in the collection of the Electors of Bavaria.

BASSANO *Virgin and Child, with St Anthony the Hermit and St Martin*

BASSANO *Virgin and Child, with St John the Baptist and St James*

TINTORETTO
Portrait of a Venetian Noble
This painting was formerly in the collection of the Duke of Radnor at Longford Castle, Salisbury. It was bought in London from Edward Fowles in 1938.

JACOPO ROBUSTI, called TINTORETTO, 1518-94
Mars and Venus surprised by Vulcan
Canvas: 53⅛" × 77 15/16" (135 × 198 cm.) Catalogue No. 9275.
(Reproduction p. 174)

The eighth book of Homer's *Odyssey* tells how Venus was once unfaithful to her husband Vulcan with the young god of war Mars; the jealous husband set a trap for the lovers, caught them in the act, and turned them over to the mockery of the gods. Tintoretto has not followed this account in all its details but has chosen to portray the scene in a highly individual way. Vulcan chances to enter the room where the couple thought themselves safe from intruders. Mars has only just enough time to hide under the table, whose cloth only half covers him. Venus has to submit to an undignified examination by her suspicious husband. As in the *Odyssey* the lovers' situation is made ridiculous, particularly by the little dog barking to attract its master's attention to Mars hiding under the table. Cupid, who was supposed to have protected the lovers from such a surprise, lies peacefully sleeping in the background.

This frivolous theme, which lends itself so well to the Venetian's innate gifts for sensual expression, is as it were sublimated by the refinement of the painting. Tintoretto has brought out the contrast between the two main characters, the old, oft-repeated theme of the ill-assorted couple. The body of the young woman, her radiant beauty delicately framed by the white drapery and dark purple coverlet, is contrasted with the rough, bent old man with his swarthy skin and grey beard, whose exercising of his legitimate rights seems somehow sacrilegious.

The diagonals formed by the two bodies are part of a dense network of parallel lines which indicate the depth of the room. This effect of perspective is heightened by the mirror reflecting the group in the foreground. This work of around 1555 already has that rhythm of composition so characteristic of Tintoretto's later works.

This canvas was at one time owned by the English painter Sir Peter Lely, who probably acquired it from the collection of the Earl of Arundel. It was purchased in 1682, on the painter's death, by the Duke of Devonshire. In the nineteenth century it passed from the collection of H. A. J. Munro to that of F. A. von Kaulbach in Munich, and was finally bought by the Bavarian state in 1925.

JACOPO ROBUSTI, called TINTORETTO, 1518–94
The Capture of Parma
Canvas: $83\frac{1}{2}'' \times 111\frac{7}{16}''$ (212 × 283·5 cm.) Catalogue No. 7306

In mid-August 1521 the young Duke of Mantua, Federigo Gonzaga, at the head of the papal forces, succeeded in recapturing the town of Parma from the French. This minor historical event provided the basis for a startling artistic vision, a turning point in the history of the painting of battles. The site of the besieged town, the strategy of the attacking forces and the realistic depiction of the fighting were all of secondary importance to the artist, who was concerned with general principles rather than individual details. This is a simple portrayal of siege, assault, bastions and entrenchments, resistance and victory, and particularly of the anonymous masses who go blindly to meet their fate, mere tools employed by the director of the battle, the commander-in-chief, the one figure who stands out as an individual personality. On the far right he surveys his infantry's advance. The troops execute a manœuvre around a fortified hill and rush like a raging torrent into the burning town through the breach opened up by the artillery, while in the background the routed enemy troops flee in disorderly haste across a bridge, dragging along with them the column of troops leading away to the other side of the walls. This S-shaped mass-movement crossing the whole picture from the right foreground to the left background is the main element, and the most fascinating one, in the composition; everything else is subordinated to it. The soldiers' uniforms and the glinting arms spread a glow of light over the column of troops, whose uniform brown-green armour is relieved only by a few strokes of colour, thus giving it the appearance of some supernatural apparition. The incomparable skill of the Venetian has, with the simplest means, transformed the harsh realities of war into a fleeting dream of colour and light.

This painting is one of the principal works of Tintoretto's late period, one of his most studied canvases, rivalling the paintings of Biblical subjects in the Scuola di San Rocco in Venice. It is one of a series of eight paintings celebrating important events in the history of the Gonzaga family. Painted between 1578 and 1580, this series remained in the palace of the Dukes of Mantua until the early eighteenth century. It is first mentioned in a catalogue of the Schleissheim collection in 1748.

TINTORETTO *Crucifixion*
This work is a sketch for the great Crucifixion of 1565 in the Scuola di San Rocco in Venice. It was moved from Schleissheim to the Hofgartengalerie in 1781, and to the Alte Pinakothek in 1909.

TINTORETTO
Investiture of Francesco Gonzaga (1433)

TINTORETTO
Battle on the Taro

ORAZIO GENTILESCHI, c. 1565–c. 1647
Two Women with a Looking-glass (Martha and Mary)
Canvas: 52$\frac{3}{8}$″ × 60$\frac{5}{8}$″ (132·7 × 154 cm.) Catalogue No. 12726

Despite the almost total lack of action in this painting, the contrast of the conflicting personalities of the two women gives it an atmosphere of tension. The fair complexion, soft fleshy face and long dishevelled hair of the right-hand figure have a strong sensuality. Her inactive nature is betrayed by her uninhibited and nonchalant posture and her free movements, giving an impression of spontaneity. The mirror and the style of her garments would seem to indicate that she is conscious of her appearance. She turns her head without moving the rest of her body, suddenly brought back from her daydreams to the world of reality by the reproachful words and gestures of the woman who has just entered, to whom she listens with an inscrutable gaze. This second figure is conceived in total contrast to the voluptuous fair-haired woman; her garments, with the shawl over her shoulders, are severely respectable, her movements sharp and precise, her features indicating a forceful will. Her thin cramped figure reflects her character: sour and austere, with a strict sense of duty that could very easily turn to narrow-mindedness and petty jealousy.

Many people have sought to discover the exact meaning of this painting, but it evokes so many ideas that any one interpretation is impossible. The opposition between the 'active life' and the 'contemplative life' and that between virtue and vice are both suggested. The most famous example of this conflict is the New Testament story of the two sisters Martha and Mary: Martha, the active sister, who complains to Christ about her sister's idleness, and Mary, the contemplative one, who forgets her household duties but whom Christ declares to have chosen the better part. According to tradition, if not to the text of the Bible, Mary is identified with the sinner Mary Magdalene. One can safely say that this painting portrays these two sisters, although the lack of clarity as to whether Mary is meant as a positive or negative character still leaves room for new interpretations. Whether the mirror should be taken to indicate vanity or self-knowledge is debatable.

The composition of the work is based on a strict, almost abstract system of vertical, horizontal and diagonal lines which restricts the freedom of movement of the figures, making them into decorative elements. The use of *chiaroscuro* contrasts with the sobriety of composition, throwing into relief the subtle and delicately blended colours – for example, the white and violet of Mary's garment, or the beige and blue of Martha's dress.

This painting, which shows the strong influence of Caravaggio, has been attributed to Artemisia Gentileschi, daughter of Orazio Gentileschi. On loan to the Kaiser-Friedrich-Museum in Berlin in the 1930s, it is now in the Alte Pinakothek as part of the bequest of Georg and Otto Schäfer.

GIOVANNI BATTISTA TIEPOLO, 1696–1770
Adoration of the Kings
Canvas: 160¼" × 83 1/16" (407 × 211 cm.) Catalogue No. 1159
Signed: GIO. B. TIEPOLO F. A. 1753

In early eighteenth-century painting the portrayal of religious themes is superficially barely distinguishable from that of profane subjects; they resemble extravagant theatrical productions with lavish eye-catching sets. Enveloped in sumptuous draperies the figures move majestically against a richly painted backcloth; the eye feasts on this triumph of beauty, which, however, does not necessarily exclude profound religious sentiment, as this work of Tiepolo's shows.

The Virgin sits regally enthroned on the steps of a ruined ancient temple, whose remains, barely sustained by beams and covered over with straw, offer her a modest shelter. Head held high and eyes staring into the distance she camly receives the homage paid to her son, 'pondering it in her heart', while behind her Joseph stands observing this strange scene with a mixture of pride and embarrassment. Joseph, like the figures in the kings' retinue on his left who, in suspicious amazement, watch their powerful masters humble themselves before a little child, is excluded from the circle of the initiated who are able to comprehend the significance of this scene. In opposition to this is the faithful devotion of the oldest king, who kneels in adoration before the Child, his bearded ascetic face contrasting sharply with the Child's pink body. His crown and jewels roll down the steps, while his page presents the royal gift, a casket full of gold pieces. The expression of the second king, holding a richly decorated alabaster receptacle in his hands, shows a trace of scepticism, but he too is already spellbound by the sight of the Child God. The tall figure of the third king, exotically and luxuriously arrayed, stands on the left with his back to us, an outsider to the scene. This progression of the participants' sentiments from cool observation to absolute ecstasy is movingly illustrated by an ascending movement, like the diagonal of a linear composition.

Tiepolo was at the height of his artistic career when in 1753, during a stay in Würzburg, he painted this work for the church of the Benedictine monastery at Schwarzach. It is one of his religious masterpieces, thanks to the virtuosity with which he has employed his rich artistic imagination to express his deep understanding of the religious theme. On the dissolution of the Schwarzach monastery in 1804, this work passed to the Munich Hofgartengalerie, and from there to the Alte Pinakothek.

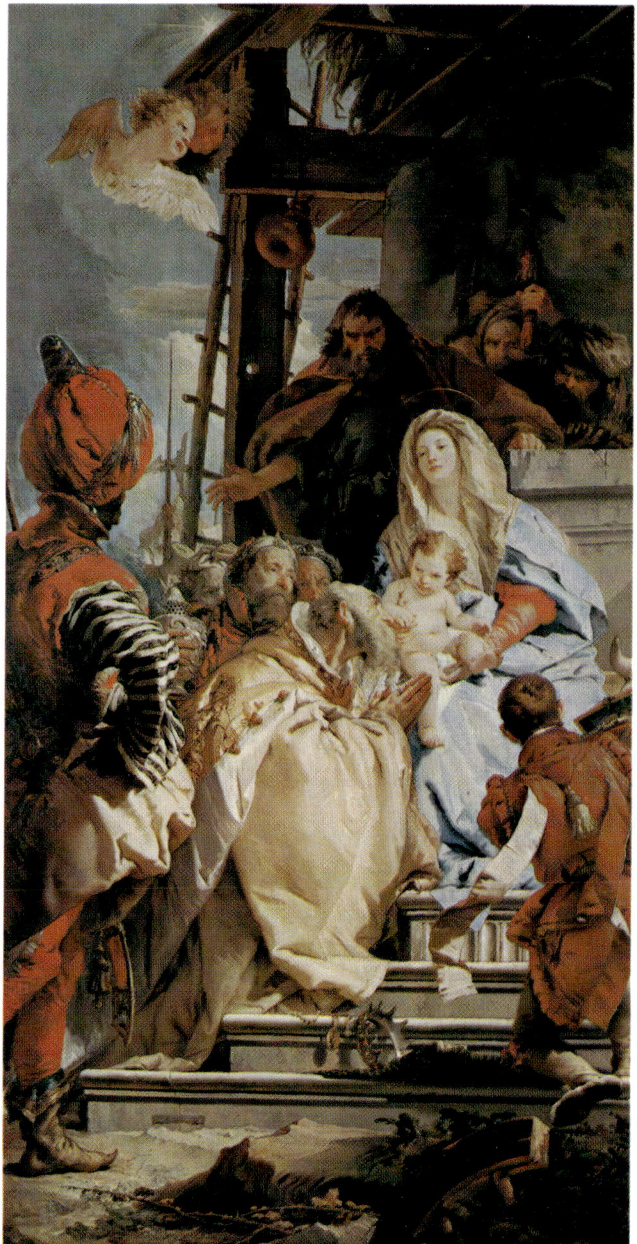

GIOVANNI BATTISTA TIEPOLO
Adoration of the Holy Trinity by Pope Clement

GIOVANNI BATTISTA TIEPOLO
Rinaldo in the Gardens of Armida
This work was painted at Würzburg between 1751 and 1755. It was moved from the Würzburg Residenz to the Alte Pinakothek in 1919.

FRANCESCO GUARDI, 1712–93
Gala Concert in Venice
Canvas: $26\frac{3}{4}'' \times 35\frac{7}{16}''$ (67·7 × 90·5 cm.) Catalogue No. 8574

When we think today of eighteenth-century Venice, the paintings of Francesco Guardi inevitably spring to mind. This is surprising, since Guardi is far from being the only famous artist who has left for posterity an image of his native town and of the action and gestures of its citizens. His contemporaries preferred Canaletto and Longhi. But none can better Guardi in the rendering of the unique and indescribable atmosphere of Venice as it strove, in a final fling of exuberant extravagance, to reassert in colour and form the radiant splendour of its historical greatness.

In 1782 Guardi received an official commission for a series of paintings depicting the festivities organized by the Republic of St Mark on the occasion of the visit of the Russian Grand Duke Paul Petrovitch, the future Tsar Paul I, and his wife. This painting of a gala concert given in the 'Sala dei Filarmonici' forms a part of the series. A female orchestra and choir have taken up their positions on the raised platform. The concert has not yet begun. The musicians tune their instruments to the sound of murmured conversations, the brushing of silk dresses and tiptoeing steps from the audience. Seats are reserved for the guests of honour opposite the orchestra along a wall decorated with a gilt-framed mirror. Two rows of chairs are set out facing each other across the room for the ladies of the aristocracy; the other spectators, including the men dressed in solemn black garments, stand beneath the gallery or walk about the room. There is no way of knowing whether the concert was held during the day (the chandeliers and light-fixtures are not lit) or whether for artistic reasons Guardi has chosen to replace the hot candlelight by an external source of light. One can, however, suppose that he has, in this as in all things, given his imagination free rein. He appears also to have rearranged the three windows on the end wall, moving the central window slightly to the right in order to emphasize the chandeliers, the central element of the composition, hovering as though weightless over the figures' heads, glittering, delicate and fragile as a dream, with all the splendour of the festivals of old. It stands for us as a symbol of the age which Guardi, through the persuasive power of his artistry, permits us to see through his eyes.

This painting was purchased in London in 1909.

GUARDI *Grand Canal near St Jeremiah*

FLEMISH SCHOOL

PIETER BRUEGEL
THE ELDER
Head of an old Peasant Woman
This portrait was moved from Schloss Neuburg to Munich in 1868. It has been in the Alte Pinakothek since 1912.

PIETER BRUEGEL THE ELDER, *c.* 1525–69
Land of Cockayne
Oak: $20\frac{1}{2}'' \times 30\frac{11}{16}''$ (52 × 78 cm.) Catalogue No. 8940
(Reproduction p. 186)

This painting was inspired, like many of Pieter Bruegel's other works, by a Flemish proverb: 'Geen ding is er gekker dan lui en lekker' (the greatest fool is an idle glutton). The Land of Cockayne, where mindless sluggards live in plenty, figures in the folklore of many European lands. Several elements of the painting serve to illustrate features of these folk tales. The scene in the right background shows how difficult it is to reach this promised land, which can be entered only by eating one's way through a mountain of gruel. The painting is decorated with a little roast pig with a knife sticking into his back, a hedge strewn with sausages, and the hut roof covered with cakes and all sorts of other goodies. In the left background a newly arrived figure lies open-mouthed, hopefully expecting a roast pigeon to fly in there and then. In the centre three glutted figures lie spreadeagled like the spokes of a wheel. They are recognizable as the peasant, the soldier and the scholar or cleric.

Bruegel painted this imaginative work in 1567, at a time when nothing could have been further from reality than the Land of Cockayne; for the Duke of Alba's Spanish troops were invading the Low Countries to put down the rebellions against Spanish rule. This work is therefore intended as the depiction of an abstract utopia. The great simplicity of the central composition, taking up the old theme of the wheel of fortune, confirms such an interpretation, although the artist's caricature of the eternal vices of sloth and debauchery is at the same time clear.

This painting, formerly in the Prague imperial collection, was carried off by the Swedes to Stockholm in 1648, and was acquired for the Alte Pinakothek in 1917.

CORNELIS VAN DALEM, *c.* 1530–?
Landscape with Farmstead
Oak: $40\frac{9}{16}''\times50''$ (103 × 127.5 cm.) Catalogue No. 12044

This work portrays a landscape of dark, softly lit ruins, the remains of a once fortified castle. A few men and animals inhabit this desolate spot where even the trees barely manage to produce their few leaves. The oppressiveness is increased by the precision of the painting. It expresses not an event or moral allegory but a mood. Painted in 1564, it has justly been awarded the title of the first mood landscape in the history of painting. Cornelis van Dalem, mentioned in contemporary documents chiefly as the master of Bartholomäus Spranger, was rescued from oblivion some years ago thanks to this painting.

He is referred to as a registered master of the Antwerp guild in 1556, but as a noble he differed from the other members of the guild in learning his trade only as a pastime, not as a full occupation, and painted only when he felt like it. This explains why his output is so small, despite the magnificence of style and colour which make Van Dalem one of the most important Flemish landscape-painters after Pieter Bruegel the Elder.

This work was acquired from the Munich collection of Hugo Bruckmann in 1954.

ROELANT SAVERY *Boar Hunt*
This work was transferred from Schleissheim to the Hofgartengalerie in 1781, and to the Alte Pinakothek in 1836.

ABRAHAM JANSSENS
Olympus
The veils covering the busts of Juno and Venus are later additions. This painting was taken from the collection of the Electors of Bavaria by Napoleon, and remained in France from 1800 to 1815.

PAUL BRIL *Tower of Babel*

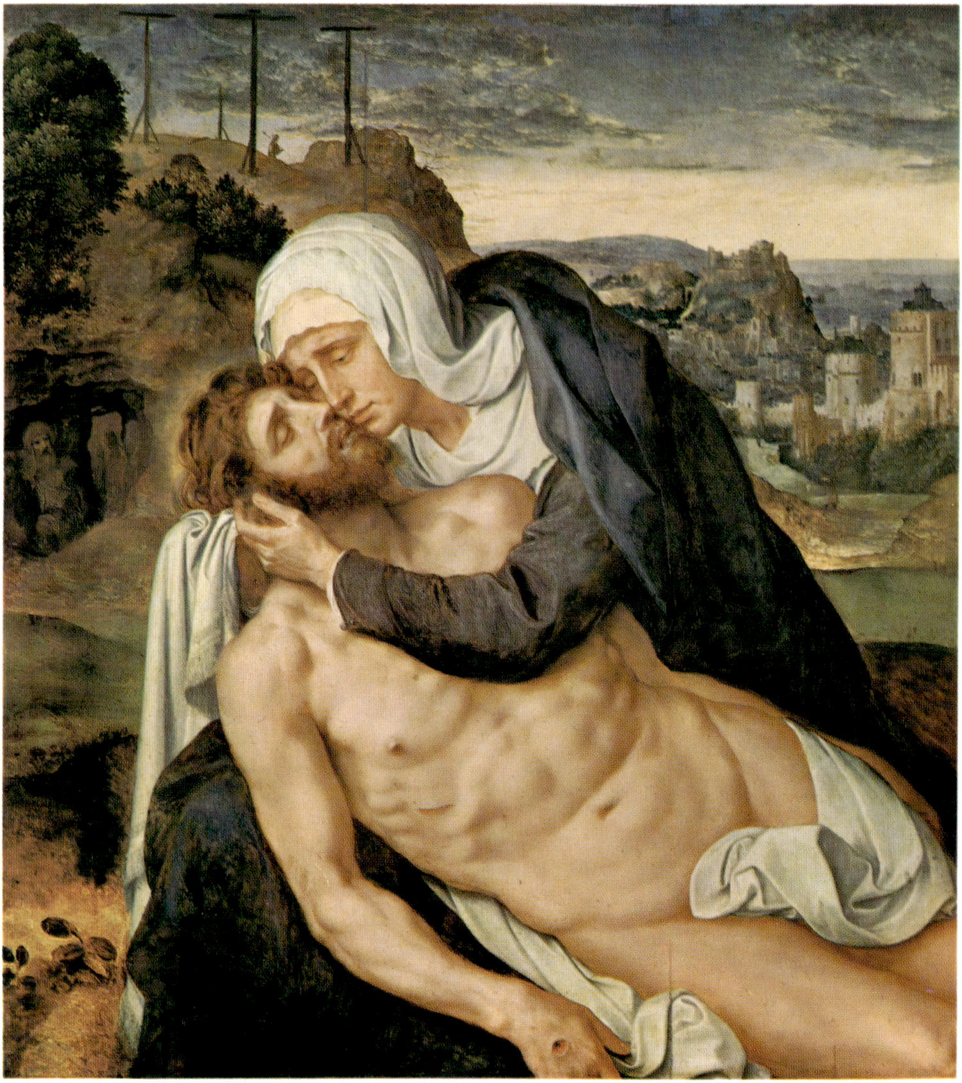

WILLEM KEY, c. 1520–68
Lamentation of Christ
Oak: 44$\frac{1}{16}$" × 40$\frac{9}{16}$" (112 × 103 cm.) Catalogue No. 539

'Now in the place where He was crucified there was a garden; and in the garden a new sepulchre, wherein was never man yet laid' (Gospel according to St John XIX, 41). In this Gospel, the Virgin, utterly desolate, laments the death of her son at the foot of Calvary. The delicate body of Christ, beautiful even in death, rests on his mother's lap. Mary bends over him, gently lifting up his head and pressing her lips to his mouth, once the source of words of consolation and hope for the world. The two figures are alone, isolated from the world around, framed against the stark Calvary, the empty crosses against the sky stressing the mood of despair. The small figures in the background make their way towards the city of Jerusalem, whose tower and walls loom in the distance. The only sympathetic witness to the scene is Joseph of Arimathaea, emerging from the Tomb on the left. The three principal elements of the theme – the group of Christ and Mary, Calvary and Jerusalem – are also the three main elements of the composition, forming three counterpointed volumes.

Willem Key, whose *Lamentation* dates from around 1550, was strongly influenced by Italian painting. Michelangelo immediately springs to mind, and in fact the figure of Christ was modelled on a drawing by Sebastiano del Piombo (in the Louvre), long attributed to Michelangelo. The Roman academic style of this painting explains its influence on the work of sculptors of Munich and south Germany, particularly on sculptures of the Pietà, from the late sixteenth to the eighteenth century.

Willem Key and Frans Floris were pupils of Lambert Lombard in Liège. Key became a registered master at Antwerp in 1542, and in 1552 was elected head of the local guild. According to Van Mander, he died on 8 June 1568, the day of the execution of Count Egmont and Count Hoorn, from grief at this tragic event.

This painting entered the Munich collections in the reign of the Elector Maximilian I.

JAN BRUEGEL THE ELDER, 1568–1625
Sermon of Christ on Lake Gennesaret
Oak: 30$\frac{11}{16}$" × 46$\frac{15}{16}$" (78 × 119 cm.) Catalogue No. 187

The princely collectors of the seventeenth and eighteenth centuries were great admirers of the rich imagination and technical precision of the paintings of Jan Bruegel. The Alte Pinakothek has over thirty of these, three of which portray a harbour with a fish market. This one of 1598, the largest and oldest, depicts a crowded 'landscape' illustrating the scene recounted in the Gospel according to St Luke, V: 'And it came to pass, that, as the people pressed upon him to hear the word of God, he stood by the lake of Gennesaret, and saw two ships standing by the lake: but the fishermen were gone out of them, and were washing their nets. And he entered into one of the ships, which was Simon's, and prayed him that he would thrust out a little from the land. And he sat down, and taught the people out of the ship.' This prelude to Simon Peter's miraculous haul of fish is set in the middle distance of the painting, almost lost in a huge crowd whose variety of races bears witness to Jan Bruegel's inexhaustible imagination. The landscape is divided into several planes, distinguished by areas of light and shadow.

Jan Bruegel has been called 'Velvet Bruegel' because of the soft luminosity of his colours. Born in Brussels, the second son of Pieter Bruegel the Elder, he studied at Antwerp, spent seven years in Italy, and became master at Antwerp in 1593. He often collaborated with Rubens (a friend of his), Rottenhammer, Joos de Momper and other artists.

This painting came to Munich with the Mannheim collection.

JAN BRUEGEL THE ELDER *Bouquet of Flowers*

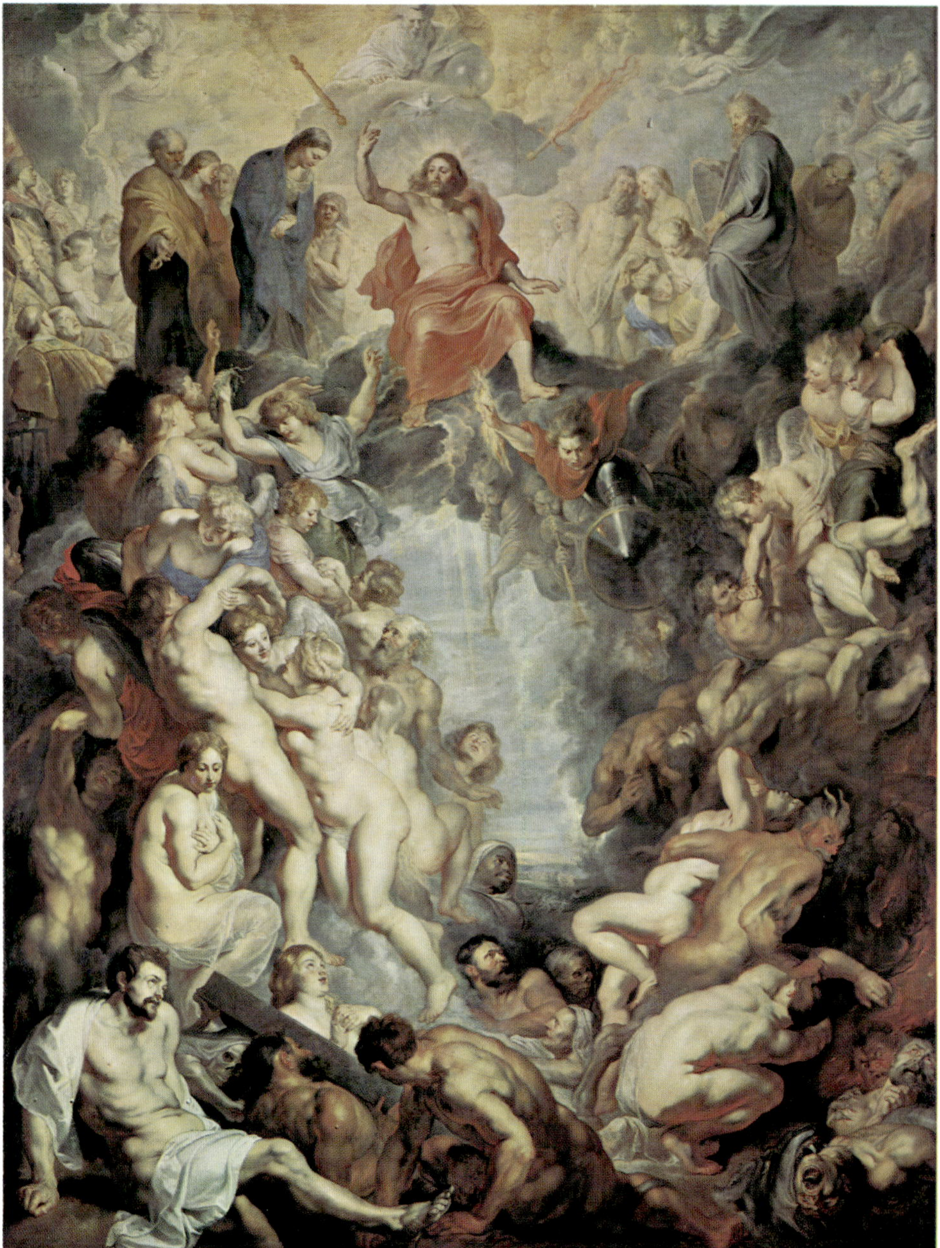

PETER PAUL RUBENS, 1577–1640
Large Last Judgment
Canvas: 237″ × 178″ (602 × 452 cm.) Catalogue No. 890

'This painting hangs in the centre of the Rubens hall, at the very heart of the Alte Pinakothek. It was commissioned, together with four other paintings, by Duke Wolfgang Wilhelm von Pfalz-Neuburg to adorn the churches of his palace. This canvas decorated the high altar of the Jesuit church at Neuburg on the Danube, the foundation stone of which had been laid by Wolfgang Wilhelm while still heir to the throne in 1608. Rubens must have received this commission shortly after the Duke succeeded to the title in 1614. The chronicle of the Neuburg Jesuit monastery refers to the painting as early as 1617, although the church was not consecrated until October 1618. 'The great painting destined for the high altar is already here. It is a magnificent work of Peter Paul Rubens, the most illustrious painter of our times; experts say that it is worth several thousand florins.' Indeed, Rubens received 3,000 florins for this work, plus the gift of a gold chain worth 200 thalers. But the Jesuits' enthusiasm for this work was short-lived. In 1653 it was covered over by an *Assumption* because its nudes were judged to be outrageously indecent for a church painting. In 1691, after long negotiations with the priests, Crown Prince Johann Wilhelm finally succeeded in acquiring it for his Düsseldorf gallery.

Of all Rubens' portrayals of the Last Judgment (most of which are at Munich) the *Large Last Judgment* is the earliest. Its composition can be compared to a bas-relief of monumental proportions. The bodies of the blessed ascending to heaven and of the damned descending into hell twist and turn in two massive columns, with only a narrow gap to indicate the abyss which separates them. Above them all, Christ sits enthroned, beside him his mother, the holy martyrs and the prophets of the Old Testament. The movements of the hands of the Supreme Judge are filled with majesty as he delivers his verdict on man, who stands there torn between hope and anguish. The ascending movement of the elect is restrained, almost deliberately slow; but the full visionary power of Rubens' artistic imagination is shown in the portrayal of the damned. The motif of Satan dragging down two women is found only in Rubens. In Rubens' Last Judgments painted slightly after this time, the blessed are left out altogether, leaving only the descent of the damned into hell, a terrible vision of a monstrous flood of human bodies falling ever downward into a raging chaos of despair.

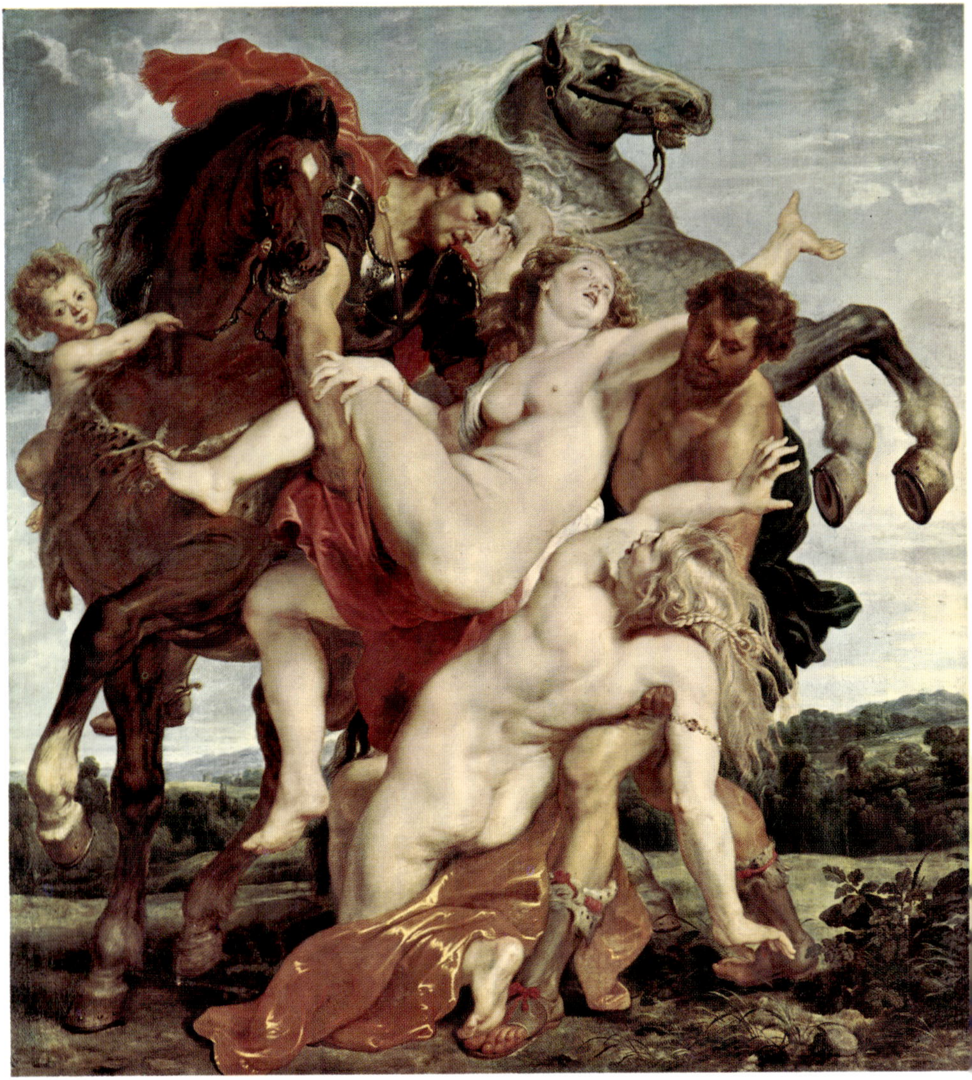

PETER PAUL RUBENS, 1577–1640
Rape of the Daughters of Leucippus
Canvas: $87\frac{3}{8}'' \times 82\frac{5}{16}''$ (222 × 209 cm.) Catalogue No. 321

Jakob Burckhardt said of this work: 'No other painter, of whatever period or school, could have created this.' Eight figures are portrayed with great imagination – the two sisters Phoebe and Hilaeira, the Dioscuri Castor and Pollux, two cherubim and two horses. Each of these couples is conceived in contrast, albeit in complementary contrast. In the middle of the painting, the women's superb bodies are fashioned in such a way that the pose of one appears to be the logical consequence of the other. The Dioscuri – who, being twins, look alike – give a similar impression: one alighted from his horse holds the bodies of the women, while the other lifts up the woman who is resisting. One is unclothed, the other clad in armour. The two spirited horses are likewise contrasted in colour, movement and direction. A marvellous rhythmic whole is thus created, independent of each individual gesture.

The massive group is enclosed in a square whose bounds are not once broken. The four human figures inscribed inside a diagonally-placed rectangle add still further to the grandiose unity of the composition. The area of ground on which the group stands is similarly rectangular. This marriage of diagonals and verticals justly deserved Burckhardt's praise.

Rubens was forty years old when he painted this mythological work. The outcome of the rape of the young girls seems to depend not on the brutality of the attack or the tenacity of the defence, but on a certain amorous accord. Leucippus, king of Argos, had two daughters, Phoebe and Hilaeira, who were betrothed to the twin brothers Idas and Lynceus. Leda's twin sons – Castor, who was mortal, and Pollux, who being begotten by Zeus was immortal – took advantage of the marriage ceremony to carry off the brides. In the ensuing chase, Castor was killed by Idas, while Pollux killed Lynceus. Zeus then sent a thunderbolt to kill Idas. In order not to be parted from his brother, Pollux begged Zeus to make him mortal. The god decided to reunite the two brothers by making them both share death and eternal life, spending one day in hell and the next on Olympus.

Rubens' painting tells us nothing of this legend, and it is thus not surprising that the subject of the work was for a long time forgotten, being rediscovered by chance in 1777 by the poet Wilhelm Heinse. It is not so much a depiction of brutal action as an image of the experience and power of love enacted by the Dioscuri, gods of light, and the glowing Hilaeira and the radiant Phoebe.

The painting came to Munich with the Düsseldorf collection.

PETER PAUL RUBENS, 1577–1640
Battle of the Amazons
Oak: 47⅝" × 64¹⁵⁄₁₆" (121 × 165 cm.) Catalogue No. 324

The outcome of the battle has already been decided. In closed ranks, brandishing their standards, the victors relentlessly drive the defeated enemy back over the bridge, which is too narrow to support this mass of men and animals.

Rubens here illustrates the fundamental, merciless violence of man's struggle against man. He has therefore chosen not a historical battle, but a mythological conflict between Greeks and Amazons. This subject was taken from the story of Hercules' labour performed for Eurystheus, King of Mycenae; his task was to bring back for the king's daughter the insignia of the Amazon queen-general Hippolyte.

This great battle painting was executed by Rubens for Cornelius van der Gheest some time before 1619. In the second half of the seventeenth century it belonged to the Duc de Richelieu. It was purchased for the collection of the Elector Palatine Johann Wilhelm in 1690 for the price of 1,800 florins, and in 1806 was transferred to Munich with the Düsseldorf gallery.

PETER PAUL RUBENS, 1577–1640
Rubens and Isabella Brandt in the Honeysuckle Bower
Canvas mounted on wood: 70" × 53½" (178 × 136 cm.) Catalogue No. 334
(Reproduction p. 200)

In autumn 1608 Rubens returned from Italy to Antwerp to see his mother who was seriously ill. Master of the Guild of St Luke since 1598, he left for Italy in May 1600, where he soon became court painter to the Duke of Mantua, Vincenzo Gonzaga. In 1603 he went at the Duke's request to Spain to deliver gifts to King Philip III and the Duke of Lerma. He spent long periods in Rome, Mantua and Genoa successively, in all of which towns he painted magnificent altarpieces and portraits. By the time he returned to Antwerp his reputation was already made, and everything was done to keep him: the town, the Spanish governors, Archduke Albert and the Infanta Isabella, all gave him commissions, and in September 1609 he was appointed court painter. But what finally decided him to settle in Antwerp was his love for Isabella Brandt. He married Isabella when she was only eighteen, on 3 October 1609. She was the daughter of a respectable Antwerp citizen, the municipal secretary Jan Brandt, whose portrait is also in the Alte Pinakothek. One daughter and two sons were born of this marriage. On his young wife's premature death on 20 June 1626 Rubens wrote to Pierre Dupuy, director of the royal library in Paris: 'As for me, I have lost an excellent companion, whom I could not but love since she possessed none of the faults of her sex; she was neither moody nor weak-willed, but so good, honest and virtuous that she was beloved during her lifetime and lamented in death by all who knew her.'

This work was painted shortly after Rubens' marriage to Isabella. The couple sit before a honeysuckle bower forming a dark backcloth. The scene has an aura of quiet, calm assurance. The two figures sit next to each other, equally tall, indicating their independence and equality. The young woman's gesture with her right hand placed on that of her husband shows her boundless trust in him. Rubens called her 'good and virtuous'; looking at this painting no one could doubt it. The delicate gentle contact of the hands forms part of an S-shaped curve passing from the man's head to the young woman's loose hand, binding the composition into a whole. The figures, set together in an oval, entirely fill the surface of the canvas, making it look almost as though it had been trimmed. 'Rubens has painted here not only an exquisite portrait of himself and his young wife, but also an image of the ideal couple' (Wolfgang Schöne).

This painting was transferred to Munich with the Düsseldorf collection.

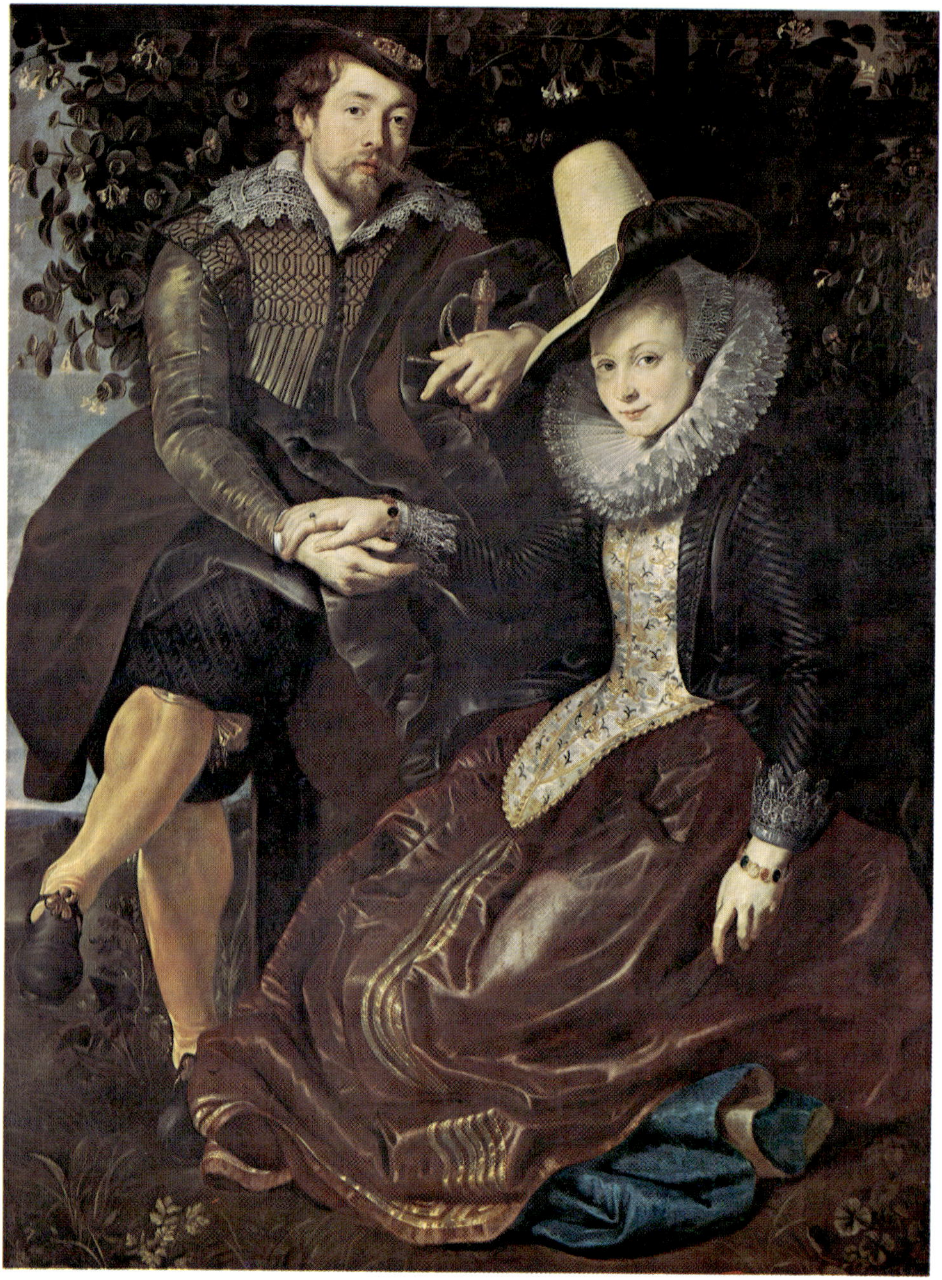

PETER PAUL RUBENS, 1577–1640
Life of Marie de' Medici: Coronation of the Queen
Oak: $21\frac{1}{4}'' \times 36\frac{3}{16}''$ (54 × 92 cm.) Catalogue No. 97

On 8 May 1625, for the inauguration of the Medici gallery in the Palais du Luxembourg, Rubens completed his most famous series of paintings on events from the life of Queen Marie de' Medici, widow of Henri IV, which was to decorate the palace.

For such an important commission, the Queen demanded to see preliminary sketches which would give her an idea of the finished product. The artist, who could hardly carry out such a number of large-scale works singlehanded, obtained permission to have a few assistants to help him. The sketches, however, had to be his own work. A first set of sketches, painted on wood, is in the Hermitage, Leningrad; these were rejected by the Queen. The court objected, on certain questions of rank, to the portrayal of the Queen's coronation, which took place in Saint-Denis on 13 May 1610. In the second set of sketches at Munich, Rubens not only changed details but draughted a totally new composition, among other things much broader in format. After this sketch, yet more changes were made until the height of perfection was reached both in the portrayal of the ceremony and in its allegorical significance.

These sketches belonged formerly to Claude Maugis, Abbot of Saint-Ambroise and Marie de' Medici's almoner. They were acquired for the Munich collections in the eighteenth century.

RUBENS
Education of Marie de' Medici

RUBENS
Reception of the Future Queen at Marseilles

RUBENS
Lion Hunt

PETER PAUL RUBENS, 1577–1640
Landscape with Cattle
Oak: 31⅞" × 41¾" (81 × 106 cm.) Catalogue No. 322

Gustav Glück declared that 'if the only works of Rubens left were the series of forty landscapes (most of which we have in the original, but some only in the form of engravings), their author would still be considered one of the world's greatest painters.' The Alte Pinakothek has two of Rubens' landscapes: the *Landscape with Rainbow* and this *Landscape with Cattle*.

A plain, gently sloping pasture bounded on the right by low brushwood and bare meadows stretches out before a pond, lying in the shadow of a cluster of tall trees. It is a simple, unpretentious slice of nature, with the milking of a herd of cows taking place in the full light in front of the patches of shade in the background. This realistic portrayal of nature involved careful study and detailed observation. In spontaneity and life it surpasses the works of other contemporary painters of landscapes and animals; the movements of the animals are conveyed with such perfection that not only did Rubens himself use this study for another painting, but it was frequently copied by his pupils and successors.

This landscape was bought from Gisbert van Ceulen by the Elector Maximilian Emanuel in 1698.

RUBENS
Drunken Silenus

RUBENS
Susanna and the Elders

JACOB JORDAENS
Satyr at the Peasant's House

JAN SIBERECHTS
Pasture-land

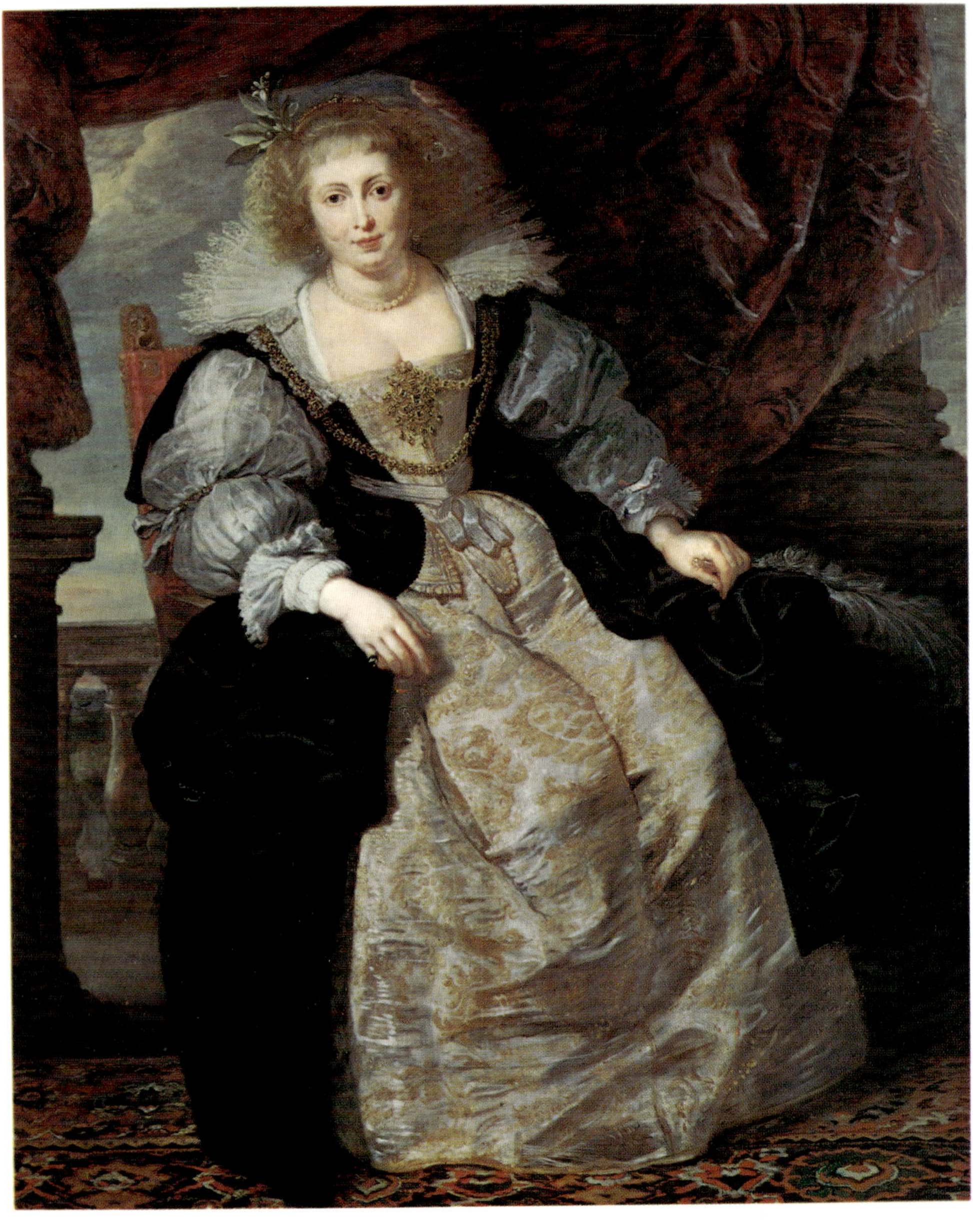

PETER PAUL RUBENS, 1577–1640
Hélène Fourment in her Wedding Dress
Oak: $63\frac{13}{16}'' \times 52\frac{3}{4}''$ (162 × 134 cm.) Catalogue No. 340

On 6 December 1630, shortly after his return from a visit to London on a diplomatic mission for the king of Spain, Rubens remarried. His second bride was Hélène Fourment, barely sixteen years old. This marriage signified a rejuvenation and a new lease of life for the fifty-year-old Rubens. His incomparable artistic genius received one last stimulus, carrying him to the peak of his career. Hélène Fourment was the personification of the type of ideal beauty created by Rubens; she became the essential substance of his art. He painted several portraits of her, the three finest of which are in the Alte Pinakothek. He painted her as the Madonna and as St Cecilia; indeed hardly a work left his studio without one figure being modelled on her. Rubens never grew tired of revealing new aspects of her beauty. As the Cardinal-Infante remarked to his brother King Philip III of Spain on seeing the *Judgment of Paris*, in which Hélène Fourment is the central figure, 'she is surely the most beautiful creature to be seen in the whole painting.'

This, the first, and probably the finest, portrait of Hélène Fourment, depicts her full-length in her wedding dress. Both bride and painting are sumptuous and radiant, with the silvers, golds and violets set off by a superb jet black. Her bearing is unaffected and modest; an invigorating freshness and gay nonchalance radiate from the pretty round face, surrounded by a lace ruff and crowned with myrtle leaves. The artist's personal feelings are clearly manifested in this painting, as in the portrait of the same period depicting Hélène putting on a glove and the one showing her with her eldest son Frans.

All three paintings were acquired by the Elector Maximilian Emanuel in 1698.

PETER PAUL RUBENS, 1577–1640
Rubens and Hélène Fourment in their Garden
Oak: $38\frac{9}{16}'' \times 51\frac{9}{16}''$ (98 × 131 cm.) Catalogue No. 313

Rubens painted two intimate scenes of his family life with Hélène Fourment, both depicting a walk. In the later painting (in the Rothschild collection, Paris) the parents watch the first steps of their child, held in a harness. The Munich painting shows Rubens on a sunny spring day taking round his garden the young wife he had married some months before. With them is Nicolas, the artist's thirteen-year-old son by his previous marriage. The clothes of the figures and the general atmosphere reflect the luxury and elegance with which Rubens loved to surround himself. This luxury and elegance are to be found in both the paintings in the Alte Pinakothek which show Rubens with his two wives, and yet, what a difference between the two paintings. In the portrait with Isabella Brandt, husband and wife appear independent of one another, the wife devoting herself freely to her husband. The family scenes of the artist's second marriage express a different sort of union: Rubens leads his young wife, clasping her arm with his left hand, showing her the way with his right.

This painting was acquired by the Elector Maximilian Emanuel in 1698.

PETER PAUL RUBENS, 1577–1640
Massacre of the Innocents
Oak: $78\frac{5}{16}'' \times 118\frac{7}{8}''$ (199 × 302 cm.) Catalogue No. 572

It is not known who commissioned this painting of the Massacre of the Innocents. Herod, having learnt of Jesus' birth, sent out a pointless and cruel decree that all children under two should be killed, hoping in this way to exterminate the new-born Christ. The king of Judea waits anxiously beneath the columns of his palace to see if his order is being properly carried out. The desperate mothers struggle to stop their children being torn away from them to be killed.

At the time when Rubens painted this work (around 1635) this scene was not just an imaginary nightmare, but a record of recent events – the Thirty Years' War, now nearing its twentieth year, was prolonged by French entry into the war in 1635. Earthly power at its most brutal is expressed as much by the imposing architecture as by the murderers. And yet, above this scene of carnage, life emerges triumphant — in the landscape bathed in light, in the green of the trees and briars growing even on the roof of the tyrant's house. An angel replies with flowers to the utter despair of a mother who lifts her empty arms up to the heavens. This work shows that, even at this time, men still believed in a celestial will ordering all earthly acts.

This painting is mentioned as being in the possession of Canon Taxis in Paris in 1642. It then passed into the collection of the Duc de Richelieu, and was acquired for the collection of the Munich Electors around 1706.

ADRIAEN BROUWER *A Taproom*
This painting was transferred from the Munich collections to Schleissheim in 1800, where it remained until 1881.

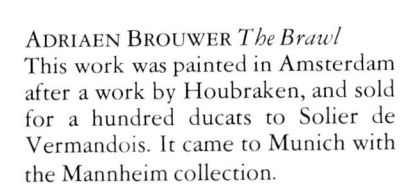

ADRIAEN BROUWER *The Brawl*
This work was painted in Amsterdam after a work by Houbraken, and sold for a hundred ducats to Solier de Vermandois. It came to Munich with the Mannheim collection.

ADRIAEN BROUWER *Peasant Quartet*

ANTHONY VAN DYCK
Portrait of a Lady

ANTHONY VAN DYCK
Portrait of a Man

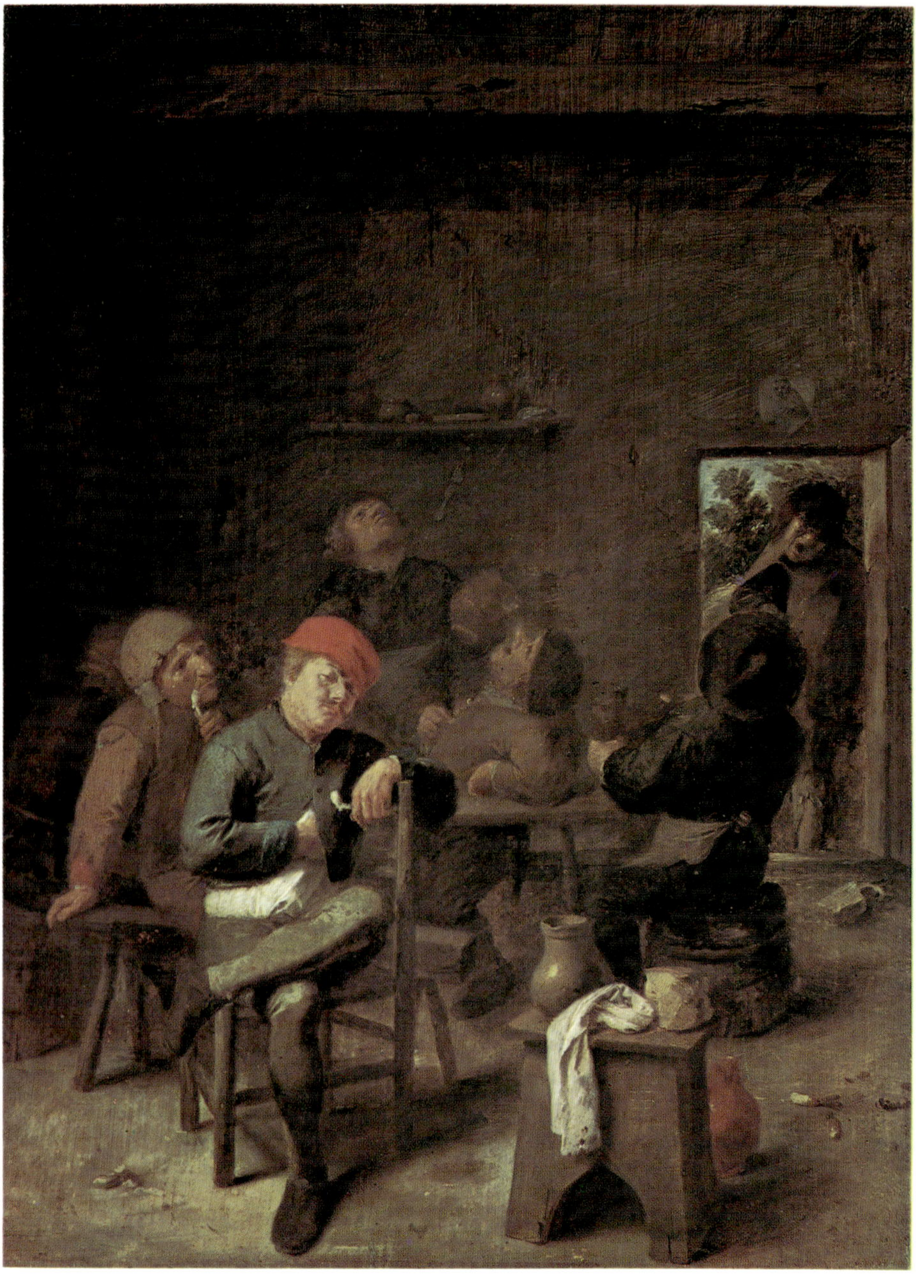

Adriaen Brouwer, 1605/6–38
Smoking Peasants
Oak: $13\frac{3}{4}'' \times 10\frac{1}{4}''$ (35 × 26 cm.) Catalogue No. 2062

The Alte Pinakothek has a great many works by Adriaen Brouwer of which this is one of the most representative. It portrays an everyday scene in an Antwerp backstreet tavern: drinkers smoking, singing, and playing cards and dice. They have traditionally been called 'peasants' rather than the more appropriate 'drinkers'. For these works (painted at Antwerp some time after 1631), Brouwer modelled his figures on real-life workers. He himself frequented these haunts and became addicted to brandy and the illegal tobacco juice, the use of which was punishable by death. It is this illegal liquor, the effects of which are shown at varying stages, which is being consumed here. One character in the full light stands out from the rest of the group; sitting on a chair, wholly given up to pleasure, he looks on with an apathetic, scathing stare. The other subtly coloured figures, who can be discerned through the smoke-laden atmosphere, form a semi-circle round the main figure, their positions illustrating the pleasures of tobacco smoking, while only the figure on the right remains in contact with the outside world.

The still-life constituted by the stool, cheese, napkin and pitcher completes the composition. These solitary individuals, cut off from one another, each with his own personality, are in this dramatic episode linked only by the studied composition. It is possible that these works of Brouwer's may form a series representing the five senses, this one being 'Taste'.

This painting has been in Munich since the eighteenth century.

ANTHONY VAN DYCK, 1599-1641
Self-portrait
Canvas: $31\frac{7}{8}'' \times 27\frac{3}{16}''$ (81 × 69 cm.) Catalogue No. 405

Eugène Fromentin described Van Dyck thus: 'A young prince of royal blood endowed with every gift of nature: beauty, elegance, talent, precocious genius, a unique education and, above all, a noble station in life... still a boy, even when grown up, foolhardy even in his last days, a libertine, gambler and money-lover, dissipated and extravagant...; with a strong constitution and a fine build but a rather feminine and delicate complexion; a Don Juan rather than a heroic type; his gay life tinged with an air of melancholy and sadness; the hurt look of a tender heart always falling in love; a passive rather than an active nature; sensual rather than passionate..., an exquisite creature in every way, sensitive to all attractions and consumed by the two most demanding passions that exist: art and women.' This description fits perfectly this portrait of the twenty-three-year-old Van Dyck. It does not show the assurance and energy of his master Rubens' self-portrait, but rather a concern for worldly recognition and acclaim.

Van Dyck became Rubens' pupil in 1617, but maintained his individual freedom in his works. Not surprisingly he remained in his master's studio even when his apprenticeship was over. In 1621 he left for a six-year trip to Italy. In Genoa particularly, he was highly regarded as an artist, and much in demand. In 1632 he was appointed official portrait painter to King Charles I in London. Success went to his head, however, and his pride and vanity eventually were the causes of his receiving no important commissions during his last years. All these characteristics are evident here in the elegantly drawn face, whose visual beauty is conveyed with the minimum of colour.

The original version of the painting was smaller than this, and the right elbow was raised with the fingers touching the shirt collar. In the second version the portrait has been enlarged, the right hand now rests on the left arm. If it was Van Dyck who made these alterations we can presume that the gold chain added later is the chain presented to him in November 1622 by Duke Ferdinand Gonzaga.

This portrait came to Munich with the Düsseldorf gallery.

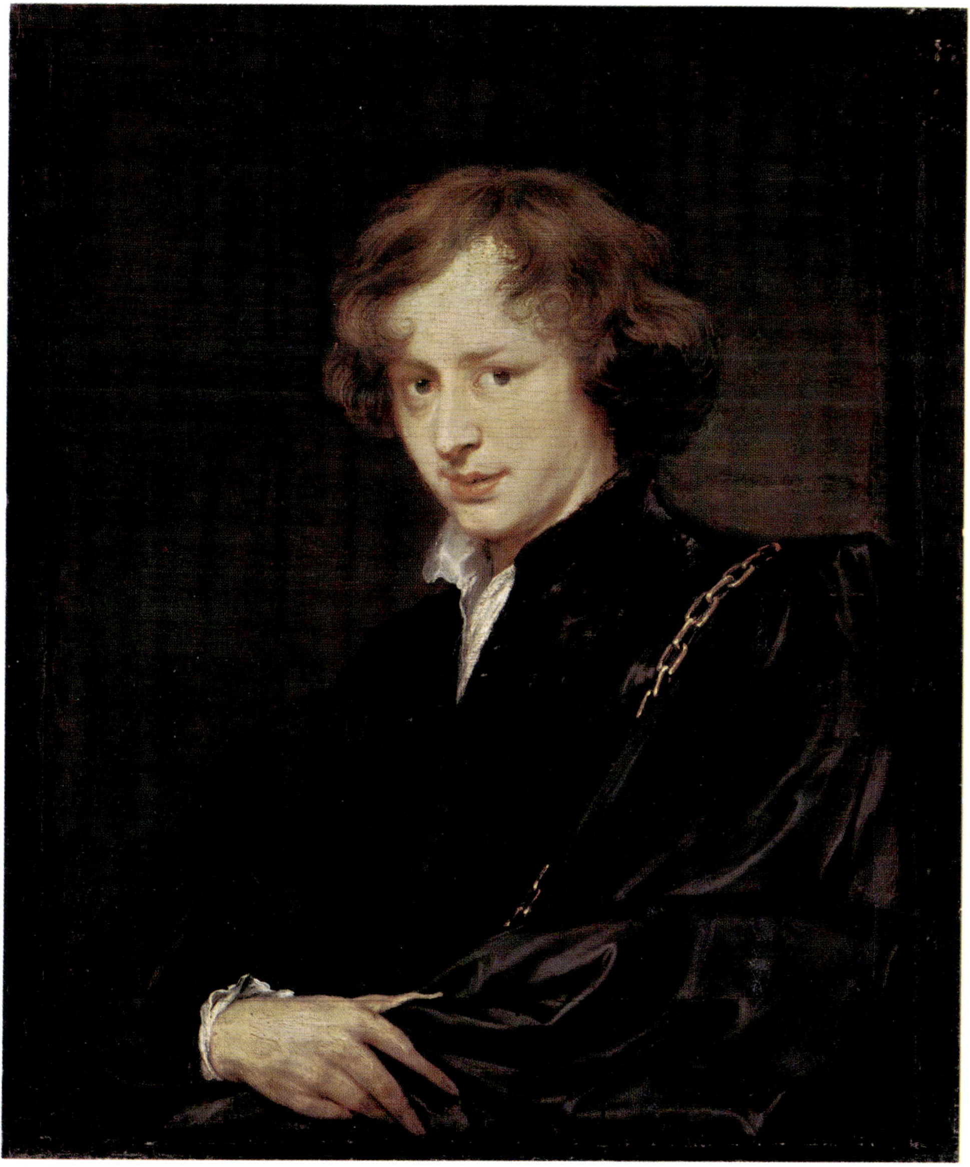

ANTHONY VAN DYCK, 1599-1641
Rest on the Flight into Egypt
Canvas: $52\frac{3}{4}'' \times 44\frac{1}{2}''$ (134 × 113 cm.) Catalogue No. 555

On his return to Antwerp in 1627 Van Dyck painted several works for churches, monasteries, rich bourgeois families and princes. Rubens occasionally acted as intermediary for him in these commissions, for example in the case of the commission for the Augustinian church at Antwerp, the main altarpiece for which Rubens painted himself. Rubens was often sent on diplomatic missions to Holland, France, Spain and England at this period, and Van Dyck was showered with commissions. During this second stay in Antwerp from 1627 to 1632, most of his works were compositions with figures. The *Rest on the Flight into Egypt* and the moving *Lamentation of Christ* are among Van Dyck's finest religious paintings. The former is a perfect example of his Italian period, showing the strong influence of Titian. 'What impressed Van Dyck in Titian was his free, masterly style, his beauty of movement and elegance of vision. From Titian he takes his aristocratic worldly elegance; but he is more playful, more delicate, more dynamic than the Venetian' (Theodor Hetzer).

The theme of rest is emphasized by the tranquillity of this painting. The centre of the work is taken up by the mother and sleeping child, enclosed in an equilateral triangle. The figure of Joseph, cautiously pointing out that it is time to set out once more, is integrated into the composition by a diagonal. This painting's delightful atmosphere of calm, lyricism and delicacy is evoked by the deep harmony of form and colour.

This work is first listed in the Munich collections in the eighteenth century.

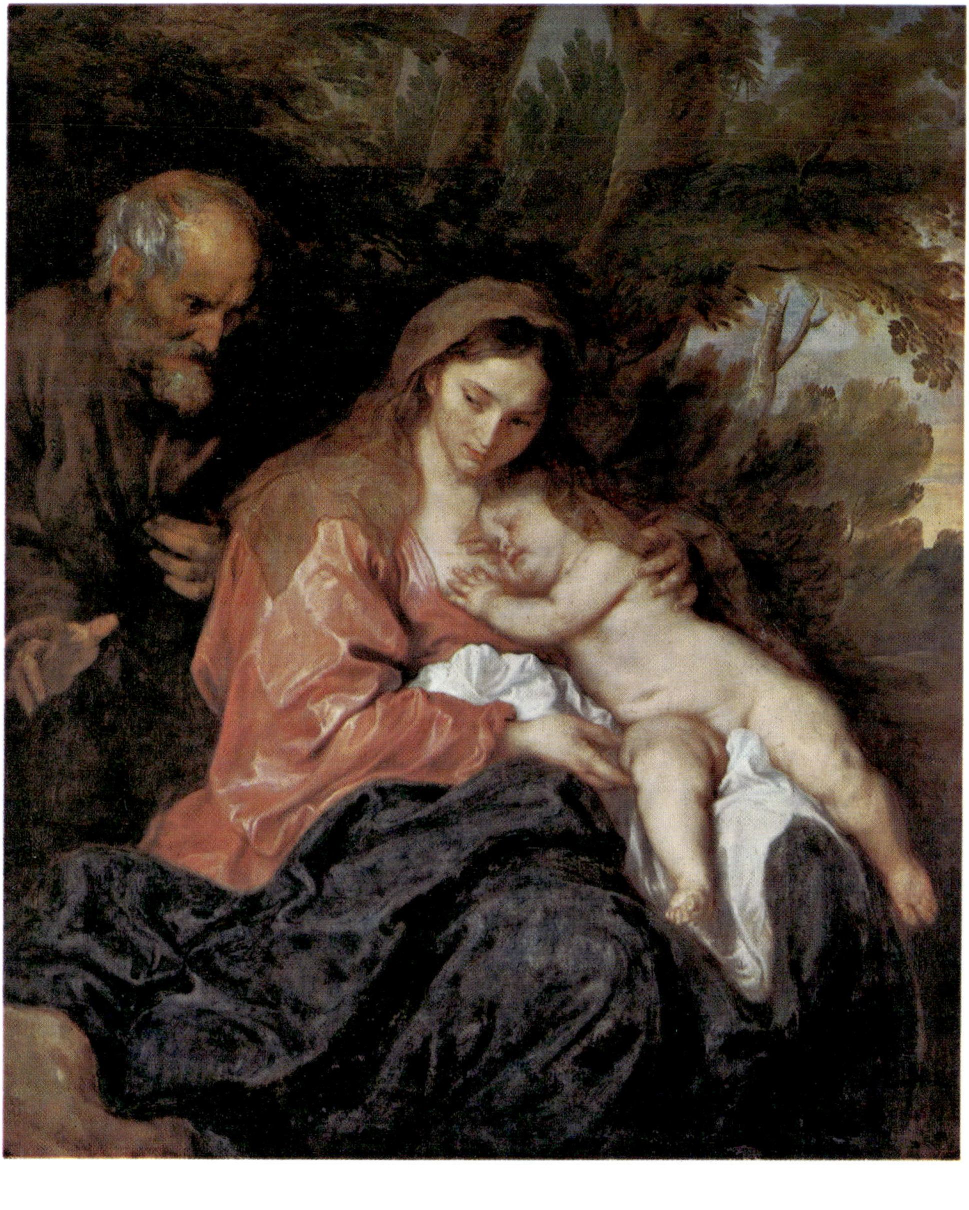

DUTCH SCHOOL

HENDRICK GOLTZIUS *Venus and Adonis*

ABRAHAM BLOEMAERT, 1564-1651
Feast of the Gods
Canvas: 39¾" × 57½" (101 × 146·5 cm.) Catalogue No. 6526

This painting is a symbolic representation of temporal delights and pleasures. A multitude of figures throng around a banqueting table set up in the open air beneath a canvas canopy to the right of the path diagonally crossing the picture. All these figures are in motion, even those retiring from the main scene of action; all are elegant and self-satisfied. They pay little attention to the drink or the music but are totally absorbed in love, the main theme of this work. Each figure is abandoned to his own pleasure. The gods sit in a closed world where nothing can disturb their tranquillity. The bright colours with which this Olympian atmosphere of serenity and joy has been conveyed lend it great charm and humour.

Despite the harsh light-effects and obvious fantasy element, the composition is in fact highly sophisticated. The yellow of the loincloth of the young man in the centre is repeated at the top left and top right, forming a triangle. On the right this yellow merges into the brilliant orange lighting up the canopy and the pale yellow of the sky. The chief focal points and the central subjects are the banqueting table and the sky. A sumptuous bright red appears in the cloak of a gallant and is repeated on the left in the robe of a girl, standing at the apex of a triangle formed by the group of four lovers. The gradations of flesh-colour range from dark brown to light brown for the men, and a greyish alabaster-white for the women, contrasting with the pale blues and greens of the landscape.

This painting was formerly in the collection of the Archbishop of Aschaffenburg.

JAN VAN GOYEN *Landscape with Farm*
This landscape was painted in 1629. Originally in the collection of the Electors of Mainz at Aschaffenburg, it entered the Alte Pinakothek in 1872.

MEINDERT HOBBEMA *Landscape*
This is an early work of the artist, acquired from M. de Vigneux at Mainz in 1792. It was transferred from the Hofgartengalerie to Schleissheim, and to the Alte Pinakothek in 1836.

ABRAHAM VAN BEYEREN
Still-life with Crab
This painting was until 1884 attributed to Willem Kalf. It was transferred from the Mannheim gallery to Schleissheim, and entered the Alte Pinakothek in 1881.

MICHAEL SWEERTS *Inn Parlour*

ADRIAEN VAN OSTADE *Brawling Peasants*

FRANS VAN MIERIS
Woman at her Looking-glass

JAN STEEN *Love-sick Woman*

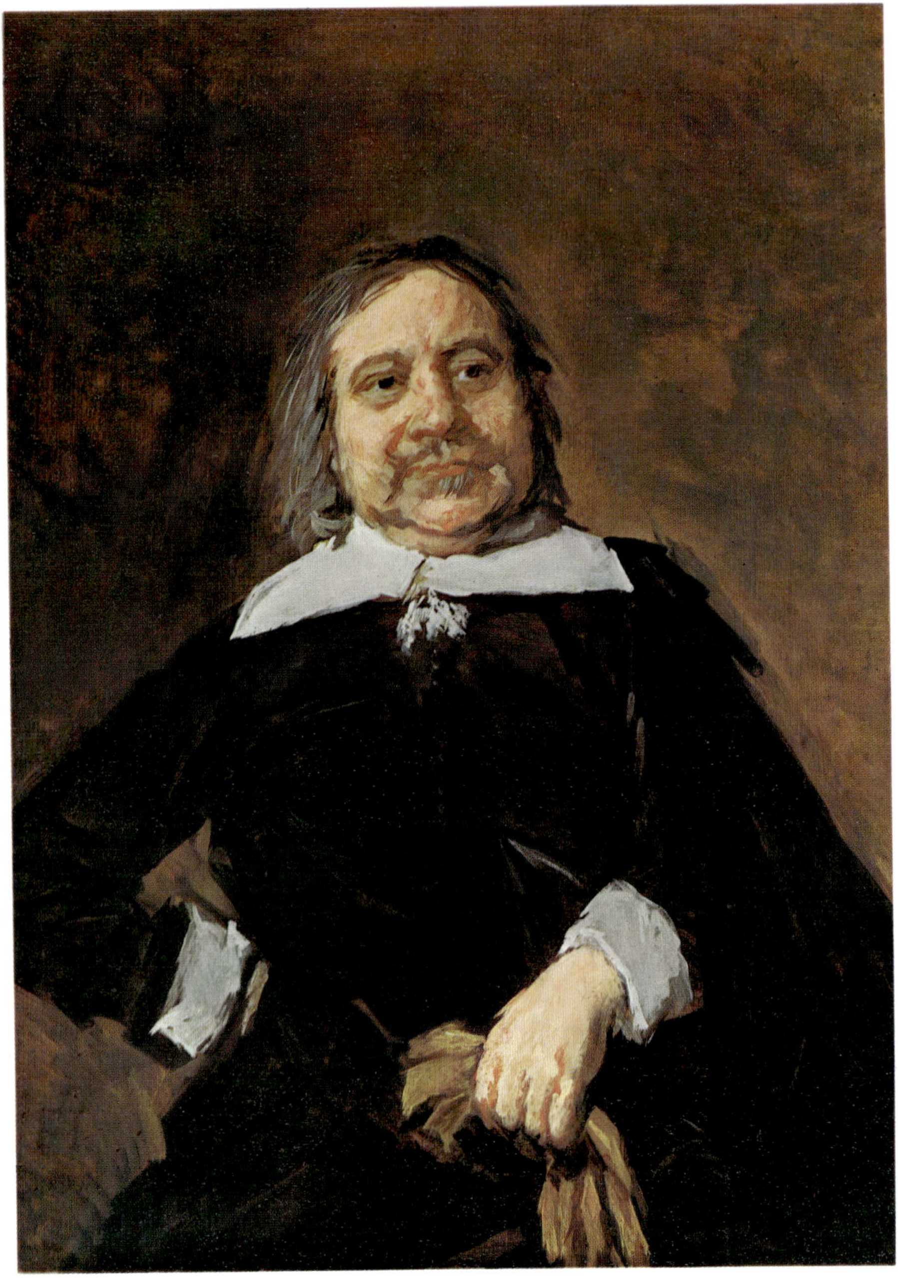

FRANS HALS, 1581/5-1666
Portrait of Willem Croes
Wood: 18½" × 13¾" (47.1 × 34.4 cm.) Catalogue No. 8402
Signed: F H.

The broad-shouldered, stocky figure sits in the foreground, his right shoulder stiffly thrust back so that the black doublet is pulled taut over his chest. This, together with the right hand on the hip, gives him a pose perfectly in keeping with his character. His plump face seems to emerge straight out of his white ruff. He leans slightly to one side, with his alert gaze fixed on some distant point above the spectator's head. He looks the epitome of the successful businessman, enterprising, energetic, crafty and unscrupulous. His expensive gloves hang carelessly from his hands, as does his cloak over his left shoulder. All that we know about Willem Croes is the date of his death; our sole evidence of his life is this one portrait, which shows him as a man of great vigour and vitality, noble-minded but with a shrewd, practical, realistic bent and a good eye for profit and gain.

Frans Hals was a superb portraitist. He painted his fellow-citizens of Haarlem, men and women, individually, in pairs, and in larger groups. In his early works he was primarily concerned with conveying their energy and vitality and, as well, their *milieu*. In later works, he sought to penetrate more deeply into their souls; his works after 1650 show him to be an expert psychologist with a great knowledge of human nature.

This portrait is generally thought to have been painted between 1658 and 1660. Despite its small format it gives an impression of weight and size. With great clarity and simplicity, Frans Hals has captured the Dutch character and way of life.

Today this artist, together with Rembrandt and Vermeer, is one of the three best-known Dutch painters, but this was not always the case. In his lifetime he fell into oblivion and died penniless in an asylum. No one bought his paintings; princes looked down on his portraits of middle- and lower-class subjects and he painted no works with religious, mythological or erotic themes. He also produced very few sketches. Although known in the eighteenth century (for example, Sir Joshua Reynolds), Frans Hals was really only rediscovered by the French impressionists. He was the first painter in the history of art to use a broad brush stroke and a full brush, and to do without a preliminary sketch, instead using bold dashes of paint to form his outlines. How Frans Hals perfected this technique can be seen in the grey hair, gloves and cuffs of Willem Croes. But what fascinated the impressionists most were his wonderful, subtly applied colours and colour values, which give his works their vitality and spontaneity. Apart from the occasional red stroke which appears in the mouth, face and hand, this portrait is made up of a whole range of greys, blacks and browns, as well as the white either contrasting with or merging into these. These colours and their varying degrees of transparency are reminiscent of Velázquez, who also made a strong impression on Manet. It was Frans Hals, Velázquez and Goya who opened up the path that was to lead to the modern techniques of impressionism.

This work was acquired from the Van Stolk collection in 1906.

REMBRANDT *Abraham's Sacrifice*

REMBRANDT *Self-portrait as a young Man*

REMBRANDT *Christ the Saviour*
This is probably the main panel in a series of paintings of saints, including a St Bartholomew which is in Downton Castle and a St James in the Willys collection. This painting of 1661 was transferred from the Aschaffenburg gallery to the Alte Pinakothek in 1916.

REMBRANDT
Adoration of the Shepherds
Another version of this work, painted the same year (1646), is in the National Gallery, London. The one here was transferred from the Düsseldorf collection to the Hofgartengalerie in 1806, and to the Alte Pinakothek in 1836.

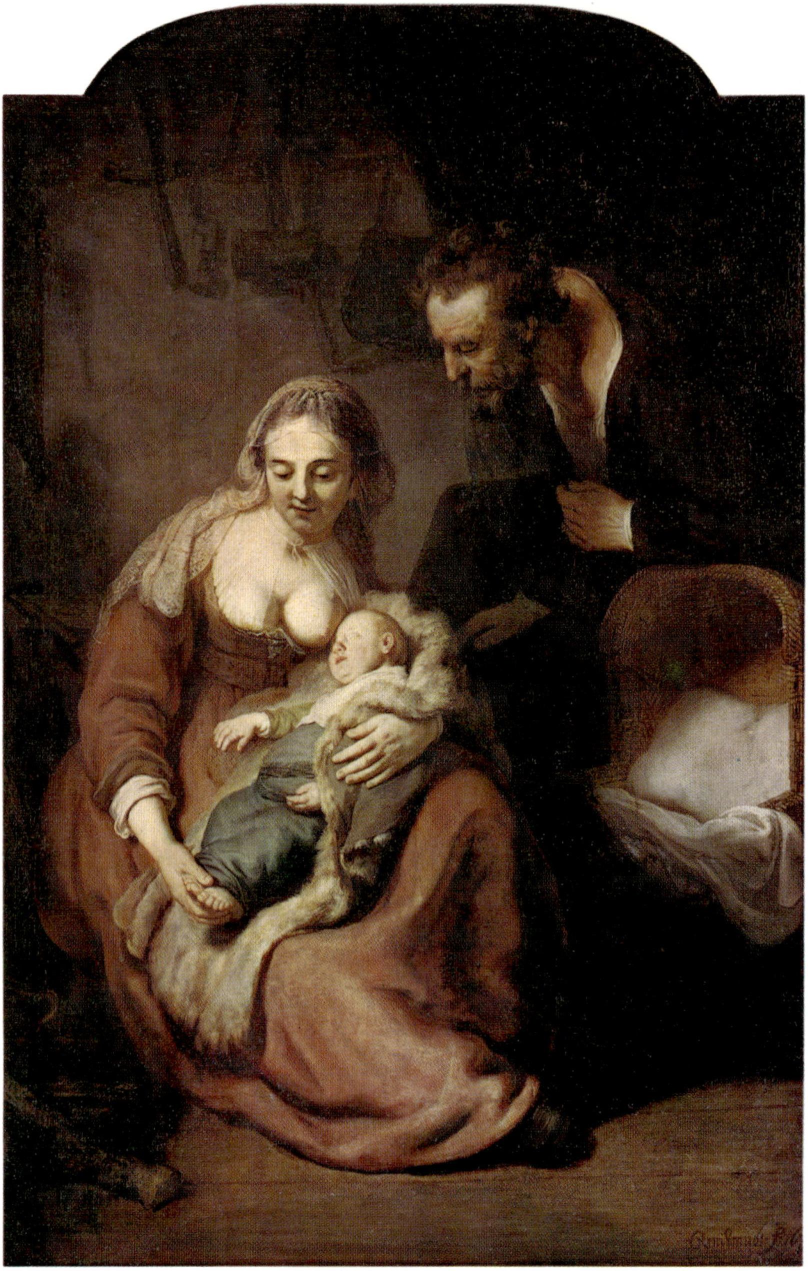

REMBRANDT HARMENSZ VAN RIJN, 1606–69
Holy Family
Canvas: $72\frac{1}{16}'' \times 48\frac{7}{16}''$ (183·5 × 123 cm.) Catalogue No. 1318
Signed and dated: Rembrandt f. 163

Rembrandt set all his religious paintings (including the drawings, of which there are an enormous number) in the framework of everyday seventeenth-century Dutch life; his Biblical characters are Dutchmen and his Jews were modelled on the inhabitants of the Joodebreedstraat in Antwerp. This Holy Family is like any petit-bourgeois Dutch family. The room is a modest one, with household utensils hanging on the wall and a typically Dutch wicker-work cradle. The high humidity in Holland explains the fur wrappings of the child and the feather pillow. But the face of the lively, harmonious mother tenderly cradling her child on her lap is transfigured. The painting is a symphony in brown, infiltrating even the dull, faded red of the Virgin's gown. The red-haired child is wrapped in a blue-green vest.

Rembrandt was roughly twenty-six when he painted this work. It already bears the unmistakable hallmark of his style, and has a warmth rare in such a large work. The Virgin's face is very like that of Rembrandt's sister Liesbeth van Rijn, whom he painted several times during this period.

This painting was auctioned at Antwerp in August 1735, and was bought from H. de Winter at Antwerp in 1760 by the court painter Lambert Krahe for the Elector Palatine Karl Theodor's Mannheim collection. It was transferred to Munich with the rest of the collection in 1799.

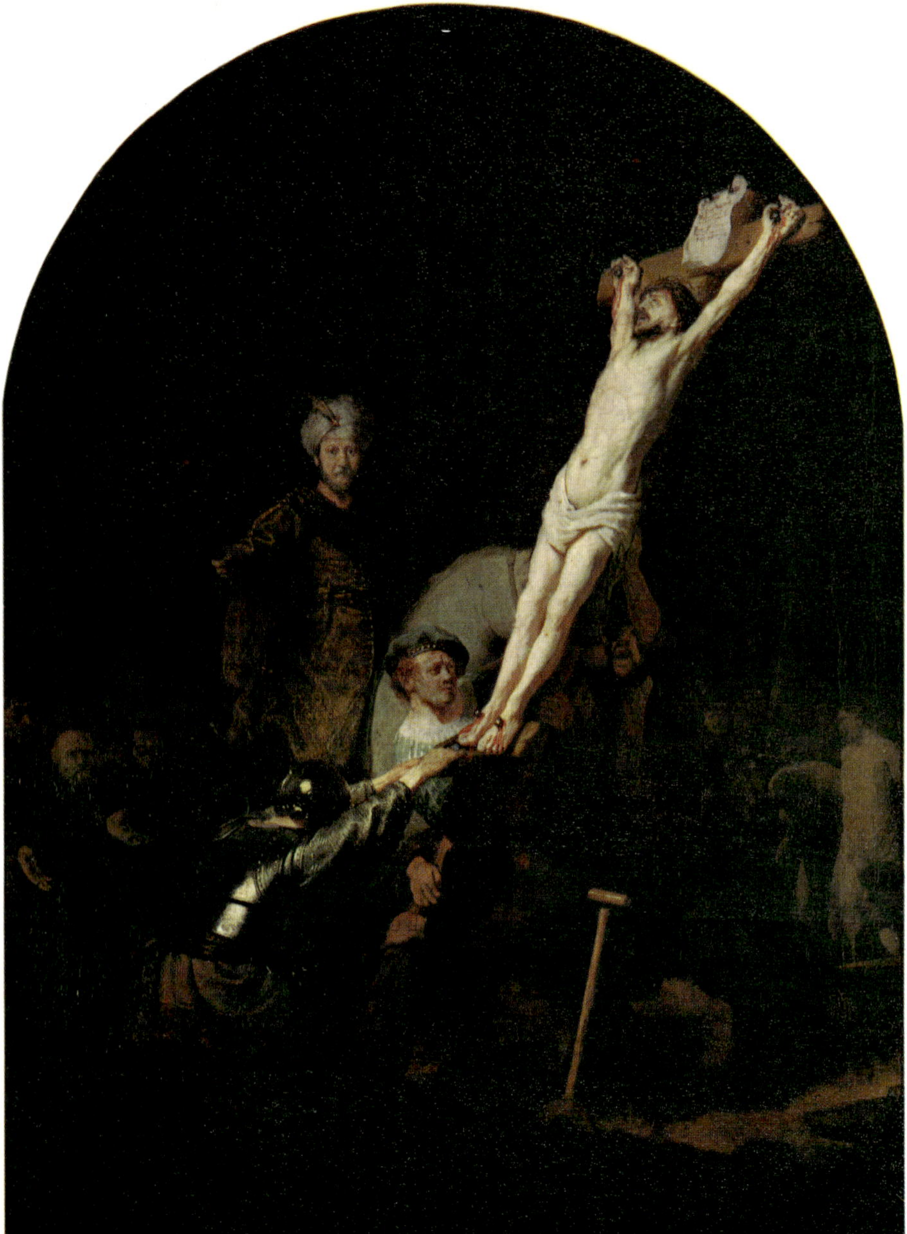

Rembrandt Harmensz van Rijn, 1606-69
Passion of Christ
Canvas: upper corners rounded, each approx. 36¼" × 28 5/16" (92 × 68 cm.)
Catalogue Nos. 394-8

The Munich series of five paintings of the Passion and some other scenes from the life of Christ took six years to paint: the *Raising of the Cross* and the *Descent from the Cross* were completed in 1633, the *Ascension* in 1636, the *Entombment* and *Resurrection* in 1639. These works formerly belonged to Prince Frederik Hendrik of Orange (d. 1647), governor of the Low Countries. According to Rembrandt's correspondence with the governor's secretary, Constantin Huyghens, it was Prince Frederik Hendrik who commissioned the *Ascension*, *Entombment* and *Resurrection*. These letters are unfortunately all that has come down to us in Rembrandt's hand. Later, around 1640, he also painted for Frederik Hendrik the *Adoration of the Shepherds* (Alte Pinakothek, catalogue no. 393) and in the same format the now lost *Circumcision of Jesus* to complete this series on the life of Christ. In 1667, these works are mentioned in the catalogue of the royal palace of The Hague. In 1719 they are listed in the catalogue of the Düsseldorf gallery – they were presumably acquired by Johann Wilhelm of the Palatinate (d. 1716). In the eighteenth century these paintings were temporarily housed in the Mannheim gallery of the later Johann Wilhelm, and were moved from Düsseldorf to Munich in 1806.

Raising of the Cross
Canvas: 37 13/16" × 28 5/16" (96·2 × 72·2 cm.) Catalogue No. 394

Bathed in light, the body of Christ stands out from the dark brown of the background. Three men are engaged in setting up the Cross. One of them leans against it from behind, the second, opposite him, hoists it up with a rope while the third in the middle steadies it with his hands. The latter, with a blue cap to match his tunic, stands caught in a shaft of light; this figure is Rembrandt himself modelled on his self-portrait of 1633. Behind him is a stout captain, mounted elegantly on his horse. His white turban makes him look like a magician; he unsheathes his sword and raises it feebly. The captain stands apart from the general activity (the figures setting up the Cross on the right and the old man on the left standing by observing the scene) and points to the spectator, as if to say: Look at this!

Descent from the Cross
West Indian cedar: $35\frac{1}{16}'' \times 25\frac{9}{16}''$ (89·4 × 65·2 cm.) Catalogue No. 395

This painting also has an imposing stout figure in a turban, casually observing the body of Christ. This time it is Joseph of Arimathaea, who is traditionally said to have buried Christ. Here he stands by as an impartial onlooker, unlike the old men opposite giving vent to their grief, and the Virgin lying stretched out unconscious on the ground. In this work too, Rembrandt participates in The Passion personally – the man in blue standing on the ladder carefully holding Jesus' right arm is the artist, based on his 1629 portrait (Alte Pinakothek, catalogue no. 11427). Albrecht Dürer also incorporated himself into the Passion of Christ.

In the *Raising of the Cross*, Rembrandt was certainly inspired by Rubens' painting of 1611 on this subject (in Antwerp Cathedral). In the *Descent from the Cross* he has copied details from another work by Rubens of 1611–14 (also in Antwerp Cathedral), an engraving of which was made shortly afterwards by Vostermann. But Rembrandt has made a substantial alteration; he has cut the number of onlooking figures by half and grouped them not in relief but in a particularly effective circle around the figure of Christ. Moreover, the various tonalities and light effects are totally different from Rubens' style. A similarity has also been noted with the *Entombment* of the Italian Bassano, a copy of which used to be in a private collection in Antwerp. This work shows how the young Rembrandt eagerly assimilated everything he saw, transforming it to his own advantage. Rembrandt often took up this theme of the Descent from the Cross in his paintings and etchings, but each time with some new variation.

A deeply religious man, he read his Bible throughout his life and drew inspiration from it for his works, bringing the ancient episodes to life by giving them new interpretations.

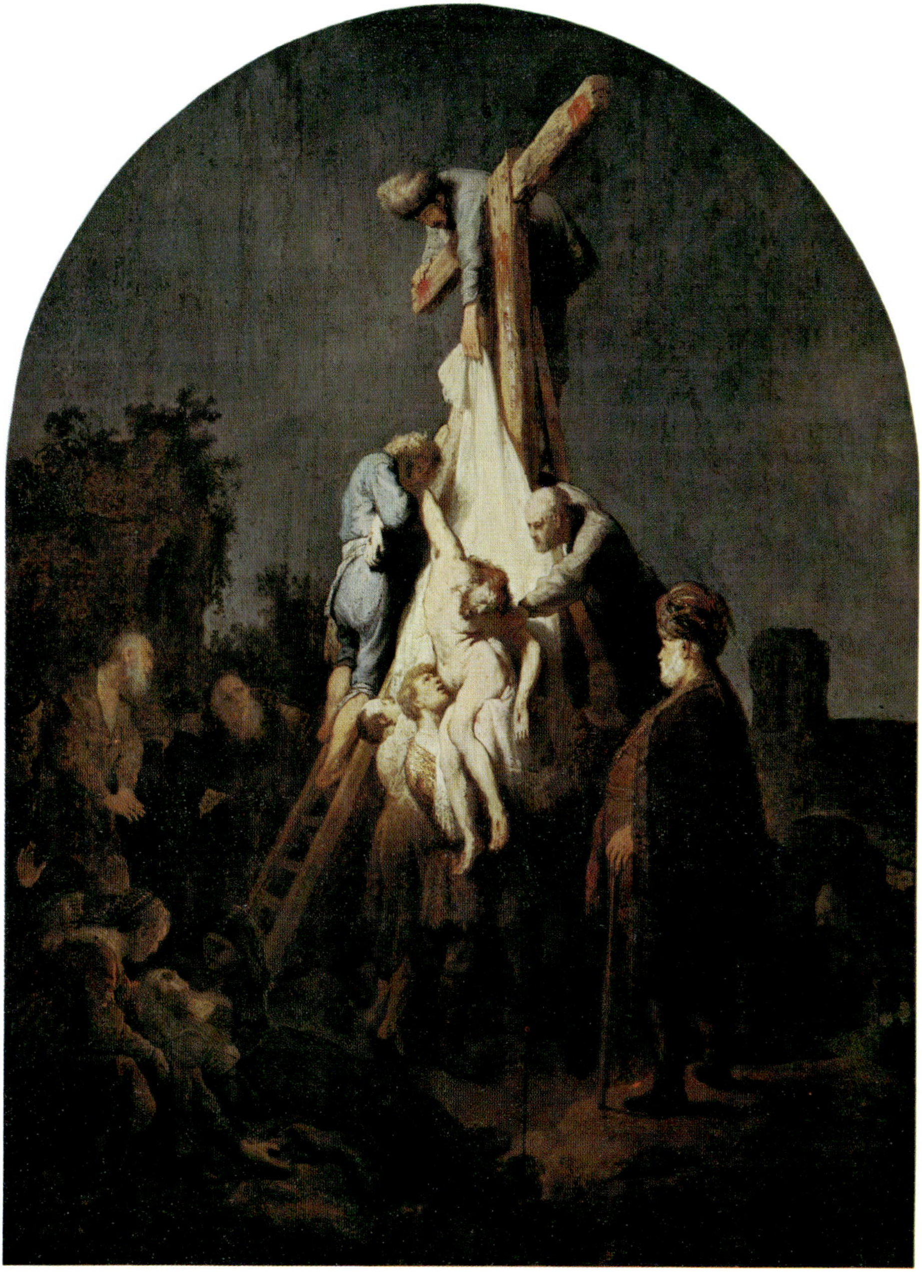

REMBRANDT *Entombment*

REMBRANDT *Resurrection*

REMBRANDT *Ascension*

FERDINAND BOL *Members of the Wine Merchants' Guild*

WILLEM VAN DE VELDE THE YOUNGER, 1633–1707
Calm Sea
Canvas: $20\frac{13}{16}'' \times 22\frac{1}{16}''$ (51·6 × 56·5 cm.) Catalogue No. 1032
(Reproduction p. 234)

This canvas is the perfect evocation of a summer's day at noon. The sun pierces through the puffy clouds; all is becalmed: the still grey water and the ships' sails. It is low tide, with not a breath of wind to swell the sails, and the grey water is so still that the rope in the centre of the painting is not even taut. The brown, beige and yellowish sails of the two fishing-boats in the foreground are reflected perpendicularly in the water. The red and blue of the Netherlands' flag provide the only bright colours in the work; the colours of the flag flying from the top of the mast of the big frigate on the left are barely visible. The ship with its two spars, the grey sky above, and the grey sea below all form a symphony in grey and brown. On the horizon to the right another frigate has just fired its guns signalling its departure; a trail of white smoke hangs over the water. In one of the ships in the foreground, three fishermen watch the frigate put out to sea, not noticing the three dolphins whose fins are sticking up above the surface of the water.

The Netherlands owed its great prosperity in the seventeenth century to sea trade with America, South Africa and the Indies. It is not surprising therefore to find a Dutch painter with a knowledge of the sea.

In early seascapes, painters were concerned only to reproduce faithfully in every detail different types of ships, or famous events such as naval confrontations or battles. Only in the mid-seventeenth century did they start to become interested in the sea itself. Willem van de Velde was the first to study sky, sea, weather and ships as an integrated whole. In his paintings he gave unique expression to the relationship between these four elements, which he set in harmony with man. His seascapes have a beauty all of their own; they reflect a deep feeling for nature which, 150 years later, still continues to move us, taking us into an ideal world created by the artist long ago by means of rigorous, sensitive observation and sober realism.

This painting belonged to the collection of King Maximilian I of Bavaria.

Philips de Koninck, 1619–88
Extensive Landscape
Canvas: 52½" × 65⅛" (133·3 × 165·7 cm.) Catalogue No. 9407

The dark-brown left bank overlooks a river lazily flowing along its winding course, with its clear waters reflecting the ochre-coloured clay rocks of the sunny right bank and the cloudy sky which takes up almost two-thirds of the surface area of the painting. The river disappears behind the trees in the centre, to form in the right background a broad estuary flowing into the sea. The other half of the landscape, comprising several horizontal lines, is dotted with isolated poplars, farms, hidden villages and a windmill. In the foreground are a few figures, two fishermen by the river's edge and the shepherds guarding their flocks on a narrow area of grass, figures which blend in perfectly with nature in this case with the dull grey-green trees and bushes. The colours of the meadows, sandbanks and silver poplars are accurately observed; only in the areas of shade do the poplars take on a bright green. Plants capable of absorbing large quantities of water are needed to fix this coastal area below sea-level. Koninck portrays them not with a sketched outline but with a light broad brushstroke, making particular use of colour. Towards the horizon the landscape merges into the beige of the sky.

Seventy extensive landscapes by Koninck are known, but none of them depicts a place which can be identified. Most seventeenth-century Dutch paintings were painted in the artist's studio, while only drawings and sketches were done in the open air. Moreover, specialization was taken to such a degree that several landscape-painters had difficulty in painting figures and would seek the aid of friends and colleagues to fill in the required people, animals and flowers. Koninck resorted to this then fashionable method. Many Dutch artists painted the polder landscapes so characteristic of their country: Hercules Seghers, Jan van Goyen, Aelbert Cuyp, Jacob van Ruisdael, Vermeer von Haarlem, etc. But only Koninck succeeded in creating powerful documents of his native land, in his finest works of the period 1654–65.

This landscape was probably painted at the beginning of this period. Previously in the Brussels collection of the Duke of Aremberg, it was acquired for the Alte Pinakothek in 1927.

JACOB VAN RUISDAEL
Forest Landscape with Marshes
This work, probably painted around 1660, was originally in the Zweibrücken gallery.

JACOB VAN RUISDAEL
Extensive Landscape with Village
This work, painted in the second half of the seventeenth century, was acquired from the collection of Prince Ernst von Sachsen-Meiningen in 1942.

JACOB VAN RUISDAEL
Sandhill Landscape
The third figure of the date is illegible, but dated works in the same style indicate that it should read 1647. This painting was presented to the state in 1823 by King Maximilian I, out of his private collection.

JACOB VAN RUISDAEL, 1628/9–82
Forest Landscape with Rising Storm
Canvas: $22\frac{1}{16}'' \times 26\frac{13}{16}''$ (55·6 × 68·2 cm.) Catalogue No. 1053
Signed J v R.

The most striking feature of this painting is the vivid yellow clay soil of the clearing hidden deep in the dark forest, suddenly lit up by lightning. A man in a red shirt is hurrying up the path round the hill to escape the flash, while a shepherd, who has already reached the area of dark, is driving his sheep down the hillside towards a pond in which an oak-tree is reflected. The path falls away so steeply to the left that the roof and chimney of a distant house appear behind the tree. On the right another rooftop, lit by the lightning, can be seen in the gulley. The central clearing is partially hidden from view by the five tall trees in the dark brown foreground. To the right, the bright green of the foliage stands out against a patch of sky that is still blue, while to the left rain is falling from dark grey clouds streaked with flashes of lightning.

The canvas is one of Ruisdael's early works (1650–55). A doctor, he was also one of the best-known seventeenth-century Dutch landscape-painters. This is typical of his work for in this rather commonplace landscape the separation of houses and path suggests a deep-rooted hostility in nature towards man. The deliberately complex composition is centred on the highly 'baroque' irruption of light which gives the painting its dramatic appeal. No other artist can paint ponds and rivers, old trees and clouds so well as Ruisdael. In his early works especially, he showed great imagination in the construction of dynamic landscapes, penetrating and giving expression to the language and life of nature. He makes the spectator feel the pull of its power over man, and it is this that gives his paintings their impact, despite their austerity.

This work entered the state collection via the Bavarian royal collection.

JACOB VAN RUISDAEL *Torrent, with Oaks and Beeches*

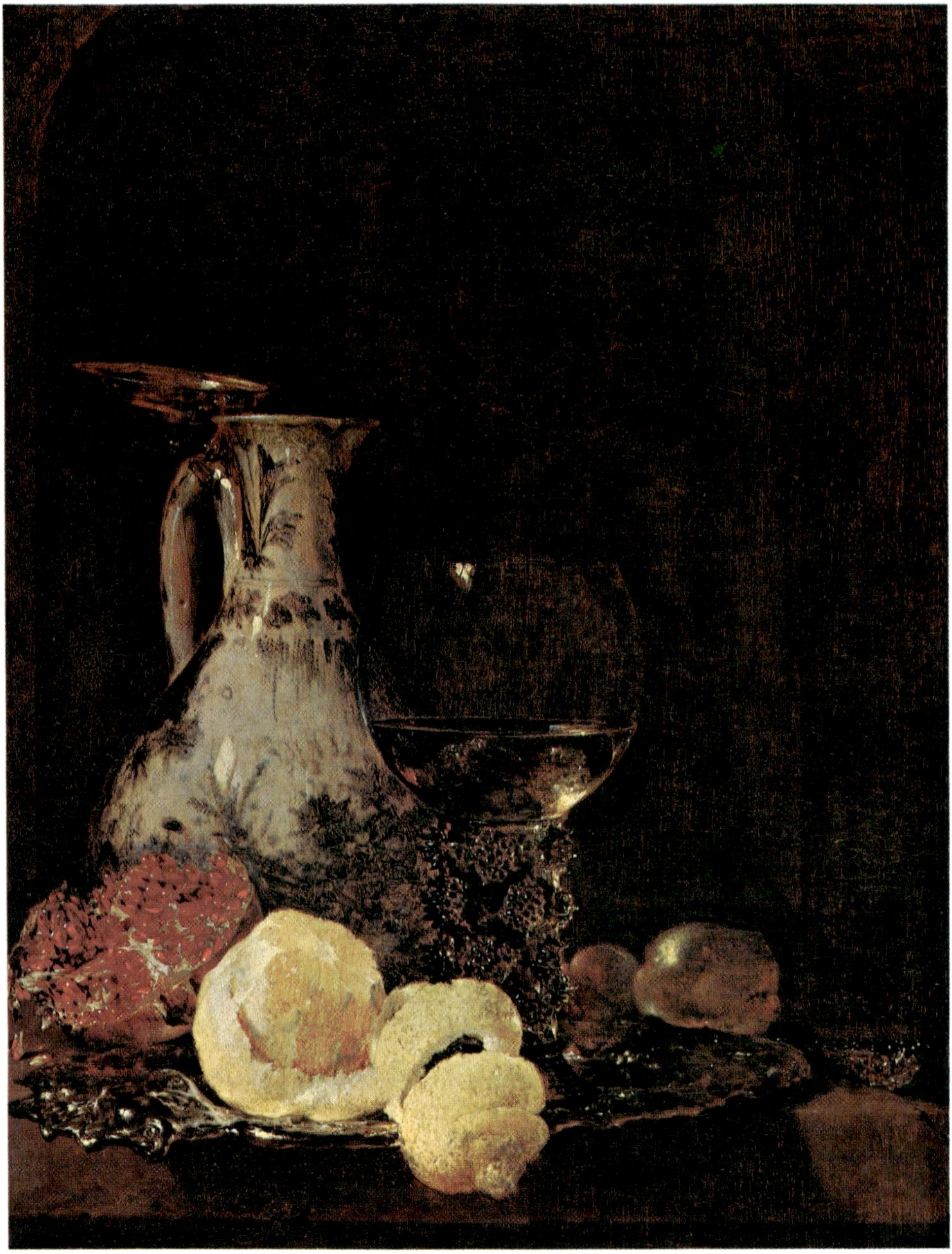

WILLEM KALF, 1622-93
Still-life with Delft Jug
Wood: $17\frac{3}{4}'' \times 14''$ (44·9 × 35·7 cm.) Catalogue No. 10763
Signed and dated: W Kalf 1653

The first object to strike us in this composition is the bright-yellow lemon with its peel curling in a corkscrew spiral and rolling over the edge of the tray and the table. Then we notice the round-bottomed jug with its metal lid raised, decorated in an even blue Chinese pattern. Between these two objects is a succulent segment of pomegranate tilted towards the left-hand edge of the picture. But the real point of focus, although the darkest object, is the glass, set on an ornately bordered tray, its contours harmonizing with the arch of the alcove dimly perceived in the dark background. Round the base of this glass is a cluster of pearly-glazed blackberries. This extraordinarily bright, translucent, spherical glass is one-third full of wine; seductive and intangible, it is given an air of mystery by the lights and colours mirrored in it: the blue of the jug, the red of the fruit and the yellow of the lemon. All these primary colours are set in the shadow like so many precious stones.

This painting was acquired from a private collection in Berlin in 1940.

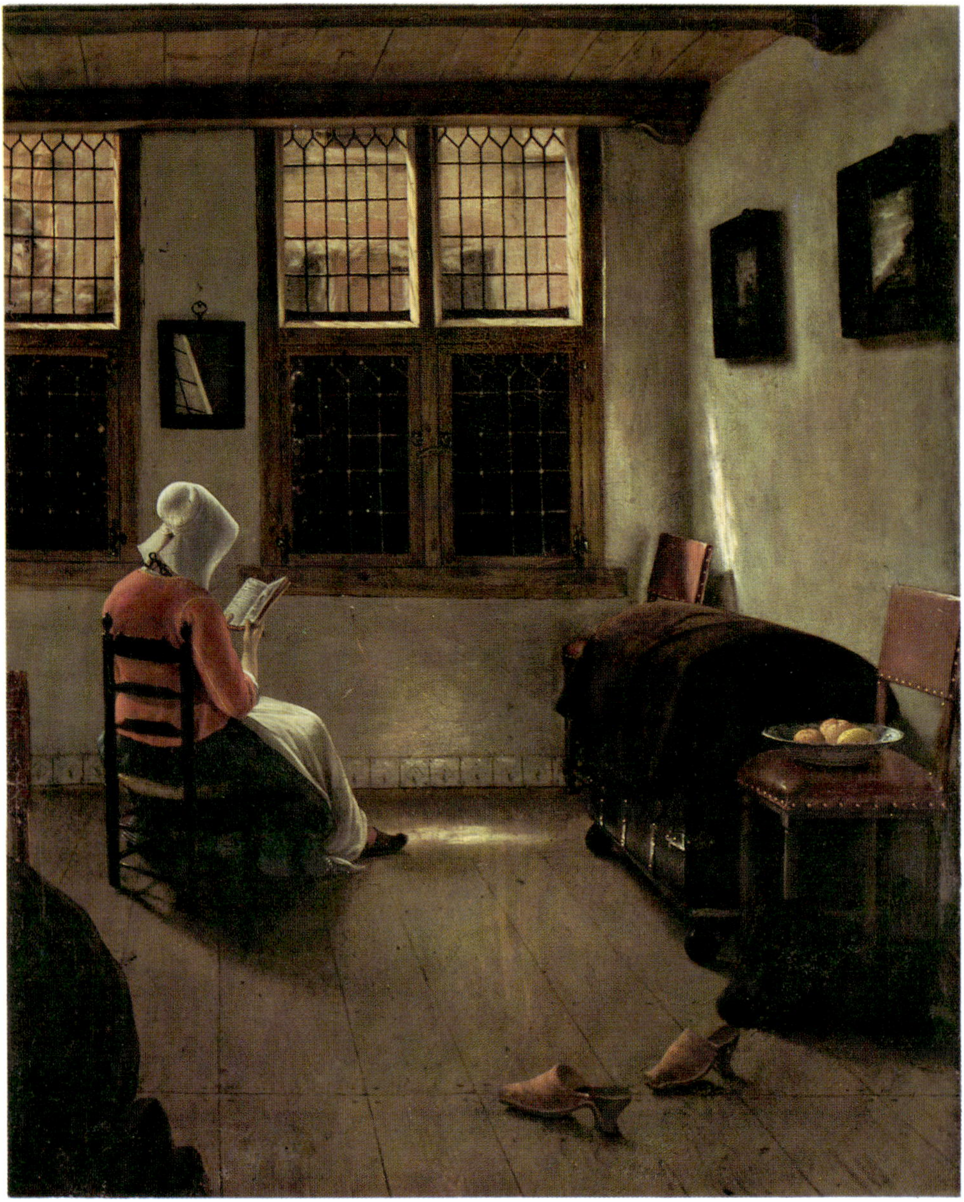

PIETER JANSSENS ELINGA, 1623–82
Woman reading
Canvas: 29¾" × 25" (75·7 × 63·5 cm.) Catalogue No. 284

In 1609 the northern Netherlands (now Holland) acquired its independence and freedom of religion. This date marks the beginnings of the country's economic and cultural growth. In seventeenth-century painting, the worldwide fame of Holland is best documented. Alongside great artists like Rembrandt and Frans Hals stand a large number of excellent painters who specialized in new subjects such as still-life, interiors, peasant scenes, landscapes and seascapes. In other words, they painted their country, the simple basic daily life of their compatriots, and they discovered the relationship between colour and light. This art, unique of its kind, was not destined for churches and princes, but for the ordinary man.

In this work, the sole decoration to the bright modest room is constituted by the mirror, the enormous chest and upholstered chairs, and the two oil-paintings hanging on the wall. The unknown woman with her back turned is absorbed in her book. The sun shines through the high window, filling the room with a soft light. Every object has its proper place and could not be moved without disturbing the peaceful atmosphere of the room. The effect of light on colour was the chief artistic problem to occupy seventeenth-century Dutch painters – a problem which was worked out and resolved in portraits, interiors and landscapes.

This work was for twenty years attributed to Pieter de Hooch, the greatest Dutch painter of interiors, but was subsequently discovered to be the work of Pieter Janssens, a painter who preferred to shun fame and glory. This is his masterpiece, and a perfect example of contemporary taste.

Painted around 1665–70, it was bought in 1791 from a dealer, de Vigneux, at Mannheim for the Hofgartengalerie, and was transferred to the Alte Pinakothek in 1836. This is one of the works Klenze had in mind when he had the idea of building small rooms into the new Pinakothek.

SPANISH SCHOOL

DOMENIKOS THEOTOKOPOULOS, called EL GRECO, 1541–1614
Disrobing of Christ
Canvas: $64\frac{15}{16}''\times 39''$ (165 × 98·8 cm.) Catalogue No. 8573

The artist has here chosen a theme rarely treated except in the Stations of the Cross: the disrobing of Christ before the Crucifixion, as described in the apocryphal gospel of Nicodemus. Christ stands in the centre of the painting, with his right hand on his chest and his left over the Cross. On the left is the Roman captain wearing the breastplate of a Spanish nobleman of El Greco's time. On the right a soldier seizes the top of Christ's tunic and is about to tear it off him. Behind the figure of Christ can be seen the heads of the two thieves, together with a crowd of Jews and Roman soldiers with halberds and pikes held high in the darkened sky. In the left foreground are three women: Christ's mother in a long black shawl, behind her Mary, wife of Cleophas, mother of James, and in front, with her back turned and her fair hair wound round her head in a plait, Mary Magdalene, who stares in horror at a slave bending down to pierce a hole in one arm of the Cross.

This work was painted around 1608–10, twenty years after El Greco's first treatment of the theme in an altarpiece for Toledo Cathedral (now in the Sacristy of Toledo Cathedral). It was probably intended as a devotional work to help put the priests in a properly pious frame of mind before Mass. The act of donning the surplice should, in itself, be a reminder of the disrobing of Christ. Mary is placed in the foreground of the painting since she is the patron saint of Toledo Cathedral.

El Greco's characteristic style is evident in the narrow elongated format, with the figures viewed slightly from below, stretching up towards the top of the canvas. A total of some nineteen figures are packed together so tightly that there is no space between them for any background landscape, thus giving the impression of an enormous crowd pressing in on Christ. The brilliant red of Christ's tunic and the vivid yellow of the two figures in the foreground brighten up the dull colours of the background figures. The most commanding figure, apart from Christ, is the distinguished-looking knight staring straight at the spectator. Unsuccessful attempts have been made to identify him; he is perhaps the donor of the painting.

This work was purchased in France in 1909.

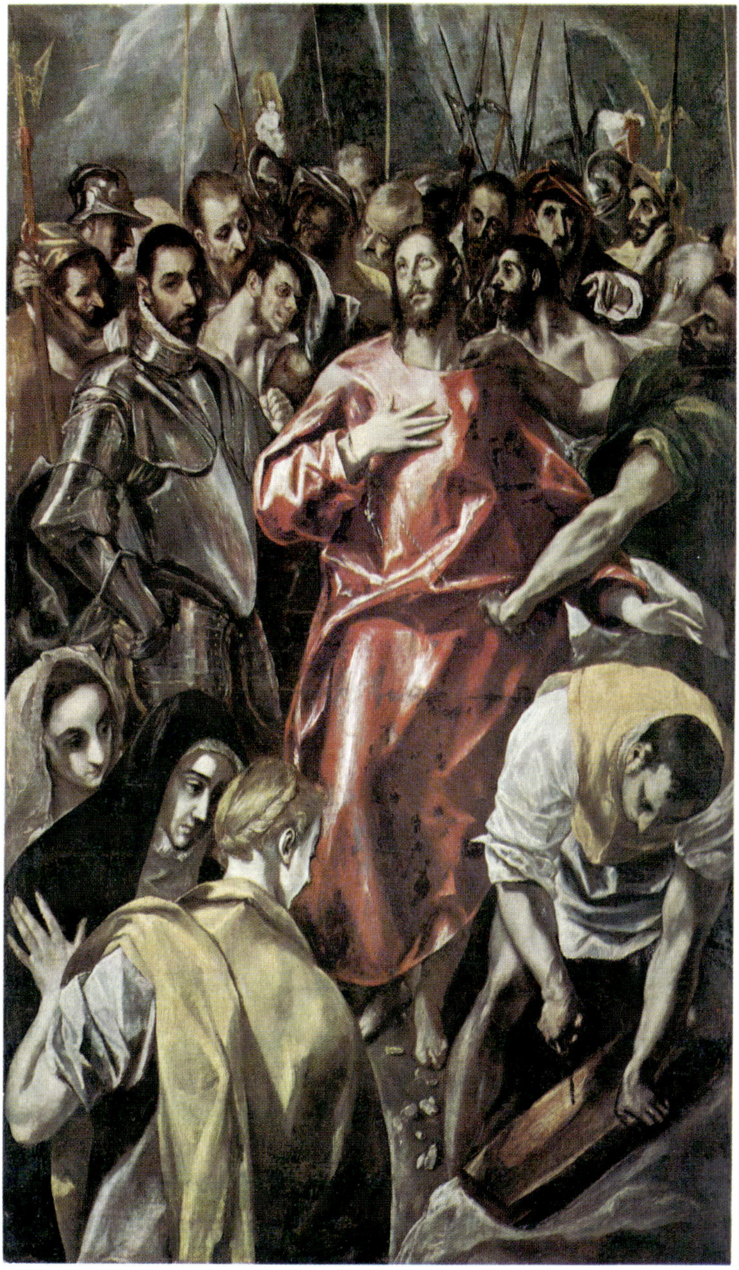

CATALAN SCHOOL
*St Louis of Anjou,
Bishop of Toulouse*

CATALAN SCHOOL
St Augustine of Hippo

RIBERA *St James*

ALONSO CANO
The Virgin appearing to St Anthony

ANTONIO DEL CASTILLO
*The Virgin and St John
returning from the Tomb*

CLAUDIO COELLO
Miracle of St Peter of Alcántara

CLAUDIO COELLO
Maria Anna of Austria, as a Widow

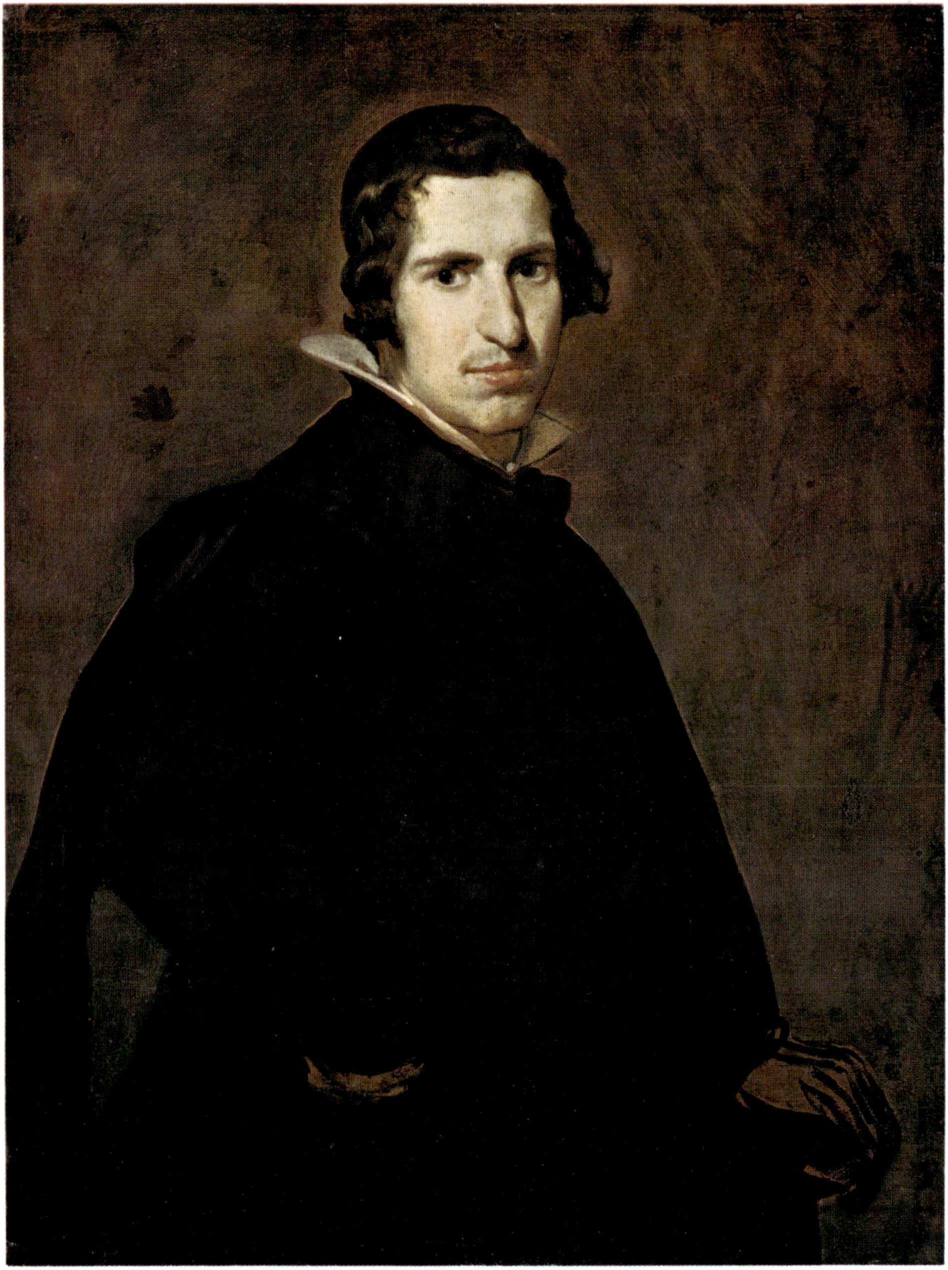

Diego Rodríguez de Silva y Velázquez, 1599–1660
Portrait of a Young Spaniard
Canvas: 35 1/16" × 27 1/8" (89·2 × 69·5 cm.) Catalogue No. 518

The young man is depicted half-length, turning towards the right with his head thrust slightly forwards; he gazes past the viewer with an absent, dreamy, rather fixed stare. The fingers of his right hand rest on his hip, while the left hand (unfinished) grasps the pommel of his sword. The head is high in the painting, and set exactly in the middle. The clear-cut outline of this figure dressed in black stands out sharply against the uniform dark background. In both composition and colour this work shows great simplicity and technical mastery, particularly in the young face, framed with dark brown wavy hair, its penetrating dark eyes contrasting with the pale complexion. The deep but reserved gaze of this figure, tinged with an air of melancholy, is unusually compelling.

The young man is wearing the black mode of dress introduced to the Spanish court by King Philip IV in 1621. The small white collar replaces the earlier ruff, which had been banned in 1623, the year that Velázquez became court painter. This portrait must therefore have been painted some time after this date, but before 1629 when the artist made his first trip to Italy in search of new sources of inspiration.

Velázquez painted many portraits in this period between 1623 and 1629, modelled on the works of earlier court painters such as Anthonis Mor and Titian. This explains why Manet, during a stay in Madrid in 1865, compared the famous portraits of Titian now in the Prado to those of Velázquez. Of Velázquez, Manet said: 'These are portraits with the real stamp of royalty – and with what means: the simplest execution imaginable, a few spots of colour.'

This excellently preserved portrait was acquired for the sum of four pistols by Heinrich von Wiser in Madrid in 1694 for the Düsseldorf collection of Johann Wilhelm von Pfalz-Neuburg. Wiser resided in Madrid as secretary to Johann Wilhelm's sister, Queen Maria Anna, wife of Carlos II of Spain (see p. 247). The painting was transferred to Munich with the rest of the Düsseldorf collection in 1806, and entered the Alte Pinakothek in 1836.

JUSEPE DE RIBERA, 1591–1652
St Peter of Alcántara meditating
Canvas: 29⅛" × 22¹³⁄₁₆" (74·4 × 58·2 cm.) Catalogue No. 909

St Peter of Alcántara (a town in the province of Estremadura) lived from 1489 to 1562; this work was painted 75 years after his death. A reformer of the Franciscan order, his own life of abstention, dedicated to contemplation and penitence, provided a shining example of austerity. He was often depicted, particularly in the seventeenth century, meditating over a skull. This painting was not known outside Spain until much later.

The friar's bald head is bent over the skull held in his hands; two profiles are close together, one as motionless as the other. There is no contrast here between the living and the dead – the old man, with his prominent cheekbones and wrinkled neck, is on intimate terms with death, the contemplation of which he uses as a means of attaining illumination. His habit takes up almost the whole picture. Patches of light fall on the saint's ascetic face and hands, as on the skull. Another source of light, from behind the saint's head, produces a sort of halo, introducing an element of mystery into this otherwise realistic painting. This spot, the most important in the whole work, is outlined with tiny brushstrokes. Ribera often used etching techniques in his paintings, being himself an enthusiastic engraver.

This work has much in common with the painting by Zurbarán illustrated on p. 256. Both of these typically Spanish works portray a monk meditating over a skull, and were painted about twenty years apart. Both have the same brown background, but the effect is different – in Ribera horizontal, rectangular and static; in Zurbarán diagonal and dynamic. But the primary difference between the two paintings is one of significance.

The painting was acquired by Karl Theodor some time between 1756 and 1780. It entered the Alte Pinakothek in 1836.

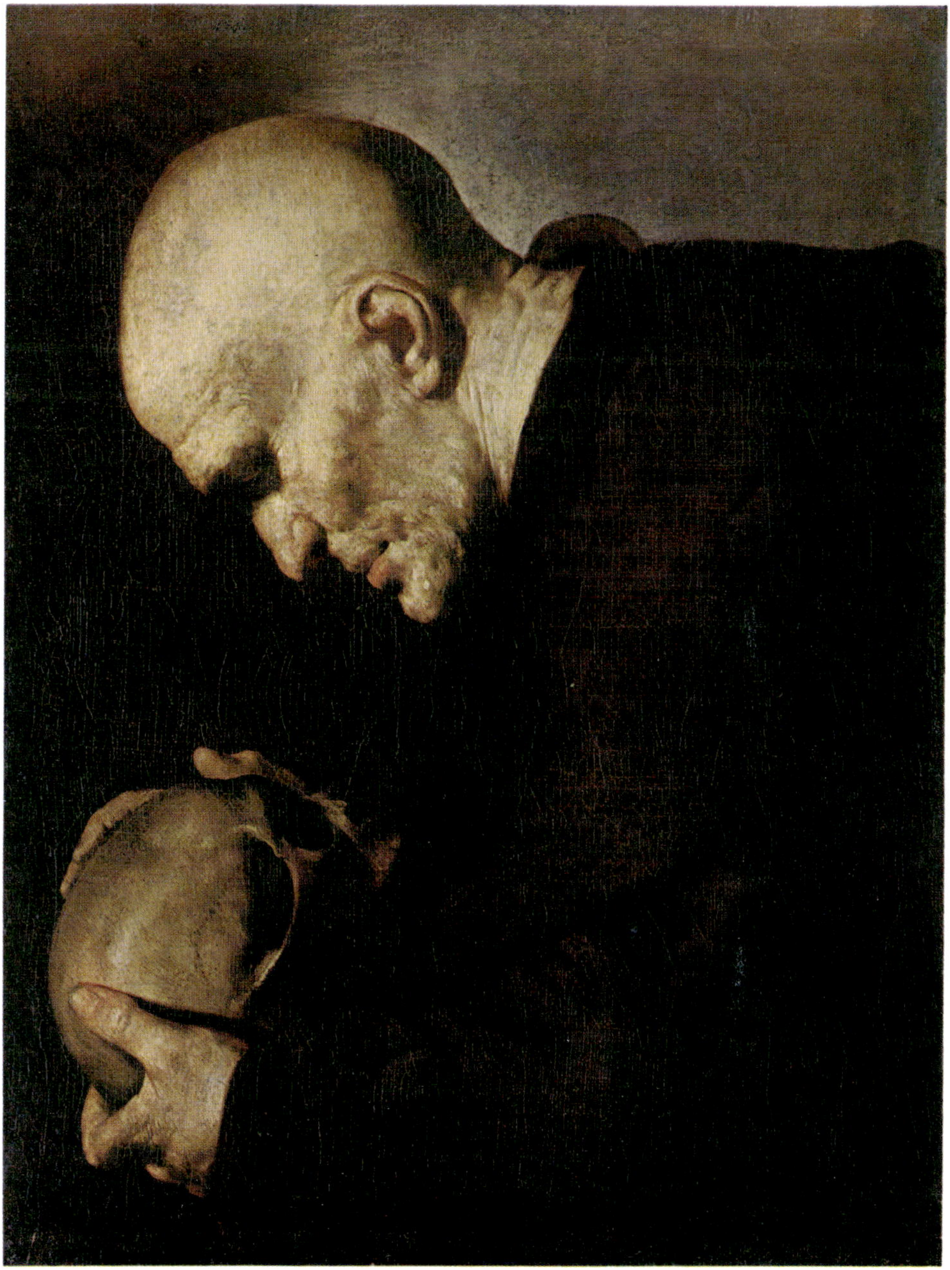

MURILLO *St Thomas of Villanueva healing a Cripple*
This work was probably painted for the Augustine monastery in Seville. It was transferred from the Hofgartengalerie to the Alte Pinakothek in 1836.

MURILLO *Domestic Toilet*
This work, painted between 1670 and 1675, was acquired from the bequest of Franz Joseph von Dufresne in 1768, and entered the Alte Pinakothek in 1836.

MURILLO *Little Fruit-Seller*

MURILLO
Boys eating Melons and Grapes

MURILLO *Pie-Eaters*

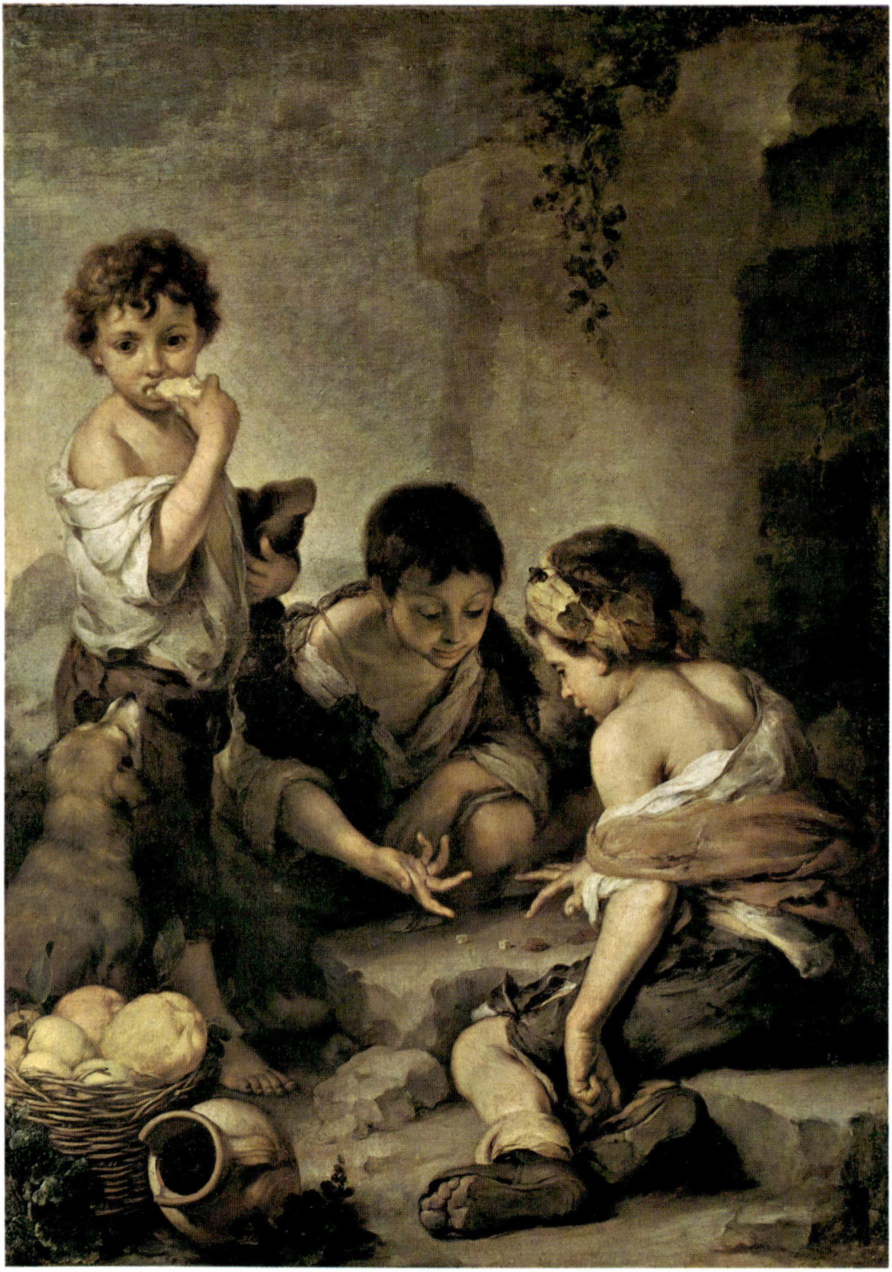

BARTOLOMÉ ESTEBAN MURILLO, 1617–82
Beggar-Boys playing Dice
Canvas: $57\frac{1}{2}'' \times 42\frac{1}{2}''$ (146 × 108·5 cm.) Catalogue No. 597

These young children run wild in the narrow dark streets of their busy town of Seville – so often celebrated in song – the town where Murillo spent all his life. In summer the streets of the town centre were covered over with sheets of canvas to shield them from the heat of the sun. Here the *chiaroscuro* effect is created by the pattern cast by the canvas above. The boys are gathered round a large block of stone, which serves as their table. Two of them are absorbed in the game, while the third gazes dreamily into the distance, oblivious even of the dog asking for some of his bread. The free, flowing composition forms a spiral, going from the worn soles of the boy's shoes in the foreground to the curly hair of the sturdy little fellow holding the hat. The Pinakothek has five of Murillo's paintings of street urchins, painted at different periods of his life but all showing the influence of the Italian Caravaggio. Apart from these popular paintings Murillo painted only religious works; his fine paintings of the Virgin and his altarpieces can still be seen in Seville. The new *genre* must have met with approval, however, for Murillo produced many works on this theme. The *Beggar-Boys playing Dice*, painted around 1670–5, is considered the best of these popular works.

Seville – the capital city of Andalusia, the richest and most fertile region of Spain – was an important port for trade with Flanders and America. The nobility and the monasteries were extremely wealthy and Murillo found no shortage of commissions. For one painting he is known to have received ten times as much as Zurbarán. Murillo was, like his beggar-boys, carefree and unpretentious, qualities which give his paintings their special charm, quite apart from any artistic merit.

Palomino, in his monograph on Murillo (1715), regretted having to say that almost all his popular works had left Spain. This painting was bought at Antwerp in 1698 by Gisbert van Ceulen for the Elector Maximilian Emanuel of Bavaria. It is mentioned in the 1748 catalogue of the Munich Residenz, and later in that of the Hofgartengalerie. It was transferred to the Alte Pinakothek in 1836.

A mezzotint engraving was made of this painting in the eighteenth century by C. Langlois. The work became popular after F. Piloty's invention of the lithograph at Munich in 1821–31, which facilitated mass-production.

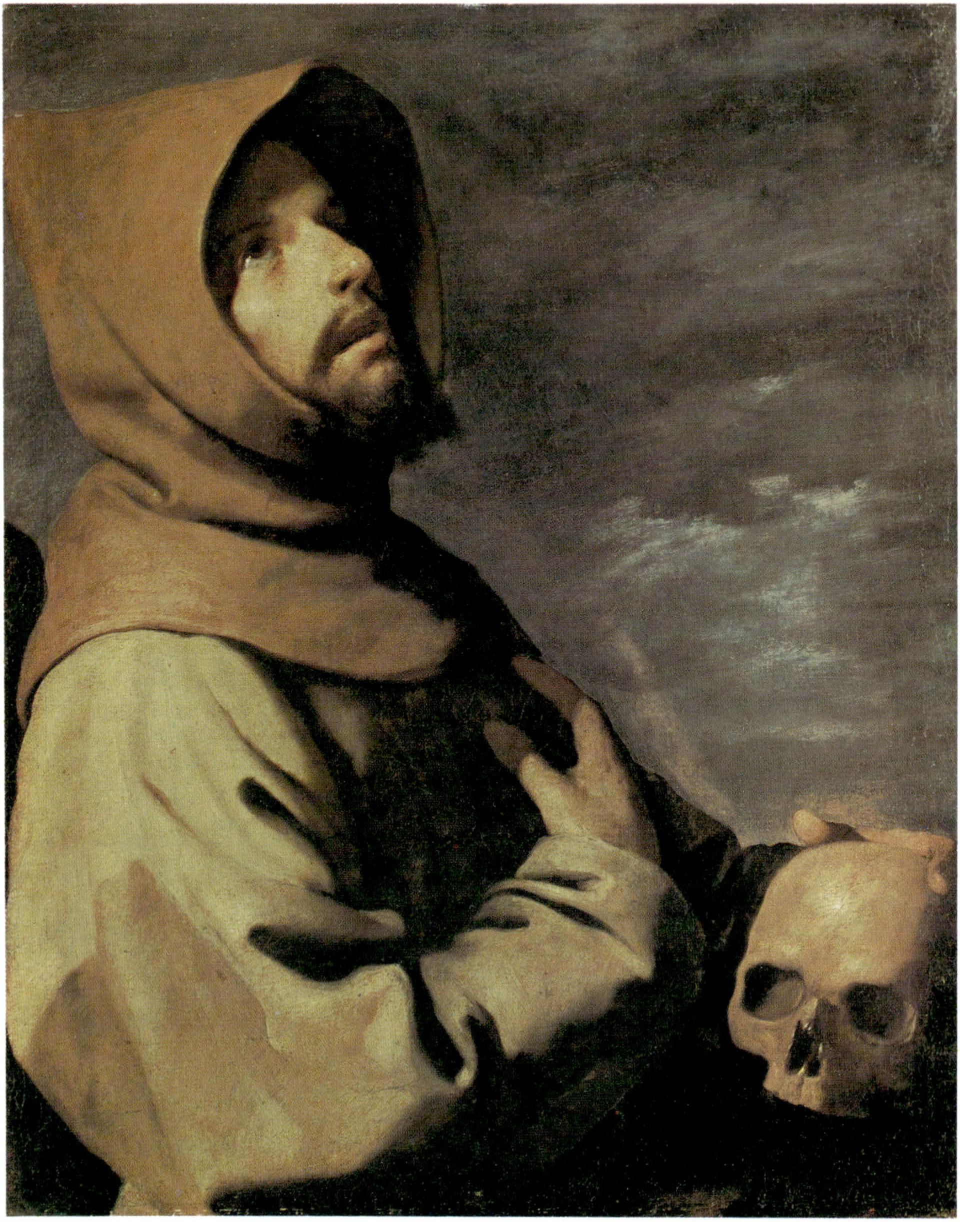

Francisco Zurbarán, 1598–1664
St Francis of Assisi
Canvas: 25⅝" × 20⅞" (64·7 × 53·1 cm.) Catalogue No. 504

The whole of the left side of the picture is taken up by the half-length figure of St Francis, hooded and dressed in sackcloth, with his head tilted slightly upwards. The composition is cut into two triangles by the diagonal going from the skull to the point of the hood. The far right-hand corner of the left triangle is occupied by the strange skull, whose black eye-sockets stare out at the spectator, and by the saint's right hand, marked with the stigmata of Christ's Passion which he had received on Mount Alverna in 1224. Hand and skull are closely linked. The right-hand triangle consists of a green-grey-blue, stormy sky and the saint's face, lit from above, gazing up into the heavens. The *chiaroscura* effect created by the hood gives the face a dramatic appeal. The saint rests his left hand on the skull, quite unafraid; his radiant face is detached from all earthly things. If one did not know that St Francis received all five of Christ's wounds, one might easily think that the actual moment of stigmatization was depicted here. The artist (who painted many religious works, particularly for monasteries – hence his nickname 'the monk painter') was well aware of the fact that St Francis lived only two years after the stigmatization, dying in 1226. According to tradition, he is supposed to have died singing. This painting was perhaps intended to signify the triumph of faith over death, or was perhaps a symbolic representation of St Francis' life spent in meditation and prayer. His face is lit with the source of that harmony which fused his life with that of all living creatures; it reminds us of Dante's opening words to his eulogy of St Francis in Canto 11 of the *Paradiso*: 'There was a sun born unto the world.'

Zurbarán, whose sublime austerity is softened in this work by the influence of Murillo, remained unknown outside Spain for fifty years. This painting is listed as being in the collection of the Electors of Mannheim in 1756. It was probably acquired by Karl Theodor in 1743 before he moved his capital to Munich, and in 1799 was transferred to the Hofgartengalerie with the rest of the Mannheim collection. It has been in the Alte Pinakothek since 1836.

GOYA
*Dona María
Teresa de Vallabriga,
Condesa de Chinchón*

FRANCISCO JOSÉ DE GOYA Y LUCIENTES, 1746–1828
Portrait of Don José Queralto
Canvas: $39\frac{3}{4}'' \times 29\frac{15}{16}''$ (101·5 × 76·1 cm.) Catalogue No. 9334
Signed and dated on the letter: Dn. Josef Queralto/Por/Goya/1802
(Reproduction p. 260)

Brown, cold, calculating eyes stare at the spectator from a face already ageing but still tinged with a gentle pink glow. His right arm is unusually positioned with the hand hidden inside the coat, throwing into relief the enormous cuff. All the important points in the painting are situated in an elongated triangle

258

placed diagonally across the picture, the horizontal side formed by the brocaded lower edging of the coat, the hand and the letter, and the apex by the grey-haired head. The painting is dominated by the free, deliberate colours of the rich brilliant uniform, signifying rank and distinction. It is as though Goya, once satisfied that he had succeeded in capturing all the pride and dignity of his model, decided to elaborate the brilliance and colour of this uniform to make it into an important visual element.

Don José Queralto was a surgeon and author of works on medicine, who died in Madrid in 1805. He served in the Navy and was director of a military hospital in South America. On his return, Carlos IV sent him abroad to pursue his medical studies, and he subsequently became a professor at the Faculty of Medicine at Madrid, as well as director of various Spanish hospitals. In 1800 he was sent to Andalusia when an outbreak of the plague occurred. All his published works deal with the subject of prophylactic measures to be applied in epidemics.

In this painting, Don José wears the uniform of a military doctor, the three stripes on his cuff signifying his rank of general.

This work belonged to the Queralto family until 1900. It was purchased for the Alte Pinakothek at a sale held in Berlin in 1925.

FRANCISCO JOSÉ DE GOYA Y LUCIENTES, 1746–1828
Still-life with Plucked Turkey
Canvas: $17\frac{11}{16}'' \times 24\frac{3}{8}''$ (45 × 62·4 cm.) Catalogue No. 8575
Signed: Goya
(Reproduction p. 261)

This still-life, composed of pinks, creams and ochres, stands out against a dark green background. The bird is propped up on the table against a reddish–brown earthenware bowl and the handle of a frying pan full of sardines. The

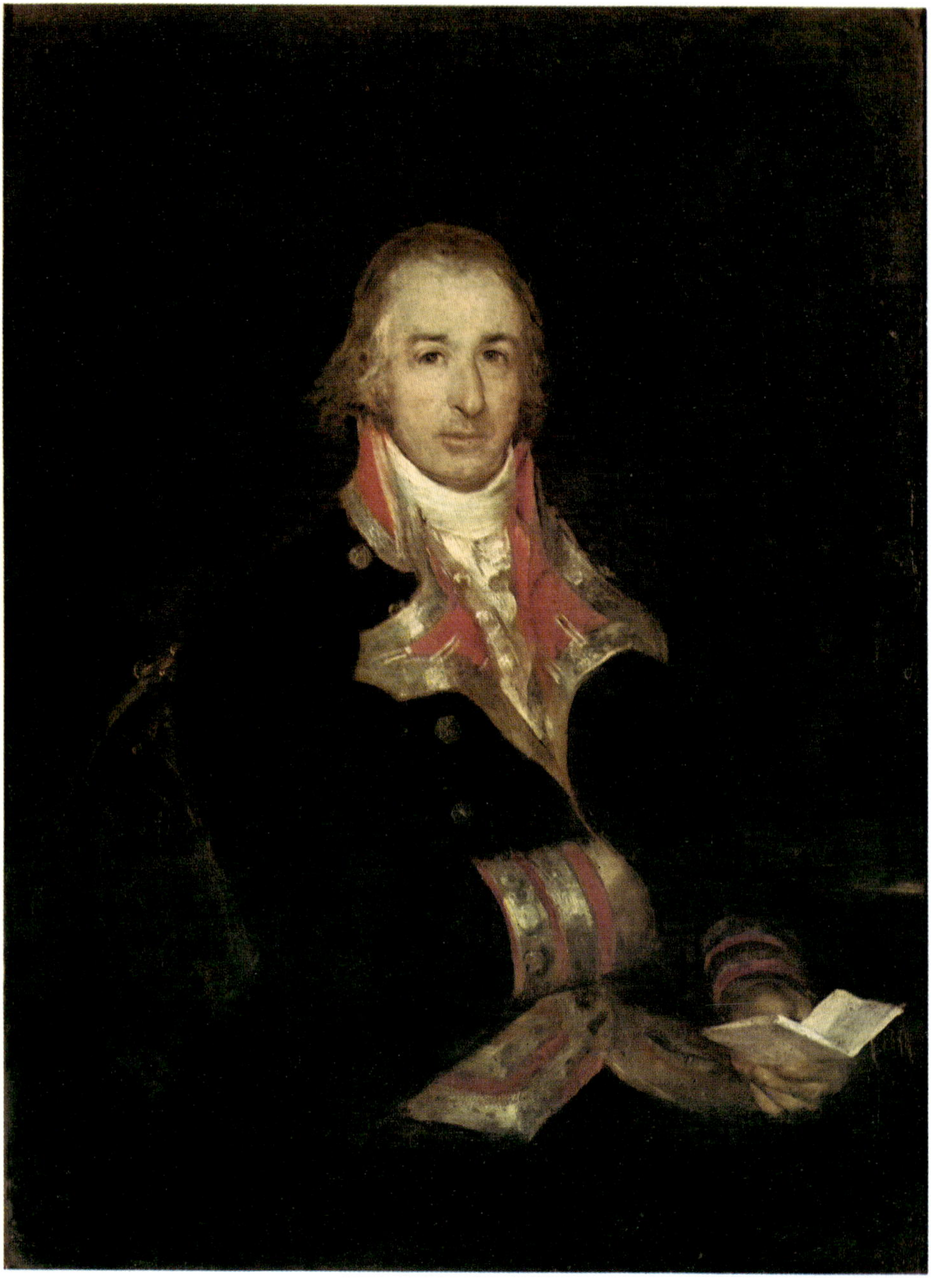

turkey's lifeless head lies in the foreground, with its neck so arranged that we can see the precise mark where its throat was cut. The aim of this painting is to convey, as realistically as possible, the fact that the bird is dead; Goya therefore shows the way it died as well as depicting it in an awkward, unnatural position, lying there plucked of its feathers. This 'rustic' subject was a favourite one with Spanish still-life painters. Here the artist has reduced the number of objects in his arrangement in order to bring out the delicate colouring and subtle shading of the plucked bird's body. The turkey has eight different kinds of meat, different in quality and in colour – Goya's painting is the first to show such a distinction. In its precise observation of detail and colour this work anticipates the nineteenth-century French impressionists, who were the first to really rediscover Goya. It is not without significance that this painting was acquired for the Alte Pinakothek by the same gallery director, Hugo von Tschudi, who acquired magnificent works by Monet, Manet and Cézanne for Munich. This still-life was probably painted between 1810 and 1820 and is therefore the most recent work in the Alte Pinakothek.

FRENCH SCHOOL

MASTER OF MOULINS, active 1475-1500
Charles II of Bourbon, Cardinal Archbishop of Lyons
Oak: $13\frac{3}{8}'' \times 10\frac{1}{4}''$ (33·9 × 25·6 cm.) Catalogue No. WAF 648

The Cardinal is portrayed half-length, in half-profile, with the ringed fingers of his hands joined in prayer, pointing in the same direction as his clear, serene gaze. His position, together with the Gothic carved choir-stalls, suggests that this painting had a companion panel probably depicting the Virgin or a saint – this is confirmed by the rounded upper edge, typical of diptychs of this kind. The rounded edge of this panel has been trimmed at some later date, but it is otherwise in its original form. The fleur-de-lys emblem of the Bourbons is carved into the choir-stalls on the left and woven into the brocade on the right. The Cardinal wears a red fur-trimmed cassock and a red cloak ('cappa magna') with an ermine-lined hood. This figure is Charles II of Bourbon (1434-88), Archbishop of Lyons, brother of Duke Pierre II of Bourbon who presented a large winged altarpiece to the cathedral of his home town of Moulins in Burgundy. It is from this altarpiece that the painter, to whom about a dozen works are attributed, takes his name. This panel shows the influence of the early Flemish masters, particularly of Hugo van der Goes, but its simple composition, clear-cut design and elegance are more characteristic of French painting. The Cardinal's long pointed nose and slanting eyes (untypical of the Bourbons) are particularly striking. Charles II belonged to the branch of Bourbons whose property was confiscated by François I and which died out in the sixteenth century; this may explain his lack of resemblance to the later Bourbon kings.

This portrait was painted some time after Charles II's nomination as Cardinal on 18 December 1476; judging by its style, probably around 1480, when the Cardinal would have been 46 years old.

The painting was acquired for the Alte Pinakothek by Ludwig I as part of the Boisserée collection.

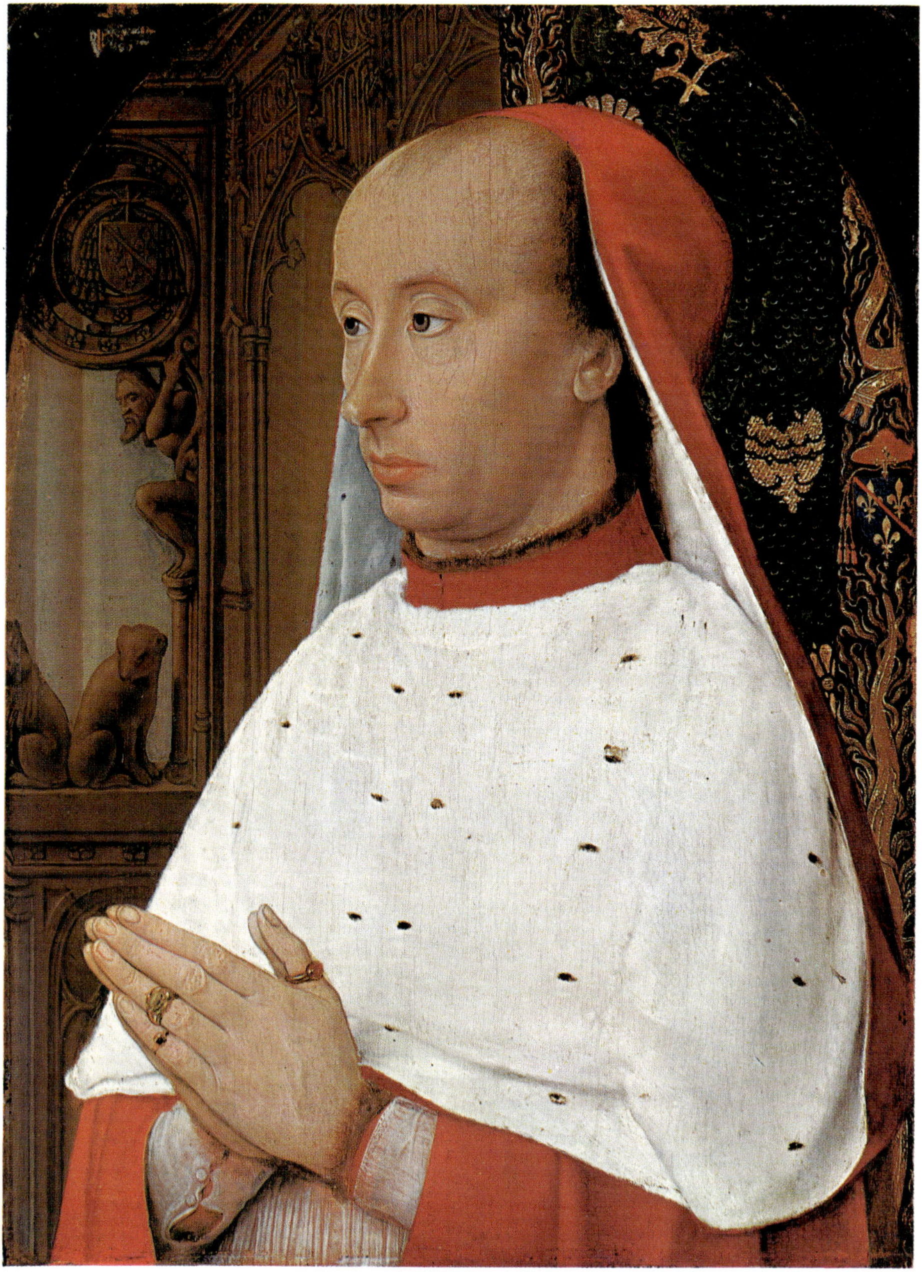

NICOLAS POUSSIN, 1594-1665
Midas and Bacchus
Canvas: 38$\frac{9}{16}$" × 51$\frac{3}{16}$" (98 × 130 cm.) Catalogue No. 528

Bacchus, a naked youth of godlike beauty, crowned with a wreath, stands before a red drapery, a wild cat at his feet. Midas, in a blue tunic and brown cloak, kneels before him. Although he wears the crown of the king of Phrygia, his gesture is that of a supplicant. The young god graciously grants him his request. To the left of Bacchus his foster-father, Silenus, lies slumped, fat, exhausted, half-asleep, with a silver wine-jar slipping from his hands.

Poussin took this episode of Midas and Bacchus from Ovid's *Metamorphoses*. This classical Latin literary work was a favourite source of themes for Italian Renaissance paintings. In Ovid's story, Silenus was carried off and taken to King Midas, who brought him back to Bacchus. In return, Bacchus asked Midas to make a wish, whereupon he asked to be given the power to change everything he touched into gold. This wish came true, unhappily for Midas since literally everything, including his food, turned into gold. Tortured by hunger, Midas begged Bacchus to deliver him from this plight. Bacchus ordered him to bathe in the river Pactolus, whereupon he was miraculously cured and from that day on the river flowed with gold dust. A river god sits in the background resting before a clump of trees, holding an urn from which issues a river. The king kneels in this river, bent so low that his head touches the ground. In the foreground two *putti* play with a little black and white goat. One of them puts on a mask to excite the animal, a detail signifying that Bacchus was also the god of tragedy. To the left, a beautiful nude Bacchante lies stretched out on blue and white draperies, like Silenus asleep, sated with the pleasures of wine and love. In front of her a drowsy *putto* seems to have fallen on his face.

Poussin went to Rome at the age of twenty-seven, and, like his younger compatriot Claude Lorraine, spent most of his life there. He not only studied the art of the ancients, incorporating into his paintings the forms of ancient sculpture, but infused these forms with new life through the freshness and delicacy of his colours and his new dream-like settings.

The nymph, the *putti* on the right, and the river god in the background show the influence of Titian's many Bacchanalia, first displayed at Rome and then in Madrid. The German painter and writer, Joachim von Sandrart, described a visit to the Villa Aldobrandini at Rome, where he saw and admired the works of artists such as Claude Lorraine, Poussin and Titian. Titian's influence is evident particularly in the use of colours, especially the contrast of reds and blues, and in their distribution. In Poussin, however, the colours are less subtle, more harsh and cold, better suited to the depiction of the measured movements of the twelve figures here.

This work must have been painted some time before 1630, since in 1631 Poussin wrote to Rubens saying he had sold a 'King Midas'. It was acquired in the early eighteenth century for the collection at Nymphenburg from where it was in 1781 transferred to the Hofgartengalerie, and in 1836 to the Alte Pinakothek.

POUSSIN *Apollo and Daphne*
This work, which forms a pair with *Midas and Bacchus* (p. 265), was painted between 1630 and 1635. It was transferred from Nymphenburg to the Hofgartengalerie in 1781, to Schleissheim in 1800, and finally to the Alte Pinakothek in 1914.

NICOLAS POUSSIN, 1594–1665
Lamentation of Christ
Canvas: $39\frac{3}{8}'' \times 57''$ (100 × 144 cm.) Catalogue No. 625

Poussin treated many different subjects: from the Old and New Testaments, from mythology, from the *Metamorphoses* of Ovid and from the epics of Tasso. But one recurring theme preoccupied him throughout, that of death: for example, *Death of Adonis*, *Death of Narcissus* (Louvre), *Death of Ajax in the Kingdom of Flora* (Dresden), *Apollo and Daphne*, where Daphne is turned into a tree (Alte Pinakothek, catalogue no. 2334).

The *Lamentation of Christ* shares this preoccupation. It is distinguished from other Lamentations by the few figures in the group gathered here in front of the tall, forbidding garden wall beneath two olive-trees and beside an ancient sarcophagus. Christ lies in the arms of the Virgin, who is supported by Mary Magdalene. Behind her, Joseph of Arimathaea makes the final preparations for the burial. On the left, St John sits in despair, raising his eyes to the heavens. On the extreme right, two little angels at Christ's feet lament his death, a traditional motif in French burial scenes. The background reveals a dismal, arid landscape, filled with huge monuments, great towers and pyramids. The austerity of this landscape, emphasized by the uniform brown, makes it look like a desert. The contrast of this brown with the reds and blues of the foreground is striking, although balance is restored by the pale turquoise of St John's shirt. The contrived composition of this painting recalls Raphael's *Entombment* in the Villa Borghese. Even more reminiscent of Raphael's style is the triangular arrangement of the four figures in the centre. There is great charm in the classical beauty of Mary Magdalene's profile, with her magnificent head of hair and the dignified movement of her arm.

All three of Poussin's works in the Pinakothek were painted around 1630, showing the variety of themes and problems which he tackled during his first few years in Italy. Poussin spoke of these problems in his many letters to his old friend and buyer M. de Chantelou, Chamberlain to Louis XIII. There is an abundance of contemporary documentation for this painter who achieved fame in his lifetime and even in his last years, despite ill-health and great hardship, continued to produce works of remarkable quality. In 1672, seven years after his death, Giovanni Pietro Bellori paid tribute to him in his book on the lives of famous painters, architects and sculptors of the time.

This painting was transferred from Schleissheim to the Hofgartengalerie, from where it passed to the Alte Pinakothek.

Claude Lorraine
Idyllic Landscape at Dusk
This work was painted for the Augsburg councillor Franz Mayer in 1676, and is a second version of an earlier work, of which Lorraine had made an engraving in 1636. It entered the Alte Pinakothek in 1836.

Claude Lorraine
Departure of Hagar and Ishmael
This was painted in 1668 for Count Waldstein. It was transferred from the Zweibrücken gallery to the Hofgartengalerie, and from there to the Alte Pinakothek in 1836.

Claude Lorraine
Hagar and Ishmael in the Wilderness
This work forms a pair with the *Departure of Hagar and Ishmael*. A replica hangs in Belvoir Castle. It was acquired by the Alte Pinakothek in 1836.

CLAUDE GELÉE, called LE LORRAIN or CLAUDE LORRAINE, 1600–82
Seaport
Canvas: $28\frac{5}{16}'' \times 38\frac{3}{16}''$ (72 × 97 cm.) Catalogue No. 381
Signed and dated: Claudio I VF Rome 1674
(Reproduction p. 270)

The spectator is attracted to this painting by the light of the sun's first rays spreading over the rippling waters, lighting up the magnificent sculptured Arch of Titus, on whose grey stone are inscribed the letters SPQR, signifying the Senate and the Roman People. Beneath this arch, several figures emerge from the darkness. On the left the brown tarpaulin covering the prow of the boat is in full sunlight, while the tops of the masts remain shrouded in the green mists of dawn. The colours, ranging through dull blues, olive-greens and greys (red is totally absent), are gentle and muted; they do not exist as separate single colours but only in relation to the colours around them.

The morning breezes cradle/The shadows of the bay. These lines of Goethe spring to mind, together with the opening lines of the poem: *And the free world feeds me/Fresh blood and nourishment./How good and kind is Nature/Who clasps me to her breast!/Our boat rocks slowly, gently/To the rhythm of the waves.* Goethe wrote his poem *On the Lake* at Zürich in 1775, a century after this work was painted. Both painter and writer saw nature as a harmonious organic whole, the manifestation of the divine, the unity of all things. Both painting and poem evoke the immensity and independence of nature and the freshness of early morning. But the position of man with regard to nature is different in the two. For Claude Lorraine, man is a part of nature. Just as the sun sends out its first rays of the day, so man prepares to go about his daily tasks. Nature will one day claim back the monuments erected by man (the three imposing towers bordering the harbour), just as she has already invaded the triumphal arch overgrown with weeds. The boats are not a discovery of man, but an integral part of the sea. Man and nature are inseparable, a world at peace with itself. Goethe, on the other hand, speaks of a certain 'nostalgia for nature': man needs nature as a balm, a source of new blood, from which, once refreshed, he will turn away again. Man and nature are two distinct, separable entities.

Claude Lorraine went to Rome at the age of thirteen, and spent most of his life there. In Rome and the surrounding countryside he found the ideal landscape: mountains, plains, fields, rivers, lakes, sea, and of course the ruins of ancient monuments. Lorraine's paintings remind us of these remains of a great past, their ruins standing as an image of eternity. Lorraine became famous at an early age, and his works were bought by all the nobles of the realm. His fame eventually grew so great that he received commissions from all over Europe. This work was painted for Franz Mayer, a town councillor of Regensburg. Lorraine had painted another version of the same theme twenty-five years before for the Archbishop of Le Mans. His other work in the Pinakothek, the *River Scene* (catalogue no. 382), was painted two years later in 1676, also for Franz Mayer, as the companion work to the *Seaport*.

Both these works were acquired for the collection of the Munich Electors. They were transferred from Schleissheim to the Hofgartengalerie in 1781, and moved to the Pinakothek at the time of its inauguration.

PHILIPPE DE CHAMPAIGNE, 1602–74
Portrait of the Vicomte de Turenne
Oak: $30\frac{11}{16}'' \times 25\frac{3}{16}''$ (78 × 64 cm.) Catalogue No. 165

The Vicomte de Turenne is depicted half-length, bare-headed, with no decorations or weapons. His face, framed in long grey curls, turns towards the right in half-profile, contrasting sharply with the black background. His striking face, with its pensive weary eyes, energetic mouth and prominent lower jaw, mirrors his life of conflict. His breastplate and wide pleated sash indicate his rank as marshal of the French Royal Army. This sumptuous white silk sash, scored with folds, exaggerates the right shoulder. The arm would look stiff and awkward if it were not for the gleaming grey and beige striped doublet. This sash and striped doublet, together with the high white collar, contrast sharply with the Vicomte's sober face, producing a striking, if not dramatic, effect which gives this superficially simple portrait a baroque quality. This is the last and best portrait of the Vicomte de Turenne. Artist and model appear to have foreseen the approach of death; both died within a year of this portrait being painted.

Henri de la Tour d'Auvergne, Vicomte de Turenne, was born at Sedan in 1611, second son of the Duke of Bouillon and, on his mother's side, grandson of William I of Orange. As a young Huguenot he fought in the wars in Flanders, Spain, Alsace and from the Lower Rhine to the Inn. His whole life was spent as a soldier, and although he rebelled against Mazarin's autocracy and fought against Prince Louis de Condé, he served his family, nation and king faithfully to the last. A Protestant for most of his life, he was converted to Catholicism in 1668, seven years before his death. He was killed in 1675 fighting against the Germans near Salzbach in Baden. Louis XIV gave orders for his grand marshal to be buried in the Abbey of Saint-Denis next to the tombs of the kings of France. Napoleon had his ashes transferred to Les Invalides, where today they rest beside Napoleon's crypt. At the time of this transfer, Lazare Carnot made a speech which ended with these words: 'What more can I say of Turenne? Here he lies in person. Of his victories? Here is the sword with which he won them. Of his death? Here is the bullet which took him from his country and from all mankind.'

This portrait was acquired by Skell for King Maximilian I of Bavaria in 1819. It was transferred from the Hofgartengalerie to the Alte Pinakothek in 1836.

VALENTIN
Crowning with Thorns
Valentin, a member of the famous Boulogne family, was born in 1594, and is thought to have been a pupil of Simon Vouet. He went to Italy at an early age, and was much influenced by Caravaggio. This work was originally in the collection of the Electors of Bavaria.

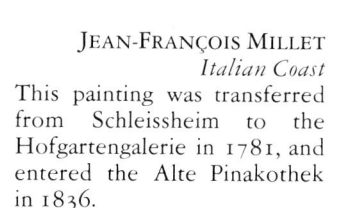

JEAN-FRANÇOIS MILLET
Italian Coast
This painting was transferred from Schleissheim to the Hofgartengalerie in 1781, and entered the Alte Pinakothek in 1836.

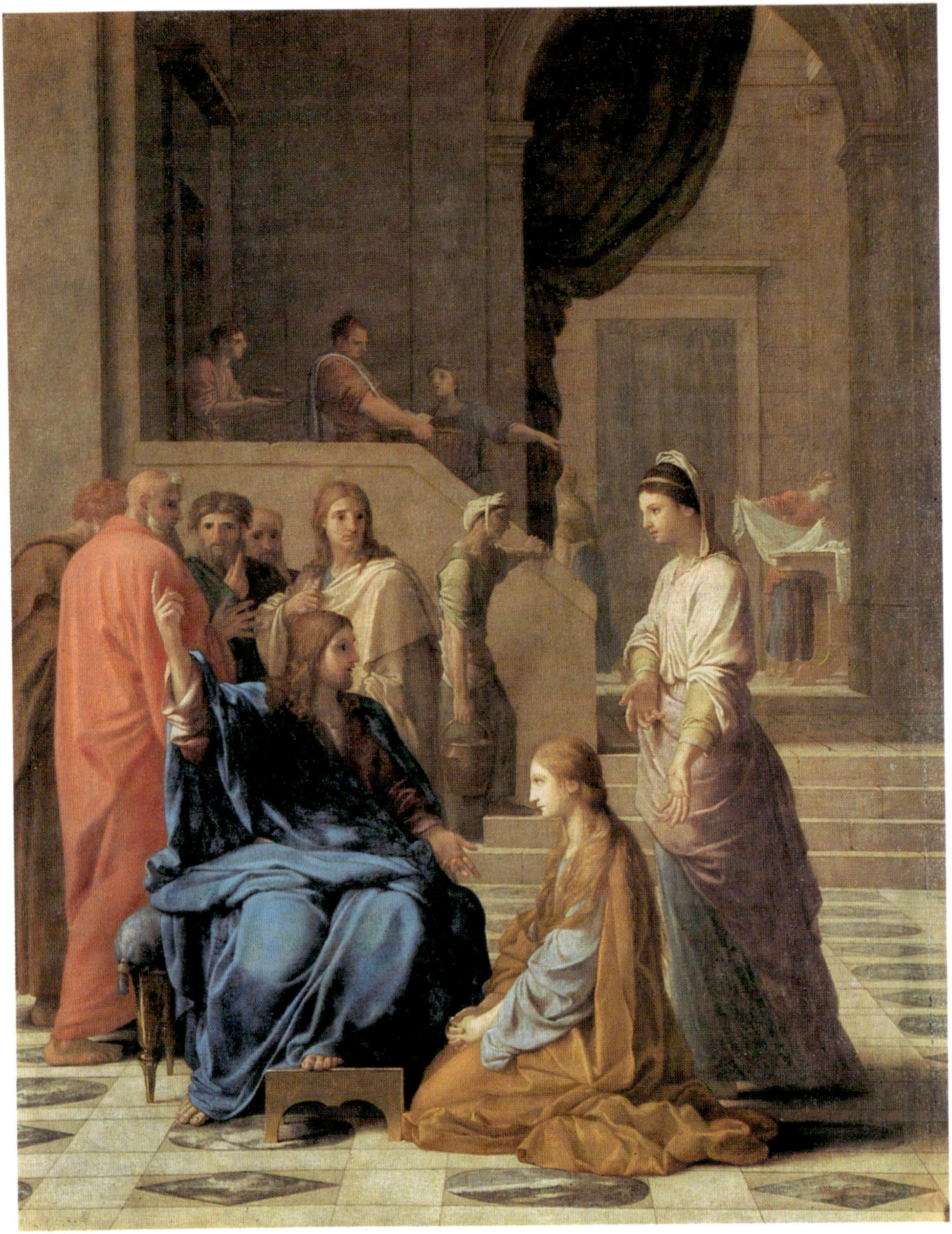

EUSTACHE LE SUEUR, 1617-55
Christ in the House of Martha and Mary
Canvas: 64" × 51 3/16" (162·5 × 130 cm.) Catalogue No. WAF 492

Christ with five of his apostles is visiting the house of the sisters Martha and Mary. Mary has drawn up a seat and a footstool for Christ, and sits at his feet listening to his every word. Martha, on the other hand, is busy summoning the servants to prepare the meal; the water-carrier in front of the balustrade and other figures on the staircase bring the food while in the right background a woman sets the table. Martha brusquely interrupts the conversation and reproaches Mary for not helping. The apostles, engrossed in the conversation, give her an angry look, John in particular. Christ solemnly raises his right hand, pointing to Mary with his left, and says: 'She has chosen the better part' (Gospel according to St Luke). This work was painted for the Church of Saint-Germain l'Auxerrois in Paris, which accounts for its format and the imposing size of the figures of Christ and St Peter, figures which might have been borrowed from Michelangelo. Christ, with his vivid blue robes and barely visible pink shirt, and St Peter, all in brilliant red, constitute the two most brightly coloured points in the canvas. The third is the golden brown cloak worn by Mary over her dull blue gown. Martha's robe is lilac while the water-carrier wears olive-green. The other pastel shades merge into each other, giving a soft, muted effect. The predominant shade of the walls of this spacious, high room is beige. The architecture matches the rigid attitudes of the figures, depicted in profile in deliberate imitation of Greek portrait-painting.

Le Sueur was a pupil of Simon Vouet at Paris, where he met Mignard and Le Brun, both about to leave for Italy, like Lorraine and Poussin before them. Le Sueur stayed in Paris, probably for lack of funds. He studied Italian painting from the collections in Paris and from Marcantonio's engravings. In 1640-1 Poussin, on a visit to Paris, noticed the young Le Sueur and invited him to come to Rome but Le Sueur declined the offer, since he was about to marry. This decision was to set his art on an entirely different course from that taken by his contemporaries. Le Sueur was already, in the seventeenth century, advocating a pure classicism that was to become generally accepted only later at the time of the Revolution and under the Empire. France has been unique in this predilection for the imitation of the Ancients, which has recurred again and again at different periods in her history. The fact that Le Sueur executed paintings, frescoes and cartoons for tapestries for the Louvre and various palaces as well as for Paris churches helps us understand why the French king showed so little interest in the powerful, dynamic, baroque style of the Italian artist Giovanni Lorenzo Bernini, an older painter than Le Sueur, when he visited Paris in 1665.

This painting was formerly in the collection of Cardinal Fesch.

JOSEPH VIVIEN, 1657–1735
Archbishop Fénelon of Cambrai
Canvas: 31⅞" × 25 3/16" (81 × 64 cm.) Catalogue No. 972

Vivien, a native of Lyons, was a pupil of Le Brun and a member of the Paris Academy. He had already built up a considerable reputation for himself when he was appointed court painter to Maximilian Emanuel, Elector of Bavaria, and to his brother Joseph Clemens, Archbishop of Cologne. Two of his many portraits in the Bavarian collections deserve special mention: the *Self-portrait before an Easel*, on which is placed the portrait of the Elector Maximilian Emanuel, and this half-length portrait of François de Salignac de la Motte-Fénelon (1651–1717), Archbishop of Cambrai.

He stands, pale and distinguished, before a brown background. Over his white surplice he wears a blue silk *mozzetta*, lined with dull red, on which rests a cross. Even though the portrait stops short at the elbows, there is a dynamic quality in the bent arms, the torso leaning to the left and the slightly tilted head. This silver-haired figure seems to be addressing us with his warm, dark eyes. His distinguished erect posture is both natural and self-assured. His face, sensitive, thoughtful, refined and spiritual, invites the spectator to discussion and reflection. Modern views of Fénelon owe as much to this portrait (of which an engraving was made in 1714 by Benoit Audran) as they do to his writings.

As a young priest, Fénelon was entrusted with the supervision of those Protestants who had been converted to Catholicism and, later, with the conversion of the Huguenots. In 1687 he published his *Traité de l'Education des Filles*. Shortly after this, in 1689, he was appointed tutor to the Duke of Burgundy, Louis XIV's grandson and heir apparent (he died, however, in 1712). To instruct and amuse this difficult child Fénelon wrote one of his most famous works, the *Aventures de Télémaque*, an epic telling the story of Telemachus' search for his father Ulysses, gone to the Trojan War. This work, which was seen as a satire on the French court, lost him Louis XIV's favour. Even later, his writings were the subject of heated argument with Bossuet and his followers. In 1695 Fénelon was appointed Archbishop of Cambrai – in his last years he devoted himself almost entirely to these duties. His works, particularly the *Lettres Spirituelles*, reveal a warm, sensitive, refined and liberal mind, a forerunner of the eighteenth century.

This portrait was transferred from Schleissheim to the Alte Pinakothek in 1836.

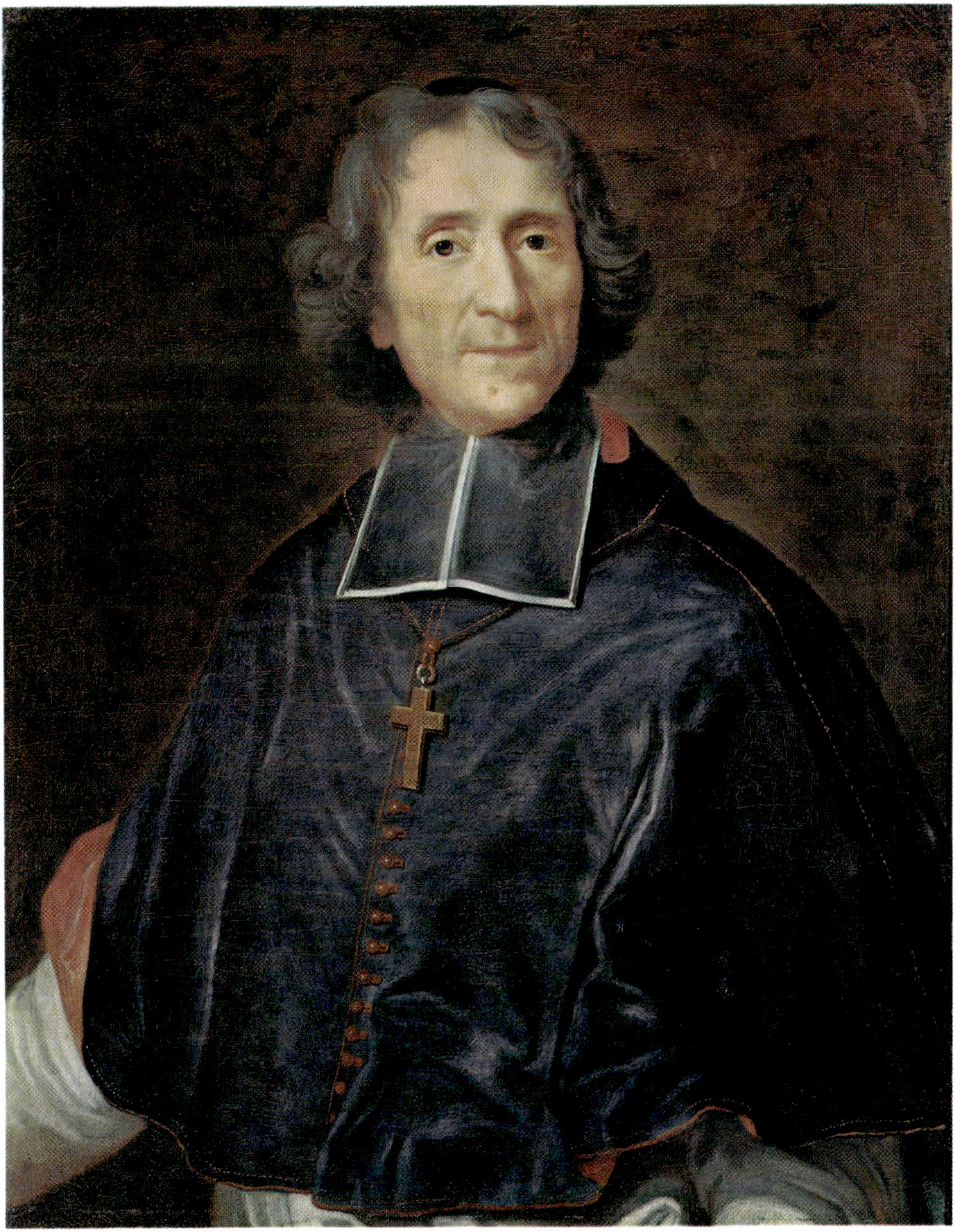

NICOLAS LANCRET, 1690-1745
The Bird Cage
Canvas: 17 5/16" × 18 15/16" (44 × 48 cm.) Catalogue No. H.u.W.4

Three elegant figures sit in a clearing on a knoll, bordered by roses and thick bushes and sheltered by a tall tree with delicately painted foliage. On the left a coquettish young woman, in the blue and red dress of a shepherdess, gracefully holds a shepherd's crook in her hand, while three docile sheep stand attentively beside her. In between her and the young man, towards whom she is leaning, lies a hunting dog sleeping. The gallant, dressed in red, yellow and blue, puts his arm round the shoulders of the pretty girl sitting beside him, wearing a pale green dress with a yellow bodice. Both are gazing intently at a bird-cage resting on the young man's right knee. What is this cage doing here in the country? Why are two small boys peeping out from behind a bush? The answer is that this is a love scene, and the bird is a symbol of the young girl's purity and virginity; if she sets the bird free she loses her honour. The game she is playing with the little bird is a dangerous one. The shepherdess also appears to have an interest in the game: the cage, in fact, holds two birds, and the colour of her garments harmonizes with those of the gallant more than does the green dress of the girl on the right. This is no doubt an eternal triangle, as the three sheep seem to indicate. The flowers and birds seem to be subtly impregnated with hidden meaning – or is this just a trick of the imagination?

In 1735 N. de Larmessin made an engraving after this work, painted four years previously; this print bore the title *Love Scene in the Bushes* and was accompanied by the following lines: 'Happy the bird who is caressed by your hands, for he is compensated for his captivity. More captive and more abject than he is the shepherd who woos you so tenderly.'

Lancret was Watteau's favourite pupil. His *genre* paintings differ from those of his master, however, in their originality and candid gaiety. This work was painted for Frederick the Great of Prussia, a fervent admirer of all things French. It remained in Potsdam Castle till 1923, and has been in the Alte Pinakothek since 1966 as part of the collection of the Bayerische Hypotheken- und Wechsel-Bank.

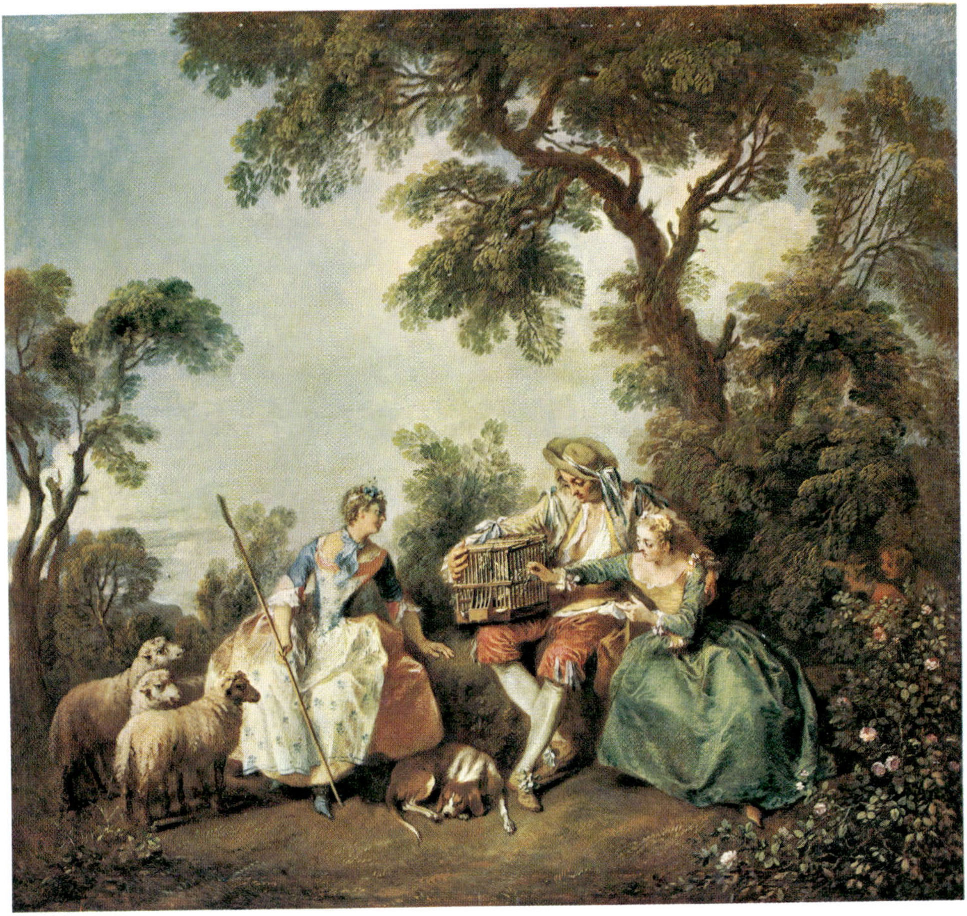

LARGILLIÈRE *Lady in festive Dress*

JOSEPH VIVIEN *Self-portrait before an Easel*

JEAN-BAPTISTE LEPRINCE *The Discreet Lover*

LOUIS TOCQUÉ
Count Palatine Friedrich Michael von Zweibrücken-Birkenfeld

Tocqué was born in Paris in 1696 and spent several years in St Petersburg and Denmark. He was a pupil of Nicolas Bertin, and was influenced by Rigaud and Largillière. The count portrayed here was considered the most handsome man of his time. This painting entered the Munich collections with the Zweibrücken gallery, and has been in the Alte Pinakothek since 1909.

PATER *Pleasures of the pastoral Life*

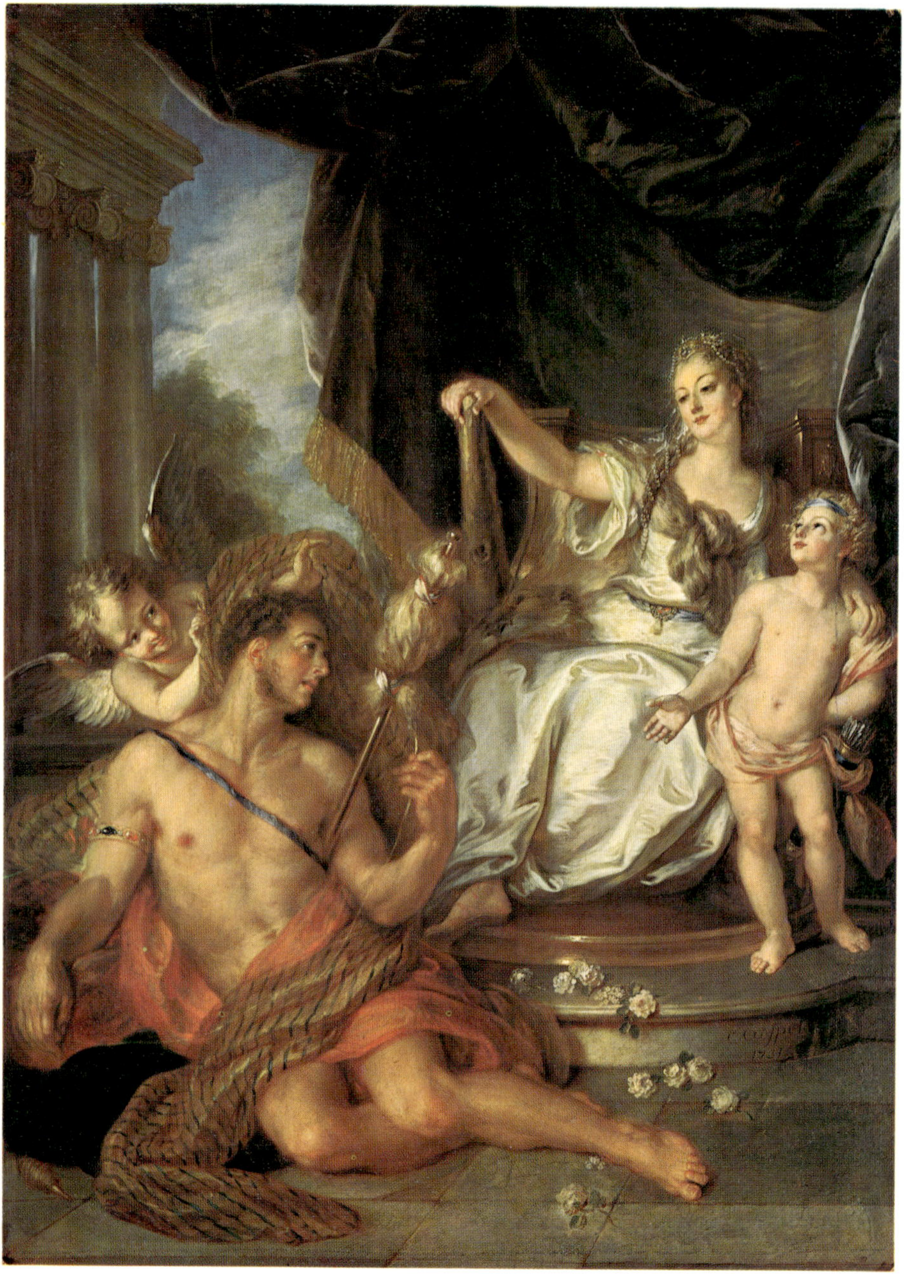

CHARLES-ANTOINE COYPEL, 1694-1752
Hercules and Omphale
Canvas: 70⅞" × 52" (179·7 × 132·8 cm.) Catalogue No. 1168
Signed and dated: C. Coypel 1731

Hercules, angered by the failure of his suit for the hand of Iole, killed her brother Iphitos. In punishment for his crime he was struck by a dreadful disease. The Oracle at Delphi, which he consulted for a remedy, instructed him to sell himself as a slave for three years. By these means he arrived unknown at the court of Omphale, Queen of Lydia. The story of Hercules and Omphale is told in late Greek literature of the Hellenistic period, with considerable variation as to the number of children born of this affair between sovereign and slave. Their love is always presented as a dionysiac scene. A fresco at Pompeii portrays Omphale holding a club and wearing Hercules' lion-skin, while Hercules is dressed up as a woman, holding a distaff and spindle and leaning half-drunk against Priapus. In Coypel's portrayal of this mythological subject, Hercules is given a more manly treatment. A *putto* helps him dress, while Omphale rests her hand on a Cupid urging her to grant Hercules her favours, which she graciously accords with her lips. She sits, in a magnificent gleaming white silk dress, half-reclining, almost lying on the royal throne which is enveloped by a huge dark green, canopy-like drapery, to the left of which is a landscape of sky and columns. The steps leading up to the throne are strewn with luxuriant flowers. Omphale is portrayed as a lady of the French court of 1730; Coypel's model was in fact Madame de Pompadour, and the Hercules prostrate before her is none other than the 21-year-old Louis XV, as his nose clearly shows.

Charles-Antoine Coypel was the last and most famous of the painters of this name. At an early age he became director of the royal collection of paintings and engravings, and favourite court painter of the Duke of Orleans. He was accorded an artist's apartment in the Louvre and became a professor and then director of the Academy, to rise still further to become Louis XV's favourite court painter. He enjoyed great favour at the court throughout his life. The author of critical works on art, he also built up an interesting private collection. His paintings are mainly historical, with a total absence of landscapes. His best-known works are the *genre* paintings such as the *Young Girl playing at being a Lady* and *Love as a Schoolmaster*. The fusion of light historical subject and *genre* painting in the *Hercules and Omphale* gives it a certain frivolity.

This painting formerly belonged to the collection of the Zweibrücken branch of the Wittelsbachs, and remained at Schloss Schleissheim until 1925.

QUENTIN DE LA TOUR
Mademoiselle Ferrand meditating on Newton
This work of around 1750–53 was exhibited in the 1753 Salon of the Paris Académie Royale. Voltaire had published his book *Idées fondamentales de la philosophie de Newton* a few years before, in 1738. This painting has been in the Alte Pinakothek since 1966 as part of the collection of the Bayerische Hypotheken- und Wechsel-Bank.

CLAUDE JOSEPH VERNET
River Scene
Claude Joseph Vernet, born at Avignon in 1712, was the pupil of his father Antoine Vernet and then of Panini. This painting was transferred from the Zweibrücken gallery to Schleissheim and has been in the Alte Pinakothek since 1935.

284

HUBERT ROBERT *Necropolis with a Temple*

HUBERT ROBERT
Old Bridge with Washerwomen
Hubert Robert, born 22 May 1753 in Paris, was the pupil of Panini. He painted in Italy from 1754 to 1765, after which he returned to Paris. Both the paintings here were purchased from a Dutch dealer in 1957.

François Boucher, 1703–70
Nude on a Sofa
Canvas: $23\frac{1}{4}'' \times 28\frac{3}{4}''$ (59 × 73 cm.) Catalogue No. 1166
Signed and dated: F. Boucher 1752

The *Nude on a Sofa* is one of the Alte Pinakothek's most famous paintings, and one of Boucher's masterpieces. Boucher was a much respected painter at the court of Louis XV, and his paintings portray the life of the court at that time with its constant festivals and entertainments of all kinds. The many sketches for this painting show how much work went into this simple portrait of a nude on a sofa in front of a wall. The young girl's position is unnatural and contrived, made extremely uncomfortable by the hard back of the sofa, and it is only with difficulty that the legs so alluringly spread out on the cushions support the arched body. The problem is resolved by the charm with which Boucher's genius has painted this movement and the details of the surrounding objects. The sofa, curtain and background wall are the same shade of olive-green, distinguished only in texture. The most striking object is the rich pink silk coverlet, but the brightest colour is in fact the blue of the silk ribbon entwined round the young girl's head and hands; blue and pink were the favourite colours of Rococo painting.

There have been many paintings of nudes in the history of art. In early paintings they formed part of a large scene or episode (for example, Danaë, Venus and Cupid, Toilet of Venus, or pastoral scenes). The nude is always depicted with other figures in a painting which has many planes and normally a background landscape. The nude remains integrated into human society and the order of the universe. This nude, however, is totally cut off from the outside world, alone, accompanied only by a sofa. Her eyes gaze into the distance, her pretty face is expressionless. The girl is Louise O'Murphy (born 1734) at at the age of fifteen. She was the mistress of Louis XV who in 1753 built a house in the deer-park near Versailles to house the objects of his fleeting passions. The first occupant of this house (sold in 1771) was Louise O'Murphy. Its inhabitants were usually replaced at short intervals, either by marrying them off or by sending them away with some settlement. Two sisters of Louise O'Murphy also sat as models for Boucher; but Louise was, along with his wife, his favourite model.

An engraving was made of this painting in 1761 by Demarteau. Originally in the Zweibrücken collection, it was moved to Schleissheim and finally, in 1910, to the Alte Pinakothek.

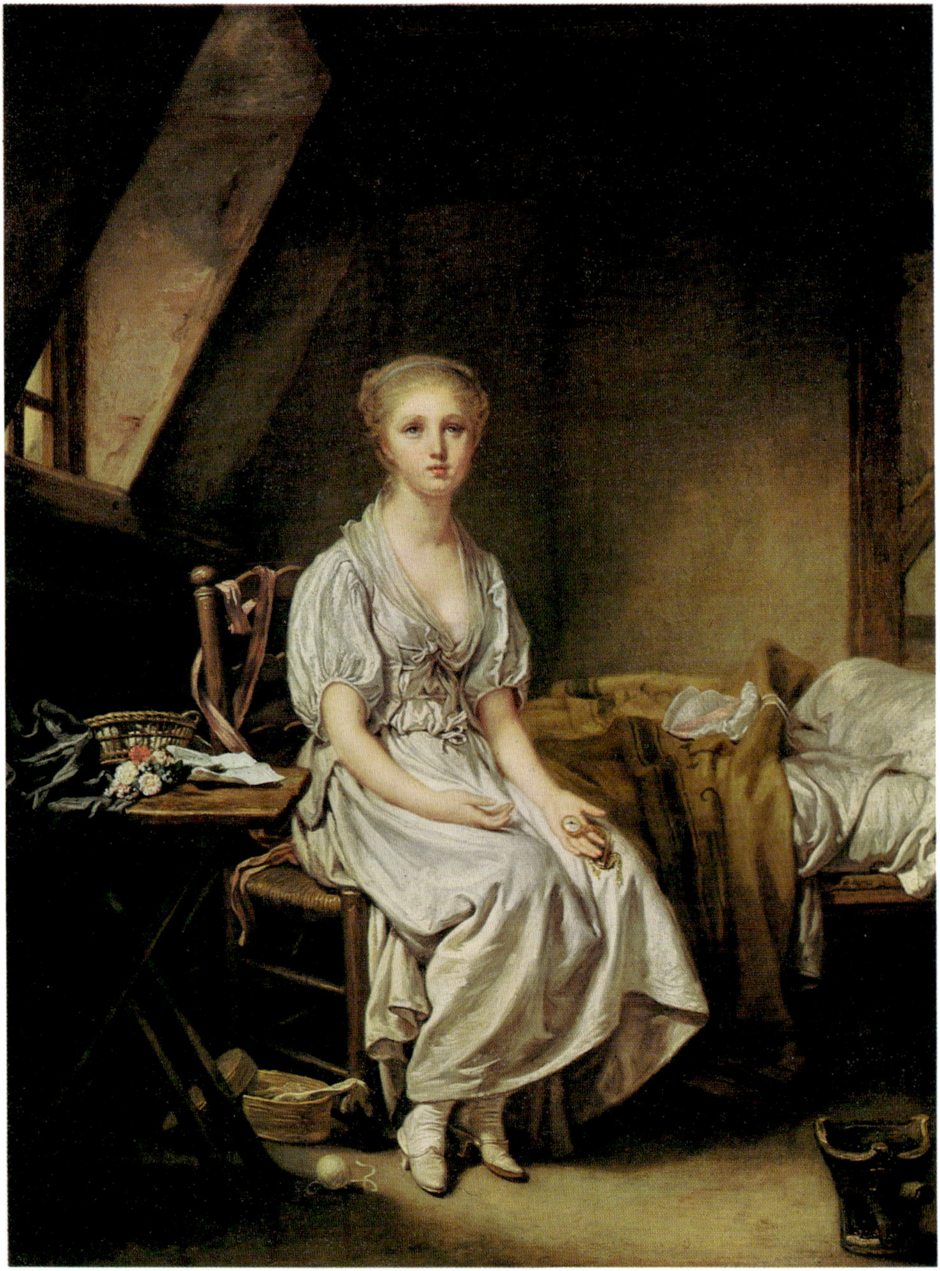

JEAN-BAPTISTE GREUZE, 1725–1805
Lament of the Watch
Canvas: 31⅛" × 24" (79·3 × 61 cm.) Catalogue No. H.u.W.3.

The principal charm of this painting is the white of the young girl's nightdress. The still-life composed by the brightly coloured flowers on the table beside her almost forms an independent painting. Needless to say, the pinks and blues so typical of Rococo paintings of women have not been forgotten here – the girl wears a blue ribbon in her hair, while pink ribbons are draped on the chair and decorate the night-cap. These colours are normally associated with a milieu of refinement and elegance but in this miserably cramped attic with faded walls they look out of place. Everything is upside down. Flowers are strewn over the table, symbolizing the transience of all things. The early morning sun enters the dark room, lighting up the unmade bed. The young girl sits on a straw-bottomed chair, holding in the hollow of her hand a gold watch whose hands are at six o'clock. She lets her arms fall back limply on to her lap and raises her tearful eyes. The meaning of the painting is clear: her lover has spent the night with her and left her for ever at daybreak. Letters and flowers announce his arrival, the gold watch his parting gift. This lover must have been some aristocrat spending the night in the miserable attic of a girl of the people. Greuze has an obvious predilection and talent for narration; this delicate tale leaves us with a strong feeling of the girl's desolation.

Beneath the visual beauty of the work and its somewhat sentimental appeal lies a bitter social criticism, which anticipates the French Revolution. Greuze's paintings were very popular and an engraving of this work was made by Massart in 1776. For Diderot, Greuze was the saviour come to rescue society from moral decay.

This painting entered the Alte Pinakothek in 1966 as part of the collection of the Bayerische Hypotheken- und Wechsel-Bank.

LIST OF ILLUSTRATIONS

The numbers in italics indicate reproductions in colour

ALBERTINELLI, MARIOTTO (1475–1515): *Annunciation*. Poplar, 65″ × 77½″ (165 × 197 cm.)   137

ALTDORFER, ALBRECHT (c. 1480–1538): *Victory of Alexander the Great over Darius, King of the Persians, at the Battle of Issus*. 1529. Wood, 62$\frac{3}{16}$″ × 47$\frac{1}{4}$″ (158·4 × 120·2 cm.)   *87*
Birth of the Virgin. Pine, 54$\frac{3}{4}$″ × 51$\frac{3}{16}$″ (139 × 130 cm.) *Susanna bathing and the Punishment of the false Accusers*. 1526. Lime, 29½″ × 24″ (75 × 61 cm.)   88
St George and the Dragon in a Wood. Lime, 11″ × 8$\frac{13}{16}$″ (28·2 × 22·5 cm.)   89
View of the Danube Valley near Regensburg. Beech, 12½″ × 8$\frac{13}{16}$″ (28 × 22 cm.)   89

AMBERGER, CHRISTOPH (c. 1505–62): *Portrait of Christoph Fugger*. 1541. Wood, 38$\frac{7}{16}$″ × 31½″ (97·5 × 80 cm.)   *110*

ANGELICO, FRA (Fra Giovanni da Fiesole) (1387–1455): *Entombment*. Wood, 14½″ × 18″ (37 × 45·5 cm.)   128
St Cosmas and St Damian: the Incitement to Idolatry. Wood, 14$\frac{15}{16}$″ × 18$\frac{1}{8}$″ (37·8 × 46·6 cm.)   *132*

ANONYMOUS VENETIAN PAINTER of the school of Giorgione: *Portrait of a Young Man*. Wood, 27$\frac{9}{16}$″ × 21$\frac{1}{4}$″ (70 × 54 cm.)   *164*

ANTONELLO DA MESSINA (c. 1430–79): *Virgin of the Annunciation*. Wood, 16½″ × 13″ (42·5 × 32·7 cm.)   *153*

BALDUNG GRIEN, HANS (1484–1545): *Portrait of the Margrave Christoph von Baden*. 1515. Lime, 18½″ × 14$\frac{1}{8}$″ (46·9 × 35·8 cm.)   102
Allegorical female Figure. Lime, 32$\frac{5}{8}$″ × 14$\frac{1}{8}$″ (82·8 × 35·9 cm.)   103
Allegorical female Figure. Lime, 32$\frac{9}{16}$″ × 14$\frac{1}{16}$″ (82·5 × 35·5 cm.)   103
Nativity. 1520. Wood, 41$\frac{5}{16}$″ × 27$\frac{9}{16}$″ (105·5 × 70·4 cm.)   *104*
Portrait of the Count Palatine Philipp. 1517. Lime, 16½″ × 12$\frac{3}{16}$″ (41·5 × 30·8 cm.)   105
Portrait of a Strasbourg Knight of St John. 1528. Lime, 22$\frac{7}{16}$″ × 16$\frac{15}{16}$″ (57 × 43 cm.)   105

BARBARI, JACOPO DE' (c. 1450–before 1515): *Still-life*. 1504. Wood, 19$\frac{11}{16}$″ × 16$\frac{9}{16}$″ (50 × 42·5 cm.)   155

BAROCCIO, FEDERIGO (1526–1612): *Noli me Tangere*. 1590. Canvas, 102″ × 72$\frac{7}{8}$″ (259 × 185 cm.)   156

BASSANO (Giacomo da Ponte) (c. 1515–92): *Virgin and Child with St Anthony the Hermit and St Martin*. Canvas, 74$\frac{3}{8}$″ × 46$\frac{7}{8}$″ (189 × 119 cm.)   172

Virgin and Child with St John the Baptist and St James. Canvas, 75⅛" × 52¾" (191 × 133 cm.)   172

BATONI, POMPEO (1708–87): *Portrait of the Elector Karl Theodor.* Canvas, 106 5/16" × 72⅞" (270 × 185 cm.)   39

BECCAFUMI, DOMENICO (1486–1551): *Holy Family with the Infant St John.* Wood, 45½" (113 cm.) diameter   137

BEHAM, BARTHEL (1502–40): *Portrait of Wilhelm IV of Bavaria.* Wood, 38½" × 28 5/16" (97.5 × 71.5 cm.)   12

BEYEREN, ABRAHAM VAN (1620/1–1674): *Still-life with Crab.* Oak, 18¼" × 24⅜" (45.5 × 62.1 cm.)   220

BLOEMAERT, ABRAHAM (1564–1651): *Feast of the Gods.* Canvas, 39¾" × 57½" (101 × 146.5 cm.)   *219*

BOL, FERDINAND (1616–80): *Members of the Wine Merchants' Guild.* Canvas, 76" × 119 11/16" (193 × 304 cm.)   233

BOSCH, HIERONYMUS (c. 1450–1516): *Last Judgment* (fragment). Oak, 23⅜" × 44⅞" (60 × 114 cm.)   115

BOTTICELLI (Sandro Filipepi) (1444/5–1510): *Pietà.* Wood, 54¾" × 81½" (139.5 × 207.3 cm.)   *142*

BOTTICINI, RAFFAELLO (1477–after 1520): *The Young Tobias with three Archangels.* Wood, 59½" × 74 13/16" (151 × 190 cm.)   141

BOUCHER, FRANÇOIS (1703–70): *Nude on a Sofa.* Canvas, 23¼" × 28¾" (59 × 73 cm.)   *286*

BOUTS THE ELDER, DIERIC (c. 1420–75): *The Betrayal.* Oak, 41⅜" × 26¾" (105 × 68 cm.)   114
Resurrection. Oak, 41⅜" × 26¾" (105 × 68 cm.)   *119*

BOUTS THE YOUNGER (?), DIERIC (c. 1448/50–91): *Small Adoration of the Kings Altarpiece,* known as the *Pearl of Brabant.* Oak. Centre panel: 24 13/16" × 24⅜" (63 × 62 cm.), each wing: 24 13/16" × 11" (63 × 28 cm.)   *121*

BRIL, PAUL (1554–1626): *Tower of Babel.* Canvas, 76⅜" × 112" (193.5 × 259 cm.)   189

BROUWER, ADRIAEN (1605/6–38): *The Brawl.* Oak, 12 3/16" × 19 5/16" (31.1 × 49.4 cm.)   210
A Taproom. Oak, 14 3/16" × 18½" (35.7 × 47.2 cm.)   210
Peasant Quartet. Oak, 16 15/16" × 22 13/16" (43 × 58 cm.)   211
Smoking Peasants. Oak, 13¾" × 10¼" (35 × 26 cm.)   212

BRUEGEL THE ELDER, JAN (1568–1625): *Sermon of Christ on Lake Gennesaret.* Oak, 30 11/16" × 46 15/16" (78 × 119 cm.)   *192*
Bouquet of Flowers. Oak, 49⅝" × 37 13/16" (125.5 × 96 cm.)   193

BRUEGEL THE ELDER, PIETER (c. 1525–69): *Head of an old Peasant Woman.* Oak, 8⅝" × 7 1/16" (22 × 18 cm.)   185

Land of Cockayne. 1567. Oak, $20\frac{1}{2}'' \times 30\frac{11}{16}''$ (52 × 78 cm.)	*186*
CANO, ALONSO (1601–67): *The Virgin appearing to St Anthony*. Canvas, $66\frac{3}{8}'' \times 43\frac{11}{16}''$ (161 × 111 cm.)	247
CASTILLO, ANTONIO DEL (1616–68): *The Virgin and St John returning from the Tomb*. Canvas, $76'' \times 49\frac{1}{2}''$ (192·5 × 126·3 cm.)	247
CATALAN SCHOOL (*c.* 1500): *St Louis of Anjou, Bishop of Toulouse*. Poplar, $71\frac{1}{8}'' \times 30\frac{11}{16}''$ (173·6 × 78·2 cm.)	246
St Augustine of Hippo. Poplar, $71\frac{1}{8}'' \times 30\frac{11}{16}''$ (173·7 × 78·4 cm.)	246
CHAMPAIGNE, PHILIPPE DE (1602–74): *Portrait of the Vicomte de Turenne*. Oak, $30\frac{11}{16}'' \times 25\frac{3}{16}''$ (78 × 64 cm.)	*271*
CIMA DA CONEGLIANO, GIOVANNI BATTISTA (1459/60–1517/18): *Virgin and Child with Mary Magdalene and St Jerome*. Wood, $31\frac{1}{2}'' \times 48\frac{7}{16}''$ (80 × 123 cm.)	*158*
COELLO, CLAUDIO (1642–93): *Miracle of St Peter of Alcántara*. Canvas, $90\frac{1}{2}'' \times 78\frac{3}{4}''$ (230 × 199·5 cm.)	247
Maria Anna of Austria, as a Widow. Canvas, $71\frac{5}{8}'' \times 52''$ (181·7 × 131·8 cm.)	247
COYPEL, CHARLES-ANTOINE (1694–1752): *Hercules and Omphale*. 1731. Canvas, $70\frac{7}{8}'' \times 52''$ (179·7 × 132·8 cm.)	*282*
CRANACH THE ELDER, LUCAS (1472–1553): *Crucifixion*. 1503. Pine, $54\frac{11}{16}'' \times 38\frac{13}{16}''$ (138 × 99 cm.)	*107*
Portrait of Johannes Geiler von Kayserberg. Beech, $11\frac{13}{16}'' \times 9\frac{1}{16}''$ (29·9 × 23 cm.)	108
Virgin and Child. Beech, $24'' \times 16\frac{1}{2}''$ (61 × 42 cm.)	108
The Golden Age. Oak, $28\frac{3}{4}'' \times 41\frac{3}{4}''$ (73·3 × 105·5 cm.)	108
Lucretia. Lime, $76\frac{3}{8}'' \times 29\frac{1}{2}''$ (194 × 75 cm.)	109
CRANACH THE YOUNGER, LUCAS (1515–86): *Venus and Cupid*. Wood, $75\frac{9}{16}'' \times 35\frac{1}{16}''$ (196 × 89 cm.)	109
CRESPI, GIUSEPPE-MARIA (1665–1747): *Massacre of the Innocents*. Canvas, $60\frac{1}{4}'' \times 83\frac{1}{2}''$ (152·5 × 212 cm.)	156
DALEM, CORNELIS VAN (*c.* 1530–?): *Landscape with Farmstead*. Oak, $40\frac{9}{16}'' \times 50''$ (103 × 127·5 cm.)	*187*
DAVID, GERARD (*c.* 1455–1523): *Virgin and Child*. Wood, $3\frac{15}{16}'' \times 3\frac{1}{8}''$ (9·7 × 7·5 cm.)	115
Christ's Farewell to the Virgin. Wood, $3\frac{15}{16}'' \times 3\frac{1}{8}''$ (9·7 × 7·5 cm.)	115
DOUVEN, FRANS (1656–1727): *Portrait of the Elector Palatine Johann Wilhelm*. Canvas, $118\frac{1}{8}'' \times 88\frac{5}{8}''$ (300 × 225 cm.)	41
DÜRER, ALBRECHT (1471–1528): *Heller Altarpiece*: Copy from Historisches Museum, Frankfurt-am-Main	23
Death of Lucretia. 1518. Lime, $66\frac{1}{8}'' \times 29\frac{1}{2}''$ (168 × 74·8 cm.)	92
Portrait of Oswolt Krel. 1499. Lime, $19\frac{3}{8}'' \times 15\frac{3}{8}''$ (49·6 × 39 cm.)	92

Paumgartner Altarpiece. Lime. Centre panel: 61" × 49⅝" (155 × 126 cm.), each wing: 61¾" × 24" (157 × 61 cm.)   93
Portrait of a Young Man. 1500. Lime, 11" × 8¼" (28 × 21 cm.)   93
Self-portrait in a Fur Coat. 1500. Lime, 26⅜" × 19 5/16" (67 × 49 cm.)   *94*
Lamentation of Christ. c. 1500. Pine, 59 7/16" × 47⅝" (151 × 121 cm.)   *96*
Four Apostles. 1526. Left panel: *St John the Evangelist and St Peter.* Lime, 84⅝" × 29 15/16" (215 × 76 cm.) Right panel: *St Mark and St Paul.* Lime, 84⅝" × 29 15/16" (215 × 76 cm.)   98

DYCK, ANTHONY VAN (1599–1641): *Portrait of a Lady.* Canvas, 82 11/16" × 53 9/16" (210 × 136 cm.)   211
Portrait of a Man. Canvas, 83¼" × 54" (211·5 × 137·5 cm.)   211
Self-Portrait. Canvas, 31⅞" × 27 3/16" (81 × 69 cm.)   215
Rest on the Flight into Egypt. Canvas, 52¾" × 44½" (134 × 113 cm.)   *217*

ELSHEIMER, ADAM (1578–1610): *Flight into Egypt.* Copper, 13 3/16" × 16⅛" (31 × 41 cm.)   112
Burning of Troy. Copper, 14 3/16" × 19 11/16" (36 × 50 cm.)   113

FERRARESE MASTER (active c. 1480–90): *Family Portrait.* Canvas, 44 1/16" × 35 7/16" (112 × 90 cm.)   *139*

FLORENTINE SCHOOL (c. 1360): *Bishop Saint with Goldfinch.* Wood, 25⅝" × 13" (65·5 × 33·5 cm.)   129

FRANCIABIGIO (FRANCESCO DI CRISTOFANO) (1482–1525): *Virgin and Child.* Wood, 26" × 19¾" (66 × 50·5 cm.)   141

GADDI, TADDEO (?–1366): *Death of Celano.* Wood, 13⅜" × 12 1/16" (34 × 30·5 cm.)   129

GENTILESCHI, ORAZIO (c. 1565–c. 1647): *Two Women with a Looking-glass (Martha and Mary).* Canvas, 52¾" × 60⅝" (132·7 × 154 cm.)   *178*

GHIRLANDAIO (DOMENICO DI TOMMASO BIGORDI) (1449–94): *Virgin in Majesty, venerated by four Saints.* Wood, 87" × 77 15/16" (221 × 198 cm.)   *144*

GIORDANO, LUCA (FA PRESTO) (1632–1705): *St Andrew's Descent from the Cross.* Canvas, 101⅝" × 77½" (258 × 197 cm.)   157

GIOTTO DI BONDONE (c. 1266–1336): *Crucifixion.* Wood, 17 11/16" × 17⅛" (45 × 43·5 cm.)   128

GOES, HUGO VAN DER (c. 1440–82): *Virgin and Child, with Angel holding the Instruments of the Passion.* Canvas, 21¼" × 17 5/16" (55 × 44 cm.)   114

GOLTZIUS, HENDRICK (1558–1612): *Venus and Adonis.* Canvas, 44⅞" × 75 3/16" (114 × 191 cm.)   218

GOYA Y LUCIENTES, FRANCISCO JOSÉ DE (1746–1828): *Portrait of Doña Maria Teresa de Vallabriga, Condesa de Chinchón.* Canvas, 63⅜" × 38½" (161·2 × 97·8 cm.)   258

Portrait of Don José Queralto. Canvas, 39¾" × 29¹⁵⁄₁₆" (101·5 × 76·1 cm.)	260
Still-life with plucked Turkey. Canvas, 17¹¹⁄₁₆" × 24⅜" (45 × 62·4 cm.)	261
GOYEN, JAN VAN (1596–1656): *Extensive Landscape with Farm.* 1629. Oak, 16¼" × 26" (41·3 × 66·5 cm.)	220
GRECO, EL (DOMENIKOS THEOTOKOPOULOS) (1541–1614): *Disrobing of Christ.* Canvas, 64¹⁵⁄₁₆" × 39" (165 × 98·8 cm.)	245
GREUZE, JEAN-BAPTISTE (1725–1805): *Lament of the Watch.* Canvas, 31⅛" × 24" (79·3 × 61 cm.)	288
GRÜNEWALD (MATHIS GOTHARDT-NEITHARDT) (*c.* 1475–1528): *St Eramus and St Maurice.* Lime, 89" × 69⁵⁄₁₆" (226 × 176 cm.)	101
Mocking of Christ. Pine, 42¹⁵⁄₁₆" × 28¾" (109 × 73 cm.)	102
GUARDI, FRANCESCO (1712–93): *Gala Concert in Venice.* Canvas, 26¾" × 35⁷⁄₁₆" (67·7 × 90·5 cm.)	183
Grand Canal near St Jeremiah. Canvas, 28" × 47¼" (71·5 × 120 cm.)	184
HALS, FRANS (1581/5–1666): *Portrait of Willem Croes.* Oak, 18½" × 13⅜" (47·1 × 34·4 cm.)	221
HOBBEMA, MEINDERT (1638–1709): *Landscape.* Oak, 20½" × 25⁹⁄₁₆" (52 × 65 cm.)	220
HOLBEIN THE ELDER, HANS (*c.* 1465–1524): *Wing of the Kaisheim Altarpiece: Presentation of the Virgin.* Pine, 70⁷⁄₁₆" × 32¼" (179 × 82 cm.)	85
JANSSENS, ABRAHAM (1575–1632): *Olympus. c.* 1615. Canvas, 41⁵⁄₁₆" × 94½" (105 × 240 cm.)	189
JANSSENS ELINGA, PIETER (1623–82): *Woman reading.* Canvas, 29¾" × 25" (75·7 × 63·5 cm.)	242
JORDAENS, JACOB (1593–1678): *Satyr at the Peasant's House.* Canvas on wood, 68½" × 80" (174 × 203·5 cm.)	205
KALF, WILLEM (1622–93): *Still-life with Delft Jug.* Wood, 17¾" × 14" (44·9 × 35·7 cm.)	240
KEY, WILLEM (*c.* 1520–68): *Lamentation of Christ.* 1553. Oak, 44¹⁄₁₆" × 40⁹⁄₁₆" (112 × 103 cm.)	190
KONINCK, PHILIPS DE (1619–88): *Extensive Landscape.* Canvas, 52½" × 65⅛" (133·3 × 165·7 cm.)	235
LANCRET, NICOLAS (1690–1745): *The Bird Cage.* Canvas, 17⁵⁄₁₆" × 18¹⁵⁄₁₆" (44 × 48 cm.)	279
LARGILLIÈRE, NICOLAS DE (1656–1746): *Portrait of a Lady in festive Dress.* 1710. Canvas, 31½" × 24¹³⁄₁₆" (80 × 63 cm.)	280
LA TOUR, MAURICE QUENTIN DE (1704–88): *Mademoiselle Ferrand meditating on Newton.* Pastel, 29" × 23¾" (73·5 × 60·3 cm.)	284

LEPRINCE, JEAN-BAPTISTE (1734–81): *The Discreet Lover*. Canvas, 29" × 36 3/16" (73·5 × 92 cm.) — 280

LE SUEUR, EUSTACHE (1617–55): *Christ in the House of Martha and Mary* Canvas, 64" × 51 3/16" (162·5 × 130 cm.) — 274

LIBERALE DA VERONA (*c.* 1445–1526/9): *Lamentation of Christ*. Wood, 51 15/16" × 34 11/16" (132 × 87 cm.) — 141

LIPPI, FILIPPINO (*c.* 1457–1504): *Intercession of Christ and the Virgin*. *c.* 1495. Chestnut, 61 7/16" × 57 7/8" (156 × 147 cm.) — 136

LIPPI, FILIPPO FRA (*c.* 1406–69): *Annunciation*. Wood, 79 15/16" × 72 13/16" (203 × 185 cm.) — *133*
Virgin and Child. Wood, 30" × 21 1/2" (76·3 × 54·2 cm.) — *135*

LOCHNER, STEPHAN (*c.* 1410–51): *Adoration of the Child*. Wood, 14 3/16" × 10 1/16" (36 × 23 cm.) — *75*
St Anthony the Hermit, Pope St Cornelius, St Mary Magdalene and a Donor. Walnut, 47 1/4" × 31 1/2" (120 × 80 cm.) — 76
St Catherine, St Hubert, St Quirinus and a Donor. Walnut, 47 1/4" × 31 1/2" (120 × 80 cm.) — 76

LORRAINE, CLAUDE (CLAUDE GELLÉE) (1600–82): *Idyllic Landscape at Dusk*. 1676. Canvas, 28 3/4" × 38 3/16" (73 × 97 cm.) — 268
Departure of Hagar and Ishmael. 1668. Canvas, 41 3/4" × 59 1/8" (106 × 140 cm.) — 268
Hagar and Ishmael in the Wilderness. Canvas, 42 1/8" × 59 1/16" (107 × 139·5 cm.)
Seaport. 1674. Canvas, 28 5/16" × 38 3/16" (72 × 97 cm.) — *270*

LOTTO, LORENZO (*c.* 1480–1556/7): *Mystic Marriage of St Catherine*. Wood, 27 15/16" × 35 13/16" (71 × 91 cm.) — *160*

MAAS, LORENZ (1845–82): *A Room in the Alte Pinakothek*. Canvas, 39 3/4" × 49 3/8" (101 × 125·7 cm.) — 64

MABUSE (JAN GOSSAERT) (*c.* 1478–1532): *Danaë*. 1527. Oak, 44 1/2" × 37 3/8" (113·5 × 95 cm.) — *123*
Virgin and Child. 1527. Oak, 12" × 9 1/2" (30 × 24 cm.) — 124

MAGNASCO, ALESSANDRO (1667–1749): *Coast Scene*. Canvas, 45 3/8" × 69" (115·5 × 175·5 cm.) — 157

MASTER OF THE LIFE OF THE VIRGIN (active at Cologne 1463–80): *Presentation in the Temple*. Oak, 33 3/8" × 42 15/16" (85 × 109 cm.) — 77
Annunciation. Oak, 33 3/8" × 41 5/16" (85 × 105 cm.) — 77
Coronation of the Virgin. Oak, 40" × 52 3/8" (101·5 × 133 cm.) — 77
Birth of the Virgin. Oak, 33 3/8" × 42 15/16" (85 × 109 cm.) — *78*

MASTER OF MOULINS (active 1475–1500): *Charles II of Bourbon, Cardinal Archbishop of Lyons*. Oak, 13 5/16" × 10 1/16" (33·9 × 25·6 cm.) — *263*

MASTER OF THE ST BARTHOLOMEW ALTARPIECE (*c.* 1450–after 1510): *St Bartholomew Altarpiece*. Centre panel: *St Agnes, St Bartholomew and St Cecilia*. Oak, 50 13/16" × 63 3/8" (129 × 161 cm.), each wing, 50 13/16" × 29 1/8" (129 × 74 cm.) — *79*

MASTER OF ST VERONICA (active 1400–20): *St Veronica with the Holy Kerchief*. Pine, 30$\frac{11}{16}$″ × 18$\frac{7}{8}$″ (78 × 48 cm.)   73

MEMLING, HANS (c. 1433–94): *St John the Baptist*. Oak, 12$\frac{7}{16}$″ × 9$\frac{1}{2}$″ (31·6 × 24 cm.)   114
Diptych: *Madonna in the Rose-bower with St George and a Donor*. Oak, each panel 19$\frac{3}{4}$″ × 11$\frac{1}{2}$″ (40 × 29 cm.)   125
The Seven Joys of the Virgin. Oak, 31$\frac{15}{16}$″ × 73$\frac{3}{8}$″ (81 × 189 cm.)   *126-7*

MIERIS, FRANS VAN (1635–81): *Woman at her Looking-glass*. Oak, 16$\frac{13}{16}$″ × 12$\frac{1}{2}$″ (42·7 × 31·3 cm.)   221

MILLET, JEAN-FRANÇOIS (1642–79): *Italian Coast*. Canvas, 41$\frac{3}{4}$″ × 46$\frac{15}{16}$″ (106 × 119 cm.)   273

MORETTO (ALESSANDRO BONVICINO) (c. 1498–1554): *Portrait of an Ecclesiastic*. Canvas, 40″ × 30$\frac{11}{16}$″ (101·5 × 78 cm.)   156

MUELICH, HANS (1516–73): *Portrait of Albrecht V of Bavaria*. 1533. Wood, 34$\frac{11}{16}$″ × 26$\frac{3}{4}$″ (87 × 68 cm.)   14

MURILLO, BARTOLOMÉ ESTEBAN (1617–82): *St Thomas of Villanueva healing a Cripple*. c. 1678. Canvas, 86$\frac{1}{2}$″ × 59″ (219·5 × 149·2 cm.)   252
Domestic Toilet. c. 1672–82. Canvas, 56$\frac{3}{8}$″ × 41$\frac{15}{16}$″ (143 × 106·5 cm.)   252
Little Fruit-Seller. 1678. Canvas, 56$\frac{3}{8}$″ × 41$\frac{15}{16}$″ (143 × 106·5 cm.)   253
Boys eating Melons and Grapes. Canvas, 57$\frac{1}{16}$″ × 41$\frac{5}{16}$″ (145 × 105 cm.)   253
Pie-Eaters. Canvas, 48$\frac{7}{8}$″ × 40″ (123·5 × 102 cm.)   253
Beggar-Boys playing Dice. Canvas, 57$\frac{1}{2}$″ × 42$\frac{1}{2}$″ (146 × 108·5 cm.)   *254*

OSTADE, ADRIAEN VAN (1610–84): *Brawling Peasants*. 1656. Oak, 17$\frac{11}{16}$″ × 14$\frac{5}{8}$″ (45 × 37·5 cm.)   221

PACCHIA, GIROLAMO DI GIOVANNI DEL (1477–after 1533): *Virgin and Child, with Angels*. Wood, 24″ × 16$\frac{1}{2}$″ (61 × 42 cm.)   140

PACHER, MICHAEL (c. 1435–98): *St Lawrence Altarpiece: Martyrdom of St Lawrence*. Wood, 40″ × 38″ (102 × 99 cm.)   80
Altarpiece of the Church Fathers: The Devil presenting the Missal to St Wolfgang. Wood, 40$\frac{9}{16}$″ × 35$\frac{13}{16}$″ (103 × 91 cm.)   80
Altarpiece of the Church Fathers: St Augustine and St Gregory. Pine. Centre panel: 83$\frac{7}{16}$″ × 78$\frac{3}{4}$″ (212 × 200 cm.), each wing 85$\frac{1}{16}$″ × 35$\frac{13}{16}$″ (216 × 91 cm.)   *82*

PALMA VECCHIO (c. 1480–1528): *Virgin and Child with St Roch and St Mary Magdalene*. Wood, 26$\frac{3}{8}$″ × 36$\frac{3}{4}$″ (67 × 93 cm.)   163

PATER, JEAN-BAPTISTE FRANÇOIS (1695–1731): *Pleasures of the Pastoral Life*. Canvas, 21$\frac{3}{8}$″ × 26″ (54·2 × 66 cm.)   281

PERUGINO (PIETRO VANNUCCI) (c. 1450–1523): *Vision of St Bernard*. Wood, 68$\frac{1}{8}$″ × 66$\frac{15}{16}$″ (173 × 170 cm.)   *148*

PIERO DI COSIMO (1462–1521?): *Legend of Prometheus*. Wood, 26″ × 46$\frac{7}{8}$″ (66 × 118·7 cm.)   140

POUSSIN, NICOLAS (1594–1665): *Midas and Bacchus*. 1632–6.
Canvas, 38$\frac{9}{16}''$ × 51$\frac{3}{16}''$ (98 × 130 cm.)   *265*
Apollo and Daphne. Canvas, 38$\frac{3}{16}''$ × 51$\frac{13}{16}''$ (97 × 131·7 cm.)   266
Lamentation of Christ. 1628–31. Canvas, 39$\frac{3}{8}''$ × 57'' (100 × 144 cm.)   *267*

PRUGGER, NIKOLAUS (*c.* 1620–94): *Portrait of Maximilian I, Elector of Bavaria*. Canvas, 80$\frac{11}{16}''$ × 47$\frac{1}{4}''$ (205 × 120 cm.)   18

RAPHAEL (RAFFAELLO SANZIO) (1483–1520): *Tempi Madonna*. Wood, 29$\frac{1}{2}''$ × 20$\frac{1}{2}''$ (75 × 52 cm.)   *149*
Madonna della Tenda. Wood, 26'' × 20'' (65·8 × 51·2 cm.)   *150*
Canigiani Holy Family. Wood, 51$\frac{9}{16}''$ × 42$\frac{1}{8}''$ (131 × 107 cm.)   *152*

REMBRANDT, HARMENSZ VAN RIJN (1606–69): *Self-portrait as a Young Man.* 1629. Oak, 6$\frac{5}{16}''$ × 5'' (15·6 × 12·7 cm.)   224
Abraham's Sacrifice. 1636. Canvas, 76$\frac{3}{4}''$ × 51$\frac{15}{16}''$ (195 × 132 cm.)   224
Christ the Saviour. 1661. Oval canvas, 30$\frac{1}{2}''$ × 25$\frac{1}{2}''$ (80 × 64·5 cm.)   225
Adoration of the Shepherds. 1646. Canvas, 38$\frac{3}{16}''$ × 28$\frac{1}{8}''$ (97 × 71·5 cm.)   225
Holy Family. 163?. Canvas, 72$\frac{1}{16}''$ × 48$\frac{7}{16}''$ (183·5 × 123 cm.)   *226*
Raising of the Cross. c. 1633. Canvas, 37$\frac{13}{16}''$ × 28$\frac{5}{16}''$ (96·2 × 72·2 cm.)   *228*
Descent from the Cross. c. 1633. Wood, 35$\frac{1}{16}''$ × 25$\frac{9}{16}''$ (89·4 × 65·2 cm.)   *231*
Entombment. 1639. Canvas, 36$\frac{3}{8}''$ × 27$\frac{1}{16}''$ (92·5 × 68·8 cm.)   *232*
Resurrection. 1639. Canvas, 36$\frac{3}{16}''$ × 26$\frac{3}{8}''$ (92 × 67 cm.)   *232*
Ascension. 1636. Canvas, 36$\frac{3}{4}''$ × 26$\frac{3}{4}''$ (93 × 68 cm.)   *232*

RENI, GUIDO (1575–1642): *Assumption*. Silk, 114$\frac{5}{16}''$ × 80$\frac{3}{8}''$ (290 × 204 cm.)   157

RIBERA, JUSEPE DE (1591–1652): *St James Major.* 1634. Canvas, 47$\frac{1}{8}''$ × 38$\frac{1}{16}''$ (119·5 × 96·8 cm.)   246
St Peter of Alcántara meditating. 164?. Canvas, 29$\frac{1}{8}''$ × 22$\frac{13}{16}''$ (74·4 × 58·2 cm.)   *251*

ROBERT, HUBERT (1733–1808): *Necropolis with a Temple*. Canvas, 15$\frac{1}{16}''$ × 18$\frac{3}{16}''$ (38·4 × 46·3 cm.)   285
Old Bridge with Washerwomen. Canvas, 9$\frac{3}{4}''$ × 13'' (24·5 × 33 cm.)   285

RUBENS, PETER PAUL (1577–1640): *Large Last Judgment*. Canvas, 237'' × 178'' (602 × 452 cm.)   *194*
Rape of the Daughters of Leucippus. Canvas, 87$\frac{3}{8}''$ × 82$\frac{5}{16}''$ (222 × 209 cm.)   *196*
Battle of the Amazons. Oak, 47$\frac{5}{8}''$ × 64$\frac{15}{16}''$ (121 × 165 cm.)   198
Rubens and Isabella Brandt in the Honeysuckle Bower. Canvas mounted on wood, 70'' × 53$\frac{1}{2}''$ (178 × 136 cm.)   *200*
Life of Marie de' Medici: Coronation of the Queen. Oak, 21$\frac{1}{4}''$ × 36$\frac{3}{16}''$ (54 × 92 cm.)   *201*
Education of Marie de' Medici. Oak, 19$\frac{1}{2}''$ × 15$\frac{1}{2}''$ (49·3 × 39·2 cm.)   202
Reception of the future Queen at Marseilles. Oak, 21'' × 34$\frac{7}{8}''$ (53·7 × 88·5 cm.)   202
Lion Hunt. Canvas, 98$\frac{1}{16}''$ × 147$\frac{5}{8}''$ (249 × 375·5 cm.)   202

Landscape with Cattle. Oak, $31\frac{7}{8}'' \times 41\frac{3}{4}''$ (81 × 106 cm.)   203
Drunken Silenus. Wood, $83\frac{3}{8}'' \times 84\frac{3}{16}''$ (212·5 × 213·5 cm.)   204
Susanna and the Elders. Oak, $31\frac{1}{8}'' \times 42\frac{15}{16}''$ (79 × 109 cm.)   204
Hélène Fourment in her Wedding Dress. Oak, $63\frac{13}{16}'' \times 52\frac{3}{4}''$ (162 × 134 cm.)   206
Rubens and Hélène Fourment in their Garden. Oak, $38\frac{9}{16}'' \times 51\frac{9}{16}''$ (98 × 131 cm.)   208
Massacre of the Innocents. Oak, $78\frac{5}{16}'' \times 118\frac{7}{8}''$ (199 × 302 cm.)   209

RUISDAEL, JACOB VAN (1628/9–82): *Forest Landscape with Marshes.* Canvas, $23\frac{5}{8}'' \times 29''$ (60 × 73·6 cm.)   237
Extensive Landscape with Village. Canvas, $23\frac{1}{4}'' \times 28\frac{3}{4}''$ (59·1 × 73·2 cm.)   237
Sandhill Landscape. Oak, $27\frac{1}{2}'' \times 36\frac{1}{16}''$ (69·7 × 91·7 cm.)   237
Forest Landscape with Rising Storm. Canvas, $22\frac{1}{16}'' \times 26\frac{13}{16}''$ (55·6 × 68·2 cm.)   238
Torrent with Oaks and Beeches. Canvas on wood, $28\frac{3}{16}'' \times 35\frac{7}{16}''$ (71·7 × 90·1 cm.)   239

SARTO, ANDREA DEL (1486–1530): *Holy Family with St John the Baptist, St Elizabeth and two Angels.* Wood, $54'' \times 41\frac{1}{16}''$ (137 × 104 cm.)   140

SAVERY, ROELANT (1576–1639): *Boar Hunt.* 1609. Wood, $9\frac{3}{4}'' \times 13\frac{3}{4}''$ (24·5 × 35 cm.)   188

SCHONGAUER, MARTIN (c. 1435–91): *Holy Family.* Lime, $10\frac{1}{4}'' \times 6\frac{11}{16}''$ (26 × 17 cm.)   84

SEGNA DI BUONAVENTURA, NICCOLÒ (?–before 1331): *St Mary Magdalene.* Wood, $17\frac{5}{16}'' \times 11\frac{1}{2}''$ (44 × 29 cm.)   128

SIBERECHTS, JAN (1627–1703?): *Pasture-land.* Canvas, $42\frac{3}{8}'' \times 33''$ (107·5 × 84 cm.)   205

SIENESE SCHOOL (c. 1340): *Assumption of the Virgin.* Wood, $30\frac{3}{4}'' \times 14\frac{3}{16}''$ (78·5 × 36 cm.)   130

SIGNORELLI, LUCA (1441–1523): *Virgin and Child.* Wood, $34\frac{11}{16}''$ (87 cm.) diameter   137

STEEN, JAN (1625/6–79): *Love-sick Woman.* Canvas, $24\frac{3}{16}'' \times 20\frac{1}{2}''$ (61·5 × 52·1 cm.)   221

STIELER, JOSEPH (1781–1858): *Portrait of Ludwig I of Bavaria.* Canvas, $90\frac{3}{8}'' \times 66\frac{15}{16}''$ (230 × 170 cm.)   2

STRIGEL, BERNHARD (1460/1–1528): *Conrad Rehlinger the Elder with his eight Children.* 1517. Wood. Left panel: $82\frac{5}{16}'' \times 39\frac{3}{4}''$ (209 × 101 cm.), right panel: $82\frac{5}{16}'' \times 38\frac{9}{16}''$ (209 × 98 cm.)   91

SWEERTS, MICHAEL (1624–64): *Inn Parlour.* Canvas, $39\frac{1}{8}'' \times 37\frac{3}{8}''$ (99·4 × 95 cm.)   221

TIEPOLO, GIOVANNI BATTISTA (1696–1770): *Adoration of the Kings.* 1753. Canvas, $160\frac{1}{4}'' \times 83\frac{1}{16}''$ (407 × 211 cm.)   181
Adoration of the Holy Trinity by Pope Clement. Canvas, $192\frac{1}{8}'' \times 100\frac{13}{16}''$ (488 × 256 cm.)   182

Rinaldo in the Gardens of Armida. Canvas, $41\frac{3}{16}'' \times 56\frac{3}{8}''$ (104·8 × 143 cm.) 182

TINTORETTO (JACOPO ROBUSTI) (1518–94): *Portrait of a Venetian Noble.* Canvas, $44\frac{7}{8}'' \times 35\frac{3}{16}''$ (114 × 89·4 cm.) 173
Mars and Venus surprised by Vulcan. Canvas, $53\frac{1}{8}'' \times 77\frac{15}{16}''$ (135 × 198 cm.) *174*
The Capture of Parma. Canvas, $83\frac{1}{2}'' \times 111\frac{7}{16}''$ (212 × 283·5 cm.) *175*
Crucifixion. Canvas, $60\frac{1}{4}'' \times 97\frac{1}{4}''$ (153 × 247 cm.) 177
Investiture of Francesco Gonzaga. Canvas, $107\frac{1}{16}'' \times 170''$ (272 × 432 cm.) 177
Battle on the Taro. Canvas, $105\frac{15}{16}'' \times 165\frac{7}{8}''$ (269 × 421·5 cm.) 177

TITIAN (TIZIANO VECELLIO) (*c.* 1488–1576): *Virgin and Child in an Evening Landscape.* Canvas, $68\frac{1}{2}'' \times 52\frac{3}{8}''$ (174 × 133 cm.) 162
Virgin and Child, with St John the Baptist and a Donor. Canvas, $29\frac{1}{8}'' \times 36\frac{3}{16}''$ (74 × 92 cm.) 162
Portrait of a Young Man. Canvas, $35\frac{1}{16}'' \times 29\frac{1}{8}''$ (89 × 74 cm.) 162
Vanity. Canvas, $38\frac{3}{16}'' \times 32''$ (97 × 81·2 cm.) 163
The Emperor Charles V. Canvas, $80'' \times 48''$ (203·5 × 122 cm.) *167*
Crowning with Thorns. Canvas, $110\frac{1}{4}'' \times 71\frac{5}{8}''$ (280 × 182 cm.) *169*

TOCQUÉ, LOUIS (1696–1772): *Portrait of the Count Palatine Friedrich Michael von Zweibrücken-Birkenfeld.* Canvas, $35\frac{1}{16}'' \times 28\frac{3}{4}''$ (89 × 73 cm.) 281

VALENTIN (JEAN DE BOULOGNE) (1594–1632): *Crowning with Thorns.* Canvas, $68\frac{1}{8}'' \times 96\frac{5}{16}''$ (173 × 245 cm.) 273

VELÁZQUEZ, DIEGO RODRÍGUEZ DE SILVA Y (1599–1660): *Portrait of a Young Spaniard.* Canvas, $35\frac{1}{16}'' \times 27\frac{1}{8}''$ (89·2 × 69·5 cm.) *248*

VELDE THE YOUNGER, WILLEM VAN DE (1633–1707): *Calm Sea.* Canvas, $20\frac{13}{16}'' \times 22\frac{1}{16}''$ (51·6 × 56·5 cm.) *234*

VERNET, CLAUDE JOSEPH (1714–89): *River Scene.* Copper, $12'' \times 17''$ (30 × 43 cm.) 284

VERONESE (PAOLO CALIARI) (1528–88): *Portrait of a Venetian Noblewoman.* Canvas, $46\frac{1}{16}'' \times 39\frac{3}{4}''$ (117 × 101 cm.) *171*
Virgin and Child with a Donor. Canvas, $40\frac{1}{4}'' \times 32\frac{1}{4}''$ (102·5 × 82 cm.) 172

VINCI, LEONARDO DA (1452–1519): *Virgin and Child.* Wood, $24\frac{7}{16}'' \times 18\frac{1}{8}''$ (62 × 46·5 cm.) *146*

VIVIEN, JOSEPH (1657–1735): *Portrait of Maximilian II (Emanuel), Elector of Bavaria.* Canvas, $92\frac{15}{16}'' \times 69\frac{5}{16}''$ (236 × 176 cm.) 30
Archbishop Fénelon of Cambrai. Canvas, $31\frac{7}{8}'' \times 25\frac{3}{16}''$ (81 × 64 cm.) 277
Self-portrait before an Easel. Canvas, $46\frac{7}{16}'' \times 37''$ (118 × 94 cm.) *280*

WEYDEN, ROGIER VAN DER (1397/1400–64): *Adoration of the Kings (St Columba) Altarpiece.* Oak. Centre panel: $54\frac{5}{16}'' \times 60\frac{1}{4}''$ (138 × 153 cm.), each wing $54\frac{5}{16}'' \times 27\frac{9}{16}''$ (138 × 70 cm.) *116-17*

ZURBARÁN, FRANCISCO (1598–1664): *St Francis of Assisi.* Canvas, $25\frac{5}{8}'' \times 20\frac{7}{8}''$ (64·7 × 53·1 cm.) *256*

INDEX OF NAMES

Adelaide of Savoy, 31
Adolph of Burgundy, 124
Alba, Duke of, 186
Albertinelli, Mariotto, 57, 137
Albrecht, Balthasar Augustin, 37
Albrecht V, Duke of Bavaria, 11, 13–16
Altdorfer, Albrecht, 11, 13, 20, 50–53, 59f, 86, 88f
Altoviti, Bindi, 56f
Amberger, Christoph, 29, 111
Angelico, Fra, 57, 128, 131f
Anna Maria Ludovica, 43
Apt, Ulrich, 27, 29
Arundel, Earl of, 43
Audran, Benoit, 276

Backhuisen, Ludolf, 41
Baldung Grien, Hans, 52f, 102f, 105, 111
Balen, Hendrick van, 42
Barbari, Jacopo de', 154
Baring, Sir Thomas, 58, 150
Baroccio, Federico, 156
Bassano, Giacomo da Ponte, 31, 172, 230
Batoni, Pompeo, 39
Battaglie, Michelangelo delle, 41
Bayersdorfer, Adolf, 62
Beauharnais family, 127
Beccafumi, Domenico, 57, 137
Bedoli, Girolamo, 27
Beham, Barthel, 11ff, 29, 111
Bellini, Giovanni, 158, 161
Bellori, Giovanni Pietro, 267
Berchem, Nicolas, 48
Bernini, Giovanni Lorenzo, 275
Bertin, Nicolas, 281

Bertram, Johann Baptist, 58
Bloemaert, Abraham, 218f
Boel, Pieter, 34, 48
Boisserée, Melchior, 58f, 63, 72, 79f, 120, 127
Boisserée, Sulpiz, 58ff, 63, 72, 79f, 120, 127
Bol, Ferdinand, 233
Bonaparte, Lucien, 55
Bordone, Paris, 45
Bosch, Hieronymus, 115
Botticelli, 57, 97, 142, 143
Boucher, François, 48, 286f
Bouts, Dieric, the Elder, 59, 63, 78, 114, 118
Bouts, Dieric, the Younger, 59, 120
Brandt, Isabella, 199
Brandt, Jan, 199
Braune, Heinz, 62f
Bretagne, Father Pierre de, 35
Breu, Jorg, the Elder, 11
Breu, Jorg, the Younger, 11
Bril, Paul, 45, 189
Bronzino, 111
Brouwer, Adriaen, 34, 42, 48, 68, 210f, 213
Bruegel, Jan, the Elder, 28, 34, 37, 42, 45, 192f
Bruegel, Pieter, the Elder, 52, 185f, 193
Bruno, Giordano, 42
Buchanan, William, 58
Buchner, Ernst, 63ff
Buonaventura, Segna di, 128
Burgkmair, Hans, 11, 27, 29, 51
Buyltink, Pieter, 127

Caliari, Carlo, 172
Canaletto, Antonio, 183
Candido, Pietro, 21
Canigliani, Domenico, 151

Cano, Alonso, 247
Canova, 54
Capelle, J. de, 40
Caravaggio, 179, 273
Carleton, Sir Dudley, 28
Carlos II, 44
Carracci, Agostino, 31
Castillo, Antonio del, 247
Catalan School, 246
Ceulen, Gisbert van, 33, 35, 203
Cézanne, Paul, 261
Champaigne, Philippe de, 53, 271f
Chardin, J-B, 48
Charles I of England, 214
Charles II of Bourbon, 262
Charles V, Emperor, 13
Christina, Queen of Sweden, 46
Churchill, John, Duke of Marlborough, 35
Cignani, Carlo, 43
Claesz, Pieter, 40, 48
Clemens of Bavaria, 48
Cleve, Joos van, 59
Coello, Claudio, 246f
Conegliano, Cima da, 58, 158f
Correggio, 27, 45, 122
Cosimo III, 43, 151
Cosimo, Piero di, 140
Coypel, Charles-Antoine, 283
Cranach, Lucas, the Elder, 21, 27, 29, 52f, 59, 65, 106, 108f, 111
Cranach, Lucas, the Younger, 109
Crespi, Daniele, 156
Crevalcare, Antonio da, 138
Croes, Willem 223f
Cuyp, Aelbert, 41, 236
Cuyp, Benjamin, 48

Dalem, Cornelius van, 187

301

Danet, 34
David, Gerard, 53, 115
Del Campo, 33
Diderot, 289
Dillis, Georg von, 7, 10, 50f, 53-8, 60f
Donatello, 134
Dörnhöffer, Friedrich, 63
Dou, Gerard, 42
Douffet, Gerard, 44
Douven, Jan Frans, 41ff
Dujardin, Karel, 42
Dürer, Albrecht, 13, 21-7, 36, 52f, 59ff, 74, 81, 83, 92f, 95, 97, 99, 111, 142, 230

Egkl, Wilhelm, 16
Elsheimer, Adam, 28, 42, 112f
Engelbrechtsen, 28, 59
Erhart, Gregor, 85
Ernst of Liège, Elector of Cologne, 28
Ernst the Pious, Duke of Saxe-Weimar, 29
Esebeck, 48
Estense, Baldassare, 138

Fabritius, Carel, 52
Ferdinand I, Emperor, 15
Ferdinand, Elector of Cologne, 28
Ferdinand Maria, Elector of Bavaria, 31
Ferrarese Master, 138
Feselen, Melchior, 11, 29
Fickler, Johannes, 15, 19f, 65
Florentine School, 129
Floris, Frans, 48, 191
Foltz, Philipp, 61
Francia, Francesco, 58
Franciabigio, 141
Frederick the Great, 279
Frederik Hendrik of Orange, 229
Fromentin, Eugène, 214
Fugger, Christoph, 111
Fugger, Johann Jacob, 15

Fugger, Raimund, 15, 111
Fyt, Jan, 34

Gaddi, Taddeo, 129
Garbo, Raffaellino del, 57
Gelder, Aert de, 41
Gentileschi, Orazio, 178f
Ghirlandaio, 57, 143, 145
Giordano, Luca, 45f, 157
Giorgione, 163, 165
Giotto, 128
Glimm, Albrecht, 21, 97
Goes, Hugo van der, 114, 262
Goethe, 38, 58, 72, 269
Goltzius, Hendrick, 218
Goltzius, Hubert, 15
Gonzaga, Federico, 175
Gonzaga, Ferdinand, 214
Gonzaga, Vincenzo, 199
Goudt, Hendrik, 113
Goya, Francisco de, 62, 224, 258-61
Goyen, Jan van, 40, 220, 236
Greco, El, 62, 244
Greuze, J-B, 289
Groeningen, Swart van, 28
Grünewald, Mathis, 52, 100, 102, 105
Guardi, Francesco, 62, 183f

Haimbl, Augustin, 25
Hainhofer, Philipp, 19
Hals, Frans, 37, 90, 223f, 243
Hanfstaengl, Eberhard, 64
Heda, Willem Claesz, 48
Heem, Jan De, 34
Heinse, Wilhelm, 197
Heller, Jakob, 24
Hemessen, Jan Sanders van, 28f
Heyden, Jan van der, 42
Heydt, Von der, 74
Hildebrand, Adolf von, 78
Hobbema, Meindert, 40, 220
Holbein, Hans, the Elder, 27, 29, 52f, 85f, 111

Holbein, Hans, the Younger, 27, 42, 111
Hooch, Pieter de, 40, 243
Huber, Wolf, 52
Huysum, Jan van, 42

Imhoff family, 22
Isenbrandt, Adríaen, 59

Jacobäa van Baden, 13
Jagerndorff, Margrave von, 26
Janssen, Abraham, 51, 189
Janssens Elinga, Pieter, 40, 243
Johann Friedrich, Duke of Saxony, 20
Johann Wilhelm, Elector Palatine, 42-6, 151, 195, 198, 249
Jordaens, Jacob, 205
Joseph Clemens, Archbishop of Cologne, 276
Joseph Ferdinand, Elector, 32, 34
Josephine, Empress, 58, 159

Kalf, Willem, 220, 241
Karl Albrecht of Bavaria (Karl VII), 35f
Karl August, Duke, 47, 49
Karl Philipp, Elector Palatine, 40, 44f
Karl Theodor, Elector Palatine, 38ff, 46f, 227, 250, 257
Karsh, Gerhard Joseph, 46
Kastner, Adolf, 85
Kerricx, Willem, 33
Key, Willem, 28, 191
Klenze, Leo von, 7-10
Koninck, Philips de, 235f
Krahe, Lambert, 40, 46, 227
Kreuznach, Conrad Faber von, 59
Kulmbach, Hans von, 111

Lancret, Nicolas, 278
Lange, Robert, 61

Langlois, C., 255
Largillière, Nicolas de, 280f
Larmessin, N. de, 278
Lasso, Orlando di, 13
Lastman, Pieter, 51
La Tour, Quentin de, 284
Le Brun, Charles, 276
Leopold I, Emperor, 32
Leprince, J-B, 280
Lespilliez, 38
Lessing, 38
Le Sueur, Eustache, 57, 275
Leyden, Lucas van, 28
Liberti, Heinrich, 33f
Lippi, Filippino, 57, 136
Lippi, Fra Filippo, 57, 133f, 136
Lochner, Stephan, 74, 76f
Lombard, Lambert, 191
Longhi, Pietro, 183
Lorraine, Claude, 36, 48, 113, 268ff
Loth, Carl, 43
Lotto, Lorenzo, 160f
Louis XV of France, 46, 283, 286f
Ludwig I of Bavaria, 10, 53–61, 66, 72, 80, 93, 118, 127, 134, 136, 143, 145, 150, 59
Ludwig X, 11

Maas, Lorenz, 64
Mabuse, Jan Gossaert, 122, 124
Maes, Nicolaes, 41
Magnasco, Alessandro, 42, 157
Manet, Edouard, 249, 261
Mander, Karl van, 24, 28, 191
Mannlich, Christian von, 47, 49, 50ff, 57
Mantegna, Andrea, 81
Maria Anna of Austria, 247, 249
Maria Antonie, 32
Martin, Kurt, 65
Martini, Simone, 131
Masaccio, 134

Massart, 289
Massys, Quentin, 28
Master of the Aix-la-Chapelle Altar, 78
Master of the Holy Family, 78
Master of Liesborn, 78
Master of the Life of the Virgin, 77, 80
Master of the Lyversberg Passion, 78
Master of Moulins, 262
Master of the Munich Crucifixion Altar, 78
Master of the St Bartholomew Altarpiece, 78f
Master of St Severin, 78
Master of St Veronica, 72
Maximilian I, Elector of Bavaria, 17–22, 24–29, 93, 109, 113, 191
Maximilian II (Emmanuel), 30–36, 203, 207, 255, 276
Maximilian III (Joseph), Elector, 36ff
Maximilian IV (Joseph of Pfalz-Zweibrücken), King Maximilian I of Bavaria, 7, 47, 49–54, 97, 99, 234, 272
Medici family, 145, 151
Medici, Francesco Maria, Cardinal, 43
Medici, Marie de', 201
Meit, Konrad, 29
Memling, Hans, 48, 59, 114, 125ff
Messina, Antonello da, 153
Metsu, Gabriel, 48
Metzger, Johann, 56f
Michelangelo, 27, 168, 191
Mieris, Frans van, the Elder, 42, 221
Mignard, 275
Mignon, 34
Millet, Jean-François, 273
Momper, Joos de, 48, 193
Monet, Claude, 261

Mor, Anthonis, 249
Morghen, Raphael, 55
Muelich, Hans, 14, 29
Munich, Elector of, 29
Murillo, Bartolomé, Estéban, 34, 37, 42, 58, 252f, 255, 257

Napoleon I, 13, 50f, 86, 189
Nasi, Bernardo and Filippo, 148
Neudorffer, Johann, 21, 97
Neveu, François-Marie, 50
Nole, Colyn de, 33
Nollet, Domenique, 36

Odescalchi, Duke, 46
Orley, Bernard van, 59
Ostade, Adriaen van, 42, 48, 221
Ott, David, 16

Pacchia, 140
Pacher, Michael, 52, 62, 80–83
Palma Vecchio, 163, 165
Palomino, 255
Panini, 284f
Pater, J-B, 281
Paul I, Czar, 183
Paumgartner, 22, 93
Perugino, Pietro, 57, 148
Petel, Georg, 46
Pey, Johann de, 86
Pfalz-Neuburg, Wilhelm of, 28, 42
Philip of Burgundy, 124
Pierre II of Bourbon, 262
Pigage, Nicolas de, 40, 48
Piombo, Sebastiano del, 191
Pleydenwurff, Hans, 52
Pontormo, 111
Poussin, Nicolas, 34, 97, 113, 264–7, 275
Prugger, Nicolaus, 18

Queralto, Don José, 258f

303

Quickelberg, Samuel, 11, 15
Raphael, 24, 27, 36, 43, 45, 55f, 58, 147–151, 266
Reber, Franz von, 61f
Reichlich, Marx, 52
Rembrandt, 40, 42, 46, 48, 62, 64, 90, 113, 122, 224f, 227, 229f, 232
Reni, Guido, 157
Reymerswaele, Marinus van, 28
Reynolds, Sir Joshua, 223
Ribera, Jusepe de, 246, 250
Richelieu, 198, 210
Rigaud, Hyacinthe, 281
Robert, Hubert, 285
Rottenhammer, Hans, 42, 193
Rubens, Nicolas, 208
Rubens, Peter Paul, 28, 33, 35, 37, 40, 42–6, 51f, 62, 68, 113, 193, 195, 197ff, 201–4, 207–210, 216
Rudolf II, Emperor, 15, 21f, 24, 28, 97, 124
Ruisdael, Jacob van, 48, 53, 236–9
Ruysch, 42
Ruysdael, Salomon van, 48

Sacrati, Umberto de, 138
Sandrart, Joachim von, 28f, 265
Sarto, Andrea del, 43, 45, 140
Savery, Roelant, 188
Schäfer, Georg and Otto, 179
Schlegel, Friedrich von, 58f, 86
Schlegel, Friedrich von, 58f, 86
Schongauer, Martin, 48, 83

Schöpfer, Hans, 11, 65
Seghers, Hercules, 35, 236
Sellaer, Vincent, 28
Siberechts, Jan, 48, 205
Sienese School, 129
Signorelli, Luca, 137
Snyders, François, 34f
Sobieski, Jan, King of Poland, 34
Soehner, Halldor, 65
Spranger, Bartholomäus, 187f
Stadler, Toni, 63
Steen, Jan, 42, 48, 221
Strada, Jacopo de, 15f, 29
Strigel, Bernhard, 59, 90, 111
Sweerts, Michael 48, 221

Teniers, David, 34, 48
Ter Borch, Gerhard, 42
Tiepolo, Giovanni Battista, 52, 180, 182
Tintoretto, 35, 51f, 168, 170, 173–7
Titian, 15f, 27, 35, 51, 58, 62, 160, 162f, 166, 168, 170, 216, 249, 265
Tocqué, Louis, 48, 281
Tongres, Nicolaus, 80
Tschudi, Hugo von, 62f, 261
Turenne, 271f

Valentin, (Jean de Boulogne), 273
Van Beyeren, Abraham, 42, 220
Van Dyck, 33, 35, 42, 45f, 68, 211, 214, 216
Van Eyck, 118
Van Goyen, Jan, 40, 220, 236
Van Soest, 33
Vélazquez, 45, 224, 229
Velde, Adriaen van de, 42, 48
Velde, Esaies van de, 48

Velde, Willem van de, the Younger, 233f
Venetian School, 165
Vernet, Antoine, 284
Vernet, Claude Joseph, 284
Verona, Liberale da, 141
Veronese, Paolo, 31, 35, 44f, 70, 172
Verrocchio, Andrea del, 147
Vinci, Leonardo da, 62, 147
Vivien, Joseph, 30, 34, 276, 280
Vos, Paul de, 33, 51
Vostermann, 230
Vouet, Simon, 275

Wael, Jan de, 33
Wagner, Martin von, 57
Wallerstein, Prince, 60
Wasserfass, Goddert von dem, the Elder, 118
Watteau, Antoine, 278
Weizenfeld, Johann Nepomuk Edler von, 37
Werff, Adriaen van der, 46
Wertinger, Hans, 13
Weyden, Rogier van der, 59, 77, 116ff, 127
Wilhelm IV of Bavaria, 11ff, 16, 29, 65, 86
Wilhelm V of Bavaria, (the Pious), 16f
Wilhelm of Cologne, 72
Willaerts, 41
Wiser, Heinrich von, 45, 249
Wolfgang Wilhelm von Pfalz-Neuburg, 28, 43, 195
Wouwermann, Philips, 34, 48
Wynants, 48

Zimmermann, Clemens, 1
Zurbaran, Francisco de, 42, 250, 255, 257

The authors stress the fact that the captions to the black-and-white pictures were written by Somogy et Cie, Paris.

ate Due